Reading Fictional Languages

Reading Fictional Languages

EDITED BY ISRAEL A. C. NOLETTO,
JESSICA NORLEDGE AND
PETER STOCKWELL

EDINBURGH
University Press

Edinburgh University Press is one of the leading university presses in the UK.
We publish academic books and journals in our selected subject areas across the
humanities and social sciences, combining cutting-edge scholarship with high
editorial and production values to produce academic works of lasting importance.
For more information visit our website: edinburghuniversitypress.com

© editorial matter and organisation Israel A. C. Noletto, Jessica Norledge and
Peter Stockwell, 2024, 2025
© the chapters their several authors, 2024, 2025

Edinburgh University Press Ltd
13 Infirmary Street,
Edinburgh, EH1 1LT

First published in hardback by Edinburgh University Press 2024

Typeset in 9 on 12pt Noto Serif
by Cheshire Typesetting Ltd, Cuddington, Cheshire

A CIP record for this book is available from the British Library

ISBN 978 1 3995 2914 3 (hardback)
ISBN 978 1 3995 2915 0 (paperback)
ISBN 978 1 3995 2916 7 (webready PDF)
ISBN 978 1 3995 2917 4 (epub)

The right of Israel A. C. Noletto, Jessica Norledge and Peter Stockwell to be identified
as the editors of this work has been asserted in accordance with the Copyright,
Designs and Patents Act 1988, and the Copyright and Related Rights Regulations 2003
(SI No. 2498).

Contents

	List of contributors	vii
	Acknowledgements	xiii
1	Introduction: reading fictional languages Israel A. C. Noletto, Jessica Norledge, and Peter Stockwell	1

PART I: Design

2	Conlanging with non-conlangers: the art of language invention in television and media David J. Peterson and Jessie Sams	17
3	On the inner workings of language creation: using conlangs to drive reader engagement in fictional worlds Benjamin Johnson, Anthony Gutierrez, and Nicolás Matías Campi	32
4	Dialects in constructed languages Harry Cook	47
5	Alien typographies in sf and the influence of Asian languages Victor Fernandes Andrade and Sebastião Alves Teixeira Lopes	63
6	Design intentions and actual perception of fictional languages: Quenya, Sindarin, and Na'vi Bettina Beinhoff	76
7	The phonaesthetics of constructed languages: results from an online rating experiment Christine Mooshammer, Dominique Bobeck, Henrik Hornecker, Kierán Meinhardt, Olga Olina, Marie Christin Walch, and Qiang Xia	93

PART II: Interpretation

8	Tolkien's use of invented languages in *The Lord of the Rings* James K. Tauber	115

9	Changing tastes: reading the cannibalese of Charles Dickens' *Holiday Romance* and nineteenth-century popular culture *Katie Wales*	133
10	Dialectal extrapolation as a literary experiment in Aldiss' 'A spot of Konfrontation' *Israel A. C. Noletto*	144
11	Women, fire, and dystopian things *Jessica Norledge*	161
12	Building the conomasticon: names and naming in fictional worlds *Rebecca Gregory*	179
13	The language of Lapine in *Watership Down* *Kimberley Pager-McClymont*	195
14	Unspeakable languages *Peter Stockwell*	213
	Index	230

List of contributors

Victor Fernandes Andrade is based at the Federal University of Bahia (UFBA), Salvador, Brazil. He is a volunteer with the research group *PRO. SOM: Estudos de Processos de Criação em Diversos Meios e Perspectivas Literárias da Literatura Irlandesa* (Studies of Creative Processes in Diverse Media and Literary Perspectives of Irish Literature), under the supervision of Prof. Eliza Morinaka. He is interested in science fiction, weird fiction, and translation studies.

Bettina Beinhoff is Senior Lecturer in Applied Linguistics and English Language at Anglia Ruskin University, Cambridge. Her research crosses sociolinguistics and second language acquisition with a particular specialism in intercultural communication and globalisation, language and identity, and she has published in all of these areas. Bettina also researches constructed languages, investigating conlangs as cultural, artistic, and linguistic phenomenon. She is Co-Director of the Anglia Ruskin Research Centre for Intercultural and Multilingual Studies (ARRCIMS) and of the Centre for Science Fiction and Fantasy (CSFF).

Dominique Bobeck is a researcher in the Institut für deutsche Sprache und Linguistik at Humboldt-Universität zu Berlin. His work focuses on phonology, morphology, optimality theory, and Semitic languages. His master's thesis in linguistics is about the influence of Semitic languages on conlangs. Furthermore, he constructed the language Horn for the Amazon Prime Original *The Gryphon*. For a German Netflix production, he developed a conlang called *Twinneð Ƙēxa*, which is going to be released between late 2024 and early 2025.

Nicolás Matías Campi is a philologist and conlanger based in Buenos Aires, Argentina. He has been conlanging since high school, and has been working with authors and clients to create conlangs since 2016. Nico's personal conlangs include the Baladian, Favrian and Delician families of languages (dozens of languages all *a priori*), Tulvan (*a priori*), and *a posteriori* languages such as Fingail (a language descended from Finnish by way of Welsh phonology) and Brest (a Germanic and Celtic hybrid language). Some of his works with authors have included Bamzooki, an animated series project with the BBC, the Karrakesh language for an Argentine movie based on Lovecraft's works and the Necronomicon, the Atlantean language for the *B.E.A.R.S.* movie project in 2020, and various conlangs for sci-fi and fantasy. He also contributed to the Na'vi dictionary translated to Spanish, the creation of the first dictionaries for both Dothraki and High Valyrian, and he was part of the development of the High Valyrian Duolingo course.

Harry Cook is based at the University of York, where he studies linguistics and German. He has been interested in fictional languages and has been a conlanger from the age of twelve; since then he has created over a dozen *a priori* languages. In 2018, he started a larger world-building project which, when complete, will feature several families of languages spread across two fictional continents.

Rebecca Gregory is Assistant Professor in Historical Linguistics and Onomastics at the University of Nottingham, where she teaches medieval literature and language, place- and personal names, and English linguistics. Her main research area is English place-names, with a particular emphasis on the influence of Scandinavian settlement on these forms. When she fancies a break from welly-clad fieldwork, Becca also enjoys diving into fictional onomastics as part of her broad interest in medieval and modern fictional worlds. She is the author of *Viking Nottinghamshire* (Five Leaves Press, 2017) and has contributed to *A New Dictionary of English Field-Names* (English Place-Name Society, 2018) as well as the co-authored *Digital Teaching for Linguistics* (Routledge, 2022).

Anthony Gutierrez (a.k.a. Credus Eldergrann) graduated from Whittier College in 2020 with a bachelors in English with a focus on creative writing and a minor in Japanese. He is currently studying for his master's in Popular Fiction at Stonecoast University, and is Principal Content Designer at Intuit in the San Francisco Bay. Anthony has been writing poetry, short stories, and attending writing conferences for about ten years. For the past two years he has been working with Jamin Johnson to create the various languages seen within his sci-fi fantasy series *The Lost Children* (languages such as Modern Standard Imperial, Alder'mane, Arbulian, Ashian, Hakdor, Western, and a possible non-humanoid language).

Henrik Hornecker is a Research Assistant in the Institut für deutsche Sprache und Linguistik at Humboldt-Universität zu Berlin. He is involved in a project editing all shorter Old Lithuanian texts known to date and making them accessible for future research. In addition to Baltic studies, the focus of his research lies in Old Germanic and Celtic linguistics. Since his youth, he has been inventing languages.

BenJamin Johnson is a language creator who has been conlanging since 1994, and working with authors, playwrights, comic writers, and graphic novelists to create conlangs for their work since 2014. Some of Jamin's personal languages include Valthungian and Northeadish (Germanic *a posteriori* languages), Gothic Romance (a Germanic and Italic *a posteriori* hybrid), and *a priori* languages such as Ox-Yew, Dlatci, and Maltcégj. He has worked with about a dozen authors to create around two dozen languages to enhance their works, including the seven Aterran languages used in Anthony Gutierrez' graphic novel *The Lost Children*, the Grayis language used in the board game *Pilots of Gallaxia* by Infinite Mind Pictures, the Braereth language (and its several dialects) used in an upcoming Kindle Vella serial by C. J. Kavanaugh, and several other projects that are still in development. In addition to creating new languages, Jamin has also taken over the curatorship of two other conlangs when their creators were no longer available to continue their development: Brooding was created by Veronica Hamilton for Riddlesbrood Touring Theatre Company in 2012 and Jamin has been developing it since 2014; Nymeran was created by Niamh Doyle in 2015 for Mythopoeia's comic *Glow*, and Jamin has been expanding on it since early 2021.

Sebastião Alves Teixeira Lopes is full Professor at the Federal University of Piauí (UFPI), Teresina, Brazil. He holds a PhD in English Language as well as English and North American Literatures from the University of São Paulo, Brazil. He has conducted postdoctoral research at the University of Winnipeg, Canada, and the University of London, UK. He is the author of several academic pieces on literature with an emphasis on postcolonial narratives.

Kierán Meinhardt is a Research Assistant in the Institut für deutsche Sprache und Linguistik at Humboldt-Universität zu Berlin, where he is working on the Old Lithuanian Etymological Dictionary. His research focuses on computer-aided metrical analysis of ancient texts. He has been crafting conlangs and code for several years.

Christine Mooshammer is Professor of Phonetics and Phonology in German Linguistics at the Institut für deutsche Sprache und Linguistik, Humboldt-Universität zu Berlin since 2013. She has published over 100 scientific papers in the areas of speech control, planning, production and errors, prosody, phonetic convergence, register and the phonological characteristic and reception of fantasy languages. She is a member of the editorial boards of *Phonetica* and the *Journal of the International Phonetic Association*.

Israel A. C. Noletto is Professor of English Language and Literature at the Federal Institute of Piauí (IFPI), Brazil. He holds a PhD in Language and Literature from the Federal University of Piauí and has been a CAPES fellow at the University of Nottingham. He is interested in literary stylistics, narrative theory and fictional languages in science fiction as a literary phenomenon and has authored several scholarly articles on glossopoesis in writers ranging from George Orwell to Ted Chiang, Jonathan Swift to Anthony Burgess, Thomas More to Suzette Haden Elgin. He has co-edited *Literatura, Memória e Cultura* (IFPI, 2021) and *Ensaios sobre teoria e crítica literária* (*Essays on Literary Theory and Criticism*) (IFPI, 2020), a collection of papers on literary criticism by scholars from Brazil, Nigeria, and Nepal.

Jessica Norledge is Assistant Professor in Stylistics at the University of Nottingham. Her research sits at the interface between English literature and English language, in stylistics and narratology. Jess has a particular interest in the style of dystopian literature and the experience of reading dystopian narratives, ranging from early utopian works through to twenty-first-century literary practice. She has published on the cognitive poetics of emotion, dystopian epistolary, unnatural and non-human minds, and worlds theories in dystopian fiction. Her books include *The Language of Dystopia* (Palgrave Macmillan, 2022) and the co-authored *Digital Teaching for Linguistics* (Routledge, 2022).

Olga Olina is researching language endangerment in urban contexts and contributing to *Berlin Spricht*, a project aimed at the documentation of linguistic diversity in Berlin. She is a language coder at *Grambank*, a joint project of the Max Planck Institute of Psycholinguistics, Nijmegen, and Max Planck Institute of the Science of Human History, Jena. Her academic interests include historical linguistics, linguistic typology, language endangerment and documentation. She has been engaged in projects researching Old Lithuanian and Yucatec Maya. She has also been a tutor of Sanskrit and Proto-Indo-European at Humboldt-Universität zu Berlin.

Kimberley Pager-McClymont is a researcher and lecturer in English Language and English for Academic Purposes at the University of Aberdeen (International Study Centre). Her research in stylistics focuses on figurative language, imagery, and conceptual metaphors, particularly the impact they have on readers and the process of characterisation. She has published on the stylistics of Brontë's *Jane Eyre*, Millhauser's *Martin Dressler*, and fetishism in Maupassant's 'La Chevelure'. Her model of pathetic fallacy appeared in the journal *Language and Literature*.

David J. Peterson is a conlanger, writer, and artist, who studied English and linguistics at UC Berkeley and UC San Diego. The inventor of numerous languages for TV, film, and novels, he is best known for creating High

Valyrian, Dothraki, and a range of minor languages for the HBO adaptation of George R. R. Martin's *Game of Thrones*. He has also created languages for Syfy's *Defiance* and *Dominion*, Netflix's *Shadow and Bone*, and the films *Dune*, *Doctor Strange*, as well as Marvel's *Thor 2: The Dark World*. His books include *Living Language Dothraki* (Zauberfeder, 2014) and *The Art of Language Invention: From Horse-Lords to Dark Elves to Sand Worms, the Words Behind World-Building* (Penguin, 2015). He co-founded the Language Creation Society and has served as its president.

Jessie Sams is a conlanger and linguistics professor at Stephen F. Austin State University, Texas. She is also the co-creator of Ménishè, the fictional language appearing in *Motherland: Fort Salem*, and the Aazh Naamori language of the vampires in *Vampire Academy*, as well as several other fictional languages such as Gnóma, Wóxtjanato, and Hiutsaθ. Together, Jessie and David Peterson host the LangTime channel on YouTube, where they create new languages in real time, including languages for mice, oppossums, reindeer, and penguins

Peter Stockwell is Professor of Literary Linguistics at the University of Nottingham and a Fellow of the English Association. He has published twenty books and 100 articles in stylistics, sociolinguistics, science fiction and applied linguistics, including *Cognitive Poetics* (Routledge, 2020), *The Language of Surrealism* (Palgrave Macmillan, 2017), *Texture: A Cognitive Aesthetics of Reading* (Edinburgh University Press, 2009), and *The Poetics of Science Fiction* (Pearson, 2000). He co-edited *The Cambridge Handbook of Stylistics* (Cambridge University Press, 2014), *The Language and Literature Reader* (Routledge, 2008), *Contemporary Stylistics* (Continuum, 2007) and *Impossibility Fiction* (Rodopi, 1996). His work in cognitive poetics has been translated into many actual languages, including Arabic, Chinese, Japanese, Polish, Persian, Russian, and Arabic.

James K. Tauber is a linguist, philologist, and software developer who uses computers to help people better understand languages and texts. He develops software and teaches Digital Humanities and Tolkien at Signum University and consults to a variety of institutions on digital texts and scholarly reading environments, especially for historical languages. James is the director of the Digital Tolkien Project and has qualifications in linguistics, Classical Greek, educational research, Germanic philology, and music theory. He is a Fellow of the Python Software Foundation and the Royal Society of Arts. Originally from Australia, James currently lives in the Boston area.

Marie Christin Walch studies linguistics at the Institut für deutsche Sprache und Linguistik at Humboldt-Universität zu Berlin and works as a research assistant at the Leibniz-Centre General Linguistics, where she is involved in projects on speech acts and discourse structure.

Katie Wales is Honorary Professor of English Language and Literature in the Faculty of Arts at the University of Nottingham. Her research interests are wide-ranging and encompass stylistics, rhetoric, Northern English dialectology, and the discourse of spiritualist mediums. She was a founder member of the Poetics and Linguistics Association (PALA) and the editor of its journal *Language and Literature*. Katie has authored nearly 100 publications in literary stylistics, applied linguistics and sociolinguistics, and her books include *A Dictionary of Stylistics* (Longman, 3rd edn, 2011), *Personal Pronouns in Present-Day English* (Cambridge University Press, 1996), and *The Language of James Joyce* (Macmillan, 1992), as well as a series of joke books for children.

Qiang Xia is a doctoral fellowship recipient at the Institut für deutsche Sprache und Linguistik at Humboldt-Universität zu Berlin. She compared the temporal aspects of conversational turn-taking in face-to-face and Zoom situations in her master's thesis. Currently, she is working on the phonetic variants of non-native addressee register.

Acknowledgements

The editors would like to thank PALA (the Poetics and Linguistics Association) and the Centre for Research in Applied Linguistics (CRAL) at the University of Nottingham for their generous financial support in bringing together the participants at the 'Reading Fictional Languages' symposium, and also the CAPES Foundation (Cocrdenação de Aperfeiçoamento de Pessoal de Nível Superior) in the Ministry of Education, Brazil, for the award of a Fellowship and travel funding. Thanks to the Language Creation Society for their support.

https://www.pala.ac.uk
https://www.nottingham.ac.uk/research/groups/cral/
https://capes.gov.br
https://conlang.org

CHAPTER 1

Introduction: reading fictional languages

Israel A. C. Noletto, Jessica Norledge, and Peter Stockwell

This introductory chapter sets out the history of fictional language creation, charting the utility and function of fictional languages across time and literary modes. It addresses existing critical accounts of glossopoesis, before moving on to present the unique mixed-methods approach taken in the collection. Reflecting on each contribution, the editors highlight the breadth and interdisciplinarity of the collection, which draws upon the work of stylisticians, narratologists, onomasts, and professional language inventors.

Fictional languages

All languages are invented, but not all languages are real. Even natural languages can be regarded as having been invented, though their origins and evolution might be dimly remembered or gradually spread over long historical sweeps of time. The creators of natural languages are usually communities of speakers, and the innovations in communication that they develop are often not contemporaneously apparent to their users. Natural languages almost always emerge because of a changed environment that is socially shared. Some other languages, however, are fictional, imagined for an equally fictional community of users, where the environment is being imagined at the same time as the language is being constructed, and such invented languages are more often acts of individual creativity. This book is about these languages that have been created for an imagined, fictional or as-yet-non-existent community of speakers, writers, or thinkers. Fictional languages might be created for an imagined fictional world, as part of the texture of a narrative, for a variety of functions, or even just as art for art's sake. Many creators of fictional languages are motivated by the process as an intellectual game, or simply as an enjoyable pastime.

In this book, we consider many different imagined languages, and explore their varied motivations, functions, and effects. We wanted to explore the creative process of language invention, and consider the nature of the imagined language, and also explore the readerly effects when a fictional language is experienced as part of the immersion into an imagined world. For these reasons, we collected together people who are actual practitioners in language construction, as well as scholarly thinkers on language, and academic researchers of linguistics and style in fiction. We began by bringing this diverse group to a symposium at the University of Nottingham in the spring of 2022, in a hybrid digital and on-campus event that allowed us a global reach of participants. We then invited all the contributors to assemble their thoughts as chapters for this book.

As a result, what you have in front of you is a book that is rather unique. It brings together researchers and practitioners from different backgrounds and disciplines; consequently, there are a range of methodological approaches in evidence. In the following chapters, you will also find a variety of writing styles and registers, from the scholarly to the less formal, encompassing personal opinion, quantitative empirical methods, stylistic analysis, theoretical explorations of concepts in language, and sociolinguistic and linguistic description. The chapters represent the end product of a process of dialogue between all of these different approaches. Of course, what unifies them all is an intense interest in language, linguistics, fiction, creation, and reading literary worlds.

Although the idea of inventing a language for a work of fiction may seem exceedingly unusual, fictional languages have been a common feature of literary worlds since Aristophanes' comedy *The Acharnian*, from 425 BCE. 'I artemane Xarxas apiaona satra', the opening line from the King of Persia's minister, Pseudartabas, apparently consists of a fake language designed to mimic Persian, with the use of a satirical namecraft, as the prefix *pseudo* implies. The play, set in the Peloponnesian War, satirises war and warmongers and uses the fake language to engender a comic effect (Conley and Cain 2006: 1). Aristophanes recognised the utility of *glossopoesis* (language invention) to give his audience both a representation of foreignness and a non-obvious subtext. So much so that he turned to the same technique sometime later in his other comedies, *The Birds* and *The Frogs*, respectively featuring a bird language and a frog language (see Wahlgren 2021: 15).

After that, sometime in the 1200s, Hildegard von Bingen's *Lingua Ignota* made the second major contribution to the phenomenon. Profoundly sensitive to music and phonaesthetics, the German abbess coined a series of unknown words (such as 'Aigonz' *God*, and 'sunchzil' *shoemaker*) allegedly according to a specific kind of religious-aesthetic effect to use in her poetry and music (Higley 2007: 63, Peterson 2015: 7). Other inventions by influential creators include Dante Alighieri's *De Vulgari Eloquentia* (around 1305), Ramon Llull's *Ars Magna* (in the early 1300s) and Jakob Böhme's *Natursprache* (1623) (see Eco 1997). These linguistic projects sought what their inventors imagined to be the original human language.

Introduction

In the period following these experiments, numerous other language creators devised their own projects, at times involving an aesthetic sense again but also often aspiring to produce a useful common tongue across the world's languages. Such a *lingua franca* existed naturalistically in the Latin across the Roman Empire, or in the original 'lingua franca' (literally the language of the Franks – the whole of Western Europe) Sabir, which was a common blend of the Romance languages used for trade between the eleventh and eighteenth centuries. Creating a functional language without the irregular historical baggage of empires or the limitations merely of trade or commerce became an attractive intellectual enterprise. The idea captivated such illustrious thinkers as Descartes, who invented unique signs for the communication of those with impaired speaking and hearing, and Leibniz, who created a universal language to express metaphysical, mathematical, and scientific concepts. From the original tongue spoken by Adam and Eve in the garden of Eden to Dalgarno's and Wilkins' philosophical languages that intended to epitomise the truth and essence of things, the sixteenth and seventeenth centuries were marked by the search for a perfect language due to profound religious tensions (see Eco 1997: 228).

In the seventeenth century, England saw the rise of rationalist thinking, which contributed to an increase in ideas such as Francis Bacon's 'characters reall'. Derived from his understanding of Chinese writing, this semiotic writing system was expected to be understood by anyone regardless of the language (see Large 1985: 5). This aspiration became widely popular towards the end of the nineteenth century, as enthusiasts of the 'International Auxiliary Language' movement began to engage in the effort to conceive a neutral means of global communication. Many offered their visions of what a *lingua franca* should look and be like. Instances include Volapük, Ido, Novial, and the most disseminated of all, Zamenhof's Esperanto.

As can be observed, language invention has generally taken one of three paths: as an art form in its own right, as a functional International Auxiliary Language, or as a literary phenomenon. While the former two have occupied people from all walks of life, intellectuals, linguists, and enthusiasts, writers have particularly deployed linguistic invention as a multipurpose narrative device. In literature, as the other components of fictional worlds, these invented languages have come to be known as fictional languages, which is our focus in this volume.

Today, Tolkien's Elvish languages, Quenya and Sindarin, are probably the most famous examples of fictional languages. These languages, beautifully intertwined with such stories as *The Silmarillion* (1977), *The Hobbit* (1937), and *The Lord of the Rings* (1954–5) trilogy, have resonated so strongly with fans that the languages gained status as artworks independently of the books. Middle-earth, the literary world created by Tolkien, however, hosts several other such languages, including Rohirric, Adûnaic, Khuzdul, and many others. Rooted in the idea that 'language is so integral to culture that a linguist can reconstruct a culture from its language', Tolkien created entire language families as a characterising device to bequeath depth to his fictional people and places (Noel 1974: 3). In science fiction, perhaps Klingon is the most well-known example, a characterising device to elaborate on the eponymous alien race from the *Star Trek* franchise. Klingon phonetics, spelling, and grammar were created to foreground the otherworldly features of its speakers (Okrand et al. 2011).

Nonetheless, many literary texts written in modern English have featured fictional languages ever since Thomas More's *Utopia* (1516). In that narrative, the Utopian language gives a semblance of authenticity and foreignness while having a thematic function in that it tends to negate the information conveyed by Hythloday, an unreliable narrator. In fact, the country's very name suggests it does not exist, for Utopia literally means not only 'good place' but also 'no place' (Noletto and Lopes 2019: 5).

Since More, many other writers have repeatedly deployed fictional languages as a multiuse stylistic device. A narrative framework known as *Reiseroman*, or the traveller's tale, showed particular patterns in invented languages from the 1600s to 1900s. Notable examples include Jonathan Swift's *Gulliver's Travels* (1726) and Edgar Allan Poe's *The Narrative of Arthur Gordon Pym of Nantucket* (1838). While the former employed many fictional languages as a disguised vehicle for its satirical message, the latter used a made-up language full of reduplications, diphthongs, and other types of phonetic stereotypes to create an atmosphere of exoticism and obscurity. These fictional languages and the mysteries embedded in them continue to interest readers and scholars even today.

More recent writers are also known for heavily relying on fictional languages for stylistic purposes. Hardly anyone would fail to recognise names such as Newspeak and Nadsat. These fictional languages, featured respectively in *Nineteen Eighty-Four* (1949) by George Orwell and *A Clockwork Orange* (1962) by Anthony Burgess, open a unique window into their narratives, reaching the reader at levels impossible for orthodox prose (Stockwell 2006: 8). Lesser-known texts have experimented with narrative, combining fluid prose and fictional dialects or idiolects of English in innovative ways that engender impressionistic effects via thematised language. Russell Hoban's *Riddley Walker* (1980) and Iain M. Banks' *Feersum Endjinn* (1994) are good examples. All these languages are anchored in the controversial belief that language can shape thought deterministically, a notion known as the Sapir-Whorf hypothesis (Sapir 1949, Whorf 1957).

In recent years, perhaps driven by the success of Tolkien's languages in movie adaptations, filmmakers have also developed a popular taste for fictional languages. This interest has extended to the world of TV series, which continue to deploy glossopoesis as a world-building tool, specifically now with the boom in online streaming platforms. However, adapting fictional languages for the big screen or television generally needs to meet new requirements. Most obviously, a detailed phonetics is more important compared with a language on the page, as now these languages would have to be pronounced by actors rather than just articulated by a reader. TV and cinema have also developed inventive writing systems as part of the set and props of the imagined world, in order to provide a stronger sense of alterity that might appeal to wider audiences. It is this scenario that has given birth to the figure of the professional *conlanger*, a practitioner (a trained or amateur linguist) whose job consists of inventing or adapting fictional languages for use in films and TV shows. Besides the previously mentioned languages of *The Lord of the Rings* (2001–3) filmic trilogy and Klingon from the *Star Trek* universe, Na'vi from *Avatar* (2009), Dothraki from *Game of Thrones* (2011–19), Heptapod B from *Arrival* (2016), Fremen and others from *Dune* (2021), and Khandaq'i from *Black Adam* (2022) form a very long list of major works featuring one or many fictional languages. Several of these are considered in this book, including from the perspective of their creators.

It is clear that, today, there is a very large community of people interested in the history, nature, functions, analysis, aesthetics, and creation of newly invented languages. This last group includes writers of fiction and screenplays, practising scholars and researchers, professional and semi-professional language creators, and hobbyists across a wide range of expertise and commitment: these are 'conlangers', and their creations are *conlangs* (constructed languages). The invention of fictional languages is also called *glossopoesis*. There are several related terms which further specify the nature and setting of the conlang. For example, an *auxlang* is an auxiliary language, created for a specific and often limited function, like Seaspeak, aviation English or PoliceSpeak – all used for clear communication between mariners, flight crew and ground staff, and border officials between Britain and France. Such auxlangs are fixed and curated by official bodies, so can be regarded as controlled natural languages (CNLs). Other auxlangs were created to have a full-spectrum function as if they were natural languages: these International Auxiliary Languages (IALs, as mentioned above) include Esperanto, Volapük, Interlingua, and several others. IALs like this often had a political and idealistic origin in aiming to enable global communication without privileging any single colonial language (to variable degrees of success).

Newly invented conlangs of all types can be more or less derivative of existing natural languages. Where there is an obvious derivation or borrowing from existing forms, the conlang is said to be *a posteriori* – created after the fact of the natural source language. This might be a simple matter of borrowing existing words or syntactic rules of grammar from a natural language and tweaking them a bit to create the conlang. Alternatively, an essentially new conlang can be created with its own vocabulary, grammatical patterns and pragmatic principles: such a conlang would be termed an *a priori* language – created from first principles. In practice, of course, the distinction is not entirely exclusive, and the definition of *a priori* and *a posteriori* conlangs can be made just in terms of whether individual words are borrowed or not, or more particularly on the basis of whether the grammar and first principles are radically new.

Other specifications of conlangs include *altlang* (a language arising from the imagined effects of an alternate history), *loglan* (a language that is entirely logical, systematic, and with no irregularities), and *artlang* (a language created for the purpose of enriching a fictional constructed world – or *conworld*). This book mainly focuses on artlangs as invented fictional languages.

Functions of invented languages

Different notions of the narrative or literary functions of glossopoesis have been proposed. For instance, in a talk given in the 1930s, later compiled and published posthumously, Tolkien outlined three directives that guided his creative process: sound and sense; sound and beauty; and language and environment. Tolkien firmly believed that some sounds are inherently more euphonic. Therefore, phonetically pleasing languages should be filled with such sounds and avoid others, a notion he termed 'phonetic predilection' (Tolkien 2016: 45). He also believed some phonemes are fitter to express specific ideas than others, a concept commonly termed phonetic or sound symbolism (Tolkien 2016: 63). Finally, for Tolkien, a fictional language should closely reflect the environment inhabited by the fictional people who speak it. This should be noticeable, for instance, in the descriptive lexicon available to a particular race of people.

For Stockwell (2006: 9), broadly speaking, fictional languages can have *elaborative*, *indexical*, and *emblematic* functions. First, glossopoesis can be applied to elaborate or further develop otherwise simpler narrative constituents, such as fictional places and characters. This also means fictional languages can themselves be explored as an index of alterity, creating a sense of otherness grounded in the readership's unfamiliarity with the foreign or alien language. Lastly, Stockwell maintained that fictional languages could serve as an emblematic medium to discuss thematically important concepts.

Revisiting Stockwell's typology, Cheyne (2008: 386) proposed that the fictional languages of science fiction are chiefly employed for characterisation, as emblems, as alien encounters or as a test for the Sapir-Whorf hypothesis. Like Stockwell, her model suggests that fictional languages can be deployed for character construction and to communicate otherness but chiefly as linguistic experiments that generally focus on the language relativity theory. Cheyne (2008: 403) argued that utterances in fictional languages are 'polyvalent, allowing authors to communicate with readers on multiple levels'.

Developing a third model, Noletto (2022: 26) has claimed that the fictional languages of science fiction can be *speculative*, *rhetorical*, *descriptive*, *diegetic*, or *paratextual*. Operating according to the stylistic features and interpretative cues common to the genre, these fictional languages can

Introduction

be viewed as the *novum* (the new concept or object) of the texts in which they appear, being thus responsible for the speculation and extrapolation expected of them (see Suvin 1979: 63). They can also be used for rhetorical purposes, that is, to help make narratives more convincing. Like Stockwell and Cheyne, Noletto also argued that glossopoesis can be used to elaborate or describe fictional places and characters by means of phonaesthetics or etymological semantics. Furthermore, Noletto argued that (as with the pattern originally created by Thomas More for *Utopia*) fictional languages can often be used to move the plot forward, interfacing theme and style. Finally, glossaries, maps, and primers frequently found in the appendices to novels can add critical information to narratives as paratexts, not written into the main body of prose but having a significant close impact on reading and interpretation (Noletto 2022: 177, and see Genette 1997: 327).

These typologies combine the descriptive account of the imagined languages with their aesthetic, experiential, and rhetorical effects on the reader. Despite being somewhat eclectic in terms of methodological approach, these models have largely drawn on stylistics and narrative theory. As 'the study of language patterns in texts and of the meaningful relationship between linguistic choice and literary interpretation' (Giovanelli and Harrison 2022: 381), an approach rooted in stylistics offers a particularly apposite methodological perspective on the creation, nature, and effect of fictional languages. Modern stylistics focuses primarily on the language of the text being studied but is also sensitive to context. Being essentially interdisciplinary in nature, stylistics also draws broadly on those areas of linguistics that encompass matters of pragmatics, narrative theory, cognition, literary criticism, and, of course, general linguistics.

Stylistics is well-represented in this book. However, we have also drawn in other traditions that can be found at the interface of language and literature: here you will find research adopting an empirical exploration of language attitudes and effects, work from an historical linguistics and onomastic perspective, studies drawing on sociolinguistics and language variation, as well as literary criticism. Our practising contributors also offer an insight into their thinking and method as they seek to create new constructed languages (*conlangs*).

The range of the book

We divide the book into two parts. The first part, on Design, collects those contributions that deal largely with the creative design, craft, and technique of fictional languages; the second part, Interpretation, deals largely with the reading, interpretation, analysis, and effects of imagined languages.

As scholars of linguistics and as professional conlangers, David J. Peterson and Jessie Sams share in their chapter the experience of working with large Hollywood and TV productions. Peterson was commissioned to create the conlangs Dothraki and High Valyrian for the series *Game of Thrones*, among many other fictional cinematic languages; Sams has similarly worked on several conlangs for TV shows such as *Motherland: Fort Salem*, *Vampire Academy*, and *Dune*. Besides describing their creative process, Peterson and Sams also account for the narrative function of their conlangs and how a fictional language can evolve during the early stages of a televisual production.

Further insights into the inner workings of the creative process are presented by the practising conlangers Benjamin Johnson, Anthony Gutierrez, and Nicolás Matias Campi. They discuss the step-by-step concerns of working as professional conlangers, creating a language for someone else's project; and they discuss the ways in which a conlang can drive readerly engagement in a fictional world. Theirs is a practical and professional perspective on the degree of technicality and complexity that would be sufficiently satisfying while still not overly burdensome for a reader. Starting with fundamental concerns, Johnson, Gutierrez, and Campi share their experiences on how they have worked on a range of conlangs to ensure a fictional language fulfils its aesthetic aims within practical constraints.

In Harry Cook's chapter, the author observes how a sociolinguistic sense of languages would lead an informed reader to expect irregular variation as a result of historical change in the fictionalised timeline of an imagined world. He suggests that an effective way of creating this rich sense of naturalistic texture is to imagine dialects of the fictional language. As a practising conlanger himself, Cook presents the depth of knowledge and creative innovation that might be required for the creation of a set of imagined dialects.

Moving on to writing systems and space opera cinema, Victor Fernandes Andrade and Sebastião Alves Teixeira Lopes produce a typographical analysis of the aesthetics of filmic *conscripts* (constructed scripts). With a corpus covering films including *Dune* and *Star Wars*, the chapter draws on the notion of Orientalism to discuss the strategy behind representations of alterity and exoticism through fictional alien languages in cinema. The chapter shows how filmic conscripts often emulate natural Asian writing systems to carry out their exotifying function, presupposed upon an assumed Western, non-Asian audience. As a result, Andrade and Lopes argue that this audience-oriented schema is rooted exclusively in Western views of 'the other', which in themselves can be ethically problematic.

As we can see from these initial chapters, in recent years the success of cinematic realisations of imagined, science fictional, and fantasy settings has led to an explosion of dystopian fantasy worlds in movies and TV series. Perhaps these have become especially prominent following the worldwide success of the cinematic adaptations of the works of J. R. R. Tolkien – one of the foremost inventors of fictional languages. In her chapter, Bettina Beinhoff explores the relation between the stated authorial design aims and the audience's actual perception of fictional languages. She asks whether Tolkien's Elvish languages really do sound pleasant and attractive, as apparently intended, and contrasts them with the language Na'vi, created for the

2009 movie *Avatar*. Using sound recordings in Quenya, Sindarin, and Na'vi and the responses of British English-speaking participants, Beinhoff discovers a strong sense of the phonaesthetics of what sounds pleasant, and also what conjures a sense of strangeness and the exotic.

The empirical method in linguistic exploration is further represented by Christine Mooshammer, Dominique Bobeck, Henrik Hornecker, Kierán Meinhardt, Olga Olina, Marie Christin Walch, and Qiang Xia with an extensive study of a set of fictional languages, in their chapter picking up the thread of phonaesthetics developed earlier by Beinhoff. Investigating the notions of euphony and cacophony, the authors designed a rating experiment among speakers of English and German to find out how different audiences perceive certain sound combinations conventionalised as aesthetically pleasant in the semiotics of glossopoesis. Significant parallels and differences were discovered across the set of fifteen literary and filmic fictional languages. This chapter sets out the design features of many fictional languages, but also of course serves as a bridge into a consideration of their analytical significance.

The second half of the book presents analytical and interpretative aspects of fictional languages. A key touchstone for anyone interested in conlangs is the invented languages of the fantasy writer, scholarly philologist, and conlanger J. R. R. Tolkien. In Chapter 8, James Tauber, the creator of the *Digital Tolkien Project*, explores the sources and meanings of several sets of fictional words in the universe of *The Lord of the Rings*. He notes the different uses of coined words, with a heavy focus on names for people and places, and he observes the extent to which a reader is partially trained to puzzle out the morphological rules of Tolkien's languages.

Katie Wales' chapter, 'Changing tastes', focuses on the interplay of context and fictional language reading, using Charles Dickens' *Holiday Romance* (1868) as a case study. Situating examples of 'cannibalese' in its original historical readerly setting and comparing the social attitudes with our own contemporary moment of reading, Wales argues for a historicised sensitivity in both reading and analysis. As she explains, reading fictional languages requires attention to intertextual relations with other types of texts and cultural or literary schemata, as well as the context of their readerly reception. Providing plenty of language samples and exploring the characters' speech patterns, Wales demonstrates how much literary glossopoesis seems to rely on referentiality to convey information beyond what is apparent on the surface level of a narrative.

Taking a different angle on dialectal innovation from Cook earlier, Israel Noletto draws on stylistics as a type of hermeneutics, in his chapter analysing Brian W. Aldiss' (1973) short story 'A spot of Konfrontation'. Aldiss devised SpEEC, a fictional dialectal extrapolation of English portrayed in the narrative as an International Auxiliary Language promoted by the European Economic Community (EEC). Noletto explores the satire's symbolism based on the assumption that Aldiss deployed glossopoesis as an experimental device for mediating style and theme while also accounting for how SpEEC may impact readability and interpretation, particularly when the historical and ideological contexts are considered.

From the practical to the idealised, Jessica Norledge's chapter explores the language of Láadan, created by Suzette Haden Elgin for her *Native Tongue* trilogy (1984–94). Elgin conceived Láadan as a perception-based women's language that was to have an existence beyond the novels. Indeed, the novels were written to promote and dramatise the language, rather than the conlang simply being an ornamentation or single aspect of the fictional dystopian world. Comparing Láadan and Orwell's Newspeak, Norledge considers whether a specific women's language is theoretically plausible; she discusses the stylistic successes and failures of Láadan within the text and in the actual world; and she considers the nature of fictional language in the genre of dystopia itself.

Several chapters across the book note the prevalence of place and personal names as part of imaginary worlds, and in her chapter Rebecca Gregory argues for the importance of what she calls a *conomasticon*, a fictional naming system as part of a fictional language. She explores the representation of literary naming in historical, post-apocalyptic, and extraterrestrial societies, considering Sandra Newman's (2014) *The Country of Ice Cream Star*, Russell Hoban's (1980) *Riddley Walker*, James Meek's (2019) *To Calais, in Ordinary Time*, Paul Kingsnorth's (2015) *The Wake*, Ursula K. Le Guin's (1974) *The Dispossessed*, and Michel Faber's (2015) *The Book of Strange New Things*. The chapter examines how names can act as worldbuilding elements and contribute to authenticity in the representation of fictional worlds.

It is clear that aspects and forms of fictional languages are also used to encode the different sorts of worldviews that are presented in such fictions. In her chapter on Lapine, the language of the anthropomorphised rabbits from Richard Adams' novel *Watership Down* (1972), Kimberley Pager-McClymont draws on foregrounding theory, Conceptual Metaphor Theory and the notion of the visibility of metaphor, to show how the language represents a rabbit-perspective on their world. She explores how Adams' stylistic choices, specifically in Lapine's figures of speech and idioms, work together to provide readers with a coherent and holistic representation of the narrative and characters. Combining her case study findings, Pager-McClymont explains how the fictional language and other metaphors that convey the rabbits' communication can be viewed as instances of pathetic fallacy.

The final chapter in the book features Peter Stockwell considering the situation in which a fictional language is presented that is designed to represent the ineffable or inexpressible. Sometimes these conlangs are minimally represented, or merely gestured at rather than realised, so they are more like *nonlangs* in the sense that they do not have any inherent described properties. However, fictional languages that are half-imagined, or only indirectly articulated, or which are pointed at but unrealised all offer different stylistic access to the ineffable, apocalyptic, mystical, or transcendental that is often the characteristic of science fictional literature.

Readings of fictional languages

Reading is an interpretation, but it is also a form of design. Reading is an act of creation as well as response. Reading can be conceived as fundamental comprehension and also a complex act of integrating the fictional experience with your own notions about the world, your life and society, and the nature of your language and thought. The act of literary and linguistic creation is itself part of an initial process of authorly reading, during which the creator shapes and reshapes the text, all while keeping a sense of the ultimate reader in mind.

We mean to encompass all of these senses of 'reading' in the title of this collection. The contributors include creators of fictional languages, analysts of fictional languages, and users of fictional languages. Several of our contributors combine different roles and practices. Above all, though, we are all readers of fictional languages. Together, we have explored the multidimensional facets of reading by considering the creative processes involved in making decisions about these artful languages, by taking a range of approaches to the description, meaning, function, and significance of constructed languages, and by researching the readerly effects of engaging with imagined languages. We hope, collectively, to have arrived at a useful map of the landscape that will enable future explorers to read other fictional languages, and more readily immerse themselves in and understand and appreciate the worlds they express.

References

Adams, R. (1972) *Watership Down*. London: Rex Collings.
Aldiss, B. W. (1979) 'A spot of Konfrontation', in *New Arrivals, Old Encounters* [original 1973]. London: Jonathan Cape, pp. 73–90.
Aristophanes (2002) *Acharnians* [original 425 BCE] (ed. S. D. Olson). Oxford: Oxford University Press.
Arrival (2016) D. Villeneuve (director). Paramount Pictures.
Avatar (2009) J. Cameron (director). 20th Century Fox.
Banks, I. M. (1994) *Feersum Endjinn*. New York: Gateway.
Black Adam (2022) J. Collet-Serra (director). Warner Brothers.
Böhme, J. (2007) *Natursprache* [original 1623] (ed. F. Brandt). Berlin: Verlag
Burgess, A. (1962) *A Clockwork Orange*. London: William Heinemann.
Cheyne, R. (2008) 'Created Languages in science fiction', *Science Fiction Studies* 35 (5): 386–403.
Conley, T. and Cain, S. (2006) *Encyclopedia of Fictional and Fantastic Languages*. Westport: Greenwood Press.

Dante Alighieri (1996) *De Vulgari Eloquentia* [original 1305] (ed. S. Botterill). Cambridge: Cambridge University Press.
Dickens, C. (1868) *Holiday Romance*. London: Chapman and Hall.
Dune (2021) D. Villeneuve (director). Warner Brothers.
Eco, U. (1997) *The Search for the Perfect Language*. New York: Wiley.
Elgin, S. H. (1984) *Native Tongue*. New York: DAW Books.
Elgin, S. H. (1987) *The Judas Rose*. New York: Women's Press.
Elgin, S. H. (1994) *Earthsong*. New York: Feminist Press.
Faber, M. (2015) *The Book of Strange New Things*. Edinburgh: Canongate.
Game of Thrones (2011–19) D. Benioff (executive director). HBO Entertainment.
Genette, G. (1997) *Paratexts: Thresholds of Interpretation* (trans. J. E. Lewin). Cambridge: Cambridge University Press.
Giovanelli, M. and Harrison, C. (2022) *Cognitive Grammar in Stylistics*. London: Bloomsbury.
Higley, S. (2007) *Hildegard of Bingen's Unknown Language: An Edition, Translation and Discussion*. New York: Palgrave Macmillan.
Hoban, R. (1980) *Riddley Walker*. London: Jonathan Cape.
Kingsnorth, P. (2015) *The Wake*. London: Unbound.
Large, A. (1985) *The Artificial Language Movement*. Oxford: Blackwell.
Le Guin, U. K. (1974) *The Dispossessed: An Ambiguous Utopia*. New York: Avon.
Llull, R. (1985) *Ars Magna* [original 1305] (ed. A. Bonner). Princeton: Princeton University Press.
Meek, J. (2019) *To Calais, in Ordinary Time*. Edinburgh: Canongate.
More, T. (1516) *Utopia* [Latin original]. Leuven: Desiderius Erasmus.
Motherland: Fort Salem (2022) E. Lawrence (creator). Gary Sanchez Productions.
Newman, S. (2014) *The Country of Ice Cream Star*. London: Vintage.
Noel, R. S. (1974) *The Languages of Tolkien's Middle-Earth. A Complete Guide to All Fourteen of the Languages Tolkien Invented*. Boston: Houghton Mifflin Company.
Noletto, I. A. C. (2022) *Language Extrapolation. Glossopoesis in Science Fiction* (unpublished PhD thesis). Federal University of Piauí, Teresina.
Noletto, I. A. C. and Lopes, S. A. T. (2019) 'Glossopoesis in Thomas More's *Utopia*: beyond a representation of foreignness', *Semiotica* 230: 1–12.
Okrand, M., Adams, M., Hendriks-Hermans, J. and Kroon, S. (2011) '"Wild and whirling words": the invention and use of Klingon', in M. Adams (ed.) *From Elvish to Klingon – Exploring Invented Languages*. Oxford: Oxford University Press, pp. 111–34.
Orwell, G. (1949) *Nineteen-Eighty-Four*. London: Secker & Warburg.
Peterson, D. J. (2015) *The Art of Language Invention: From Horse-Lords to Dark Elves, the Words Behind World-Building*. New York: Penguin Books.
Poe, E. A. (1838) *The Narrative of Arthur Gordon Pym of Nantucket*. New York: Harper and Brothers.
Sapir, E. (1949) *The Selected Writings of Edward Sapir* (ed. D. G. Mandelbaum). Berkeley: University of California Press.
Stockwell, P. (2006) 'Invented language in literature', in K. Brown (ed.) *Encyclopedia of Language and Linguistics* (2nd edn). Oxford: Elsevier, pp. 3–10.
Suvin, D. (1979) *Metamorphoses of Science Fiction. On the Poetics and History of a Literary Genre*. New Haven: Yale University Press.
Swift, J. (1726) *Gulliver's Travels*. London: Benjamin Motte.
The Lord of the Rings (2001–3) P. Jackson (director). New Line Cinema.
Tolkien, J. R. R. (1937) *The Hobbit*. London: George Allen and Unwin.

Tolkien, J. R. R. (1954–5) *The Lord of the Rings*. London: George Allen and Unwin.
Tolkien, J. R. R. (1977) *The Silmarillion*. London: George Allen and Unwin.
Tolkien, J. R. R. (2016) *A Secret Vice* (eds D. Fimi and A. Higgins). London: HarperCollins.
Vampire Academy (2021) J. Plec and M. MacIntyre (creators). Universal Television.
Wahlgren, Y. (2021) *The Universal Translator: Everything You Need To Know About 139 Languages That Don't Really Exist*. Cheltenham: History Press.
Whorf, B. L. (1957) *Language, Thought, and Reality: Selected Writings of Benjamin Lee Whorf* (ed. J. B. Carroll). Cambridge: MIT Technology Press.

Part I
Design

CHAPTER 2

Conlanging with non-conlangers: the art of language invention in television and media

David J. Peterson and Jessie Sams

In this opening chapter, David Peterson and Jessie Sams present a personal account of language creation as inspired by their work as professional conlangers. Drawing upon their experiences of working for Hollywood and international streaming services such as Netflix and HBO, Peterson and Sams uncover the art of language invention in television and media. Offering behind-the-scenes insights into the creative process from the moment of hiring through to on-set interaction, they consider the role and position of the professional conlanger in multimedia production, offering invaluable guidance and advice for the aspiring fictional language creator.

Since its inception, language creation has largely been a solitary endeavour. Though language itself, as humans use it, relies crucially on a community of users, a created language struggles to find any kind of community of users – if, indeed, such a community is even sought. For the most part, humans are content to have language on hand as a tool – a necessary evil for the functioning of human society, and nothing to make a fuss over. This is likely due to the steep learning curve faced by the learner of any language, natural or otherwise. The sheer volume of memorisation, leaving grammar aside, is something that can't be mastered in a day, or even a month. Whatever benefits a new language may offer, learning one requires a serious investment of time and effort and is an enterprise undertaken neither lightly nor frivolously.

The very nature of Hollywood is at odds with the usual process of language construction. There has been no serious study on the matter (and we doubt whether such a study could be undertaken), but, from experience, it takes a good six to twelve months to take a conlang from its infancy to some semi-stable state with a decent-sized vocabulary. Taking all the projects of both authors into consideration, the average amount of time a professional conlanger receives before major translations are demanded is about a month and a half. To put it directly: a professional conlanger rarely, if ever, receives adequate time to create a language capable of handling serious translation. This doesn't take concerns of quality into account. Language creation is an art, and high-quality art often requires greater time and care than art which is merely sufficient.

Complicating matters further is the fact that working on a multimedia production makes one a *de facto* collaborator in an environment where there exists a clear and strict hierarchy. Collaborating with another conlanger is difficult enough, but directors, script writers, set designers, cinematographers, producers – these are not conlangers. The professional conlanger often finds themself in a bizarre position: they have been hired to create a language by those who do not understand what's involved in such a process, and know very little about language, yet the specific individual(s) who hired them will undoubtedly know more about it than the rest of the crew. In our experiences, a professional conlanger is treated most often with either indifference or outright annoyance. A script writer may be annoyed by a comment from the location scout that the scene they wanted to take place on the castle balcony at dawn won't work, because the castle is facing the wrong direction and the whole thing will be covered in shadow, but at least they will understand what a location scout is, and they will appreciate their role on the film. A script writer often won't have heard of language creation and will have no sympathy for someone whose role they don't understand commenting that the line of dialogue they want to be cut mid-word won't work in translation because the verb in the conlang comes at the end of the sentence and won't have been uttered yet if cut off after three words.

Despite the drawbacks, language creation in Hollywood appears to be here to stay, as the number of professional conlanging jobs has steadily increased since *Avatar* hit the big screen in late 2009. Though there are still only a handful of conlangers who have gotten the opportunity to create a language for big or small screen productions, that number, too, has steadily increased and will likely increase in the future as knowledge of language creation spreads. However, Hollywood likes to stick with the names it already knows and nepotism is as strong as ever, so if a director or writer knows what language creation is and happens to know a friend, child, or nephew of theirs does it, that can often be enough to launch a new career. Yet, it's useful to consider where we are at, in terms of language creation in Hollywood, and where we might go. After all, it's better to be a language creator working in Hollywood right now than it was in 1984, but there is a lot of room for improvement. And so we have devised some questions for a would-be professional language creator to consider as they look towards a potential career working in the entertainment industry.

How do I get in?

It is not without regret and a bit of embarrassment that we admit there is absolutely no definite way to become a professional language creator. It's been more than a decade since the Language Creation Society (LCS) put together a competition to decide who would create the Dothraki language for HBO's *Game of Thrones*, yet that still stands as the most visible and democratic method of assigning a language creation job. At present, the best advice remains for a conlanger to be alive at the time of a potential job and hope they are contacted directly by someone connected to the production.

In 2012, David Peterson (one of the authors) created the LCS Jobs Board as president of the LCS. The hope was that major productions would learn about the Jobs Board and come to think of it as a kind of guild portal – a place for hiring a high-quality language creator without having a particular one in mind. Though the Jobs Board still exists, it is completely unknown in the entertainment industry. It has gotten a number of conlangers jobs – particularly in print media – but none as large as *Game of Thrones*. There are a number of reasons the Jobs Board has not been as successful as its creator would have hoped, but that lies beyond the scope of this chapter.

To date, the most successful method of obtaining a job as a language creator in Hollywood has been as follows:

- Have a previous high-profile job with, perhaps, some press, so that one's name is actually known.
- Have a personal connection to one of the producers and/or the show runner of a television show, or the producers or the director of a film.
- Have a website claiming some tenuous connection to language creation and have someone involved with the production find it by Googling.
- Work at a university as a linguistics professor and have someone working in production email you or your department asking if anyone there can create a language.
- Be the subject of a news story where one demonstrates some familiarity with an established created language like Klingon or Na'vi.
- Already be working on the production in some other capacity (for example as an actor or writer) and be able to claim some tenuous connection to anything having to do with linguistics, language creation, or language in general.
- Know a language creator who has had a high-profile job, demonstrate your worth to that language creator, and have them pass a job to you directly.

The same advice one might give a teenager asking the question, 'How do I get famous?' would generally serve in this instance. It would behoove a would-be professional conlanger to continue creating languages and follow advice from those instructing would-be influencers on how to create a personal brand and market themselves.

We suggest two potential futures for creating a path to professional conlanging. The first involves establishing a studio. Just as Walt Disney Studios, rather than Walt Disney himself, is responsible for films like *Sleeping Beauty* and *Cinderella*, so might a conlang studio with a number of conlangers involved in the process be responsible for future professional conlangs. Provided the conlangers work well together (a difficult, though achievable task), a team could produce higher-quality work faster than an individual. While conlangs are often personal statements, just like paintings or novels, they don't have to be. Just like films, television shows, or video games, they can be a single artist's vision that is carried out by many different artisans. A conlang studio like this would have the added advantage of immediate familiarity in the entertainment industry. Productions are used to working with art studios, special effects studios, and virtual effects studios. It would be no stranger for them to hire a conlang studio than a conlanger. And that conlang studio would then become an employer – a persistent entity with the ability to offer conlangers steady work. For such a studio to be financially viable, it has to be fairly small or has to take the majority of the jobs because, no matter how many films or shows are in production, only a tiny percentage require a conlang.

A second potential future lies in certification. For instance, some entity, whether it be a non-profit organisation like the LCS or a for-profit entity with a bigger presence in Hollywood, could create a certification process that ensures those who have achieved a certain level are a high enough quality conlanger to handle any industry job. At present, there is no such process, and Hollywood generally asks for no qualifications (or, when they do, the qualifications they seek are often irrelevant, e.g., having a tiny bit of familiarity with more than four languages or having heard of Klingon). The presence of such a process, though, could signal to producers that they wouldn't have to do any work on their part to assess qualifications of an individual: that would be done for them. Eventually, it could become a *de facto* prerequisite for any professional work. At that point, the certification would become a form of advertisement for one's services. One needn't try to market oneself, nor have a presence on whatever social media platform is hot: it would suffice to give one's name, location, email, and certification.

The description above doesn't paint the current situation as very rosy, yet it is as accurate as we can make it. This is where we're at right now. Perhaps we can work together to make it better.

What constraints are there on language creation?

Though there are constraints that curtail some of a conlanger's artistic freedom while creating a language on a production, those constraints are, for the most part, limited to the creation process itself, and are settled before production begins. To go into detail, we will separate *a priori* and *a posteriori* conlangs. Though many of the constraints are common to both, the differences are important enough to merit separate discussions.

The terms *a priori* and *a posteriori*, as they apply to conlanging, are different from their usages in other arts and sciences. An *a priori* conlang is one where the vast majority of the grammatical structures and vocabulary have been decided upon or created by the author. An *a posteriori* conlang is one where the grammar and vocabulary have been inherited from one or more languages. For example, if a conlanger decided to create a brand-new Romance language by applying different sound changes to Latin, as with Andrew Smith's Brithenig or Jan van Steenbergen's Wenedyk, then it shouldn't be a surprise if all or nearly all of the vocabulary is derived from Latin – indeed, one would be quite surprised to find otherwise. Similarly, if one wants to create a brand-new language, it wouldn't be surprising to find that *tloffek* is the word for 'book'. It would be rather surprising if the word for 'book' were *libre*, on the other hand, as it looks rather a lot like Latin *liber*. Perhaps one coincidence could be brushed aside, but if the bulk of the vocabulary 'coincidentally' looks very similar to another language, it's hard to argue that it's anything other than either an *a posteriori* language, or, more likely, a sloppy *a priori* language. The source of vocabulary and grammar is quite crucial when it comes to an entertainment franchise employing a conlang, as it often depends on whether the work is being adapted from another source or created from scratch.

In many ways, it's easier to create an *a priori* conlang for a television show or film. There is little in terms of expectation, either from the production team or the future fanbase, and the conlanger is free to do what they wish. It does, however, mean the conlanger will possess less authority over how their conlang is used on screen. This might seem paradoxical to an outsider – if the conlanger creates every aspect of a language, how could they not be the ultimate authority? In practice, what this means is that if the actors make mistakes, or the conlanger's wishes aren't honoured, the conlanger will be pressured to accept whatever made it on screen. After all, it will be what everyone in the world has seen on TV or in the movie theatre versus what the conlanger is saying is accurate. This is a battle a conlanger generally does not win, and the production knows that.

In terms of sound, with regard to a spoken language, the most common request we receive is that the language be 'exotic', either melodious or aggressive, depending on the character of the speakers, and extraordinarily easy for the all-English-speaking cast to pronounce. These mandates are rather nebulous in nature and quite often at odds with one another. It's doubtful that there could be a language that sounds 'exotic' to an English speaker that would be easy for a monolingual English speaker to pronounce, yet this is often precisely what we're called on to do.

We have the most success in creating a phonology that features a minimal number of sounds that are foreign to English speakers married with a phonotactic structure that diverges sharply from English. Below, for example, is the set of sounds used in Méníshè, the language of the witches of Freeform's *Motherland: Fort Salem*, presented in the International Phonetic Alphabet (IPA):

Stops: p/b, t/d/t', k/g/k', ʔ
Affricates: tʃ/dʒ/tʃ'
Fricatives: f/v, s/z, ʃ/ʒ, x/ɣ, h
Approximants: ɾ/l
Glides: w, j
Nasals: m, n, ɲ, ŋ
Vowels: i/iː, e/eː, a/aː, o/oː, u/uː

With the set above, the ejectives were something the American/Canadian cast hadn't worked with before. They would have heard [x] and maybe [ɣ] in second language study (both occur, in some form, in French and Spanish), and would be somewhat familiar, and the phonotactics are such that neither [ŋ] nor [ɲ] ever begins a word. As a result, there were really two sets of 'challenge' sounds – the ejectives and the velar fricatives – and our expectations were that these sounds would be done nearly right a lot of the time, and if they weren't, they would be replaced by nearby sounds that were 'close' (for example, non-ejective versions of the ejective consonants, and perhaps [h] or [g] or [k] for the velar fricatives). In general, this is the best a professional conlanger can hope for: a pronunciation that's close enough most of the time.

Beyond this, the biggest issue the professional conlanger faces is names. With an *a priori* language, chances are new characters will require new names which will likely be in the conlang. Writers tend to pay little attention to the phonotactic structure or phonetic inventory of a created language when generating names for characters they create, and are often hostile to critiques from the language's creator (to provide a hypothetical example, so as to protect the real individuals who have made similar requests, insisting that a character's name be 'Samantha' because their sister's name is 'Samantha', despite the fact that the language in question lacks [θ] and coda consonants). It is good practice for the conlanger working on the project to generate a large list of hypothetical names at the outset for writers to draw from. Provided the list is sought out and can be located at the appropriate time, there is a chance it might actually be used, as happened with the name of the Dothraki character Kovarro in HBO's *Game of Thrones*. Sometimes a production will be responsive to feedback from the conlanger, as happened with David Peterson working on Syfy's *Defiance*, but such instances are rare.

Creating an *a posteriori* language for an adaptation brings separate challenges that exist somewhat independently from the usual concerns that come with working on a major production. It is well documented that J. R. R. Tolkien created the bulk of his languages prior to publishing his *Lord of the Rings* trilogy. Where names don't match up with the language strictly, it was he who made the changes, so he, as both author and conlanger, is able to exert ultimate control, and the production simply has to turn to the author's own work to answer questions regarding pronunciation and nomenclature. The majority of science fiction and fantasy authors do not create full languages – or even partial ones – before creating the names and invented words used in their books. Focusing solely on the novel adaptations one or both of us have worked on, none of the ten authors below went about creating a full conlang, or even a well-documented conlang sketch. A list of these authors, along with the relevant works that were adapted, is given below:

- Leigh Bardugo (*Shadow and Bone, Siege and Storm, Ruin and Rising, Six of Crows, Crooked Kingdom*)
- L. Frank Baum (*The Wonderful Wizard of Oz, The Marvelous Land of Oz, Ozma of Oz*)
- Terry Brooks (*The Sword of Shannara, The Elfstones of Shannara, The Wishsong of Shannara*)
- Richelle Mead (*Vampire Academy, Frostbite, Shadow Kiss, Blood Promise, Spirit Bound, Last Sacrifice*)
- Frank Herbert (*Dune, Dune Messiah, Children of Dune*)
- George R. R. Martin (*A Game of Thrones, A Clash of Kings, A Storm of Swords, A Feast for Crows, A Dance of Dragons, Fire and Blood*)
- Kass Morgan (*The 100*)
- Matt Ruff (*Lovecraft Country*)
- Andrzej Sapkowski (*The Witcher, Sword of Destiny, The Last Wish, Blood of Elves, Time of Contempt, Baptism of Fire, The Tower of the Swallow, The Lady of the Lake, Season of Storms*)
- Brian K. Vaughan (*Paper Girls*)

Reviewing the list above, one might be surprised to learn there are no actual created languages in use in these works, though there are innumerable created languages referred to, complete with names, words, and full sentences – even the occasional discussion of grammar. All these can be found in one or more of the works above, yet all were created more or less off the cuff. There are a number of strategies modern authors use as they attempt to 'fake' the work that a conlanger does (to make it look like Tolkien without having to do the work of Tolkien, so to speak), and a study on the subject would prove entertaining. When push comes to shove, none of the work that was done is able to handle the kind of translation that is demanded by a television show or film that requires conlang dialogue.

A conlanger presented with the above often finds themselves in an unenviable position. If a work is being adapted, it often has a loyal and devoted fanbase, much of which has become quite attached to the gibberish and/ or language-adjacent elements present in the work. It's up to the conlanger to decide how to turn that material into a functioning language that isn't burdened by wildly unpredictable exceptions that happen to account for the work's most famous words and phrases and no others. The best scenario one can hope for is what David Peterson was presented with in adapting George R. R. Martin's *A Song of Ice and Fire* book series. Focusing on the Dothraki language, there were fifty-six words and names present in the first three books in the series, in addition to a couple of full sentences and a handful of nominal phrases. A conlanger in this position has a clear set of steps to follow to go from assorted book material to a full language. These steps are presented below, using Dothraki as an example:

Step 1: Collect all language material, including author notes, if present (though this material is usually non-existent). Arrange the material in list form, both as individual words and as phrases and sentences. This step resulted in the above-mentioned list of Dothraki material.

Step 2: Analyse the material phonologically. There is rarely a pronunciation guide for invented material in a book (and, when it is present, it is often less than helpful), so it is up to the conlanger to use their own skills and insight to determine how words ought to be pronounced. With Dothraki, David Peterson was guided by a few simple principles:

- First, he took into consideration that Martin is a monolingual speaker of American English, and furthermore, the audience he was writing for, at least initially, is primarily an English-speaking audience. This, he reasoned, would guide the author's choices in terms of romanisation, while also offering insight into how readers would pronounce what they read.
- Second, he took into consideration that the author knew he was representing a non-English language, which meant that the presence of non-English sounds was not off the table.
- Third, he elected to treat the author's spellings as sacrosanct, which meant that outside of non-controversial changes for the sake of consistency, if a word was spelled differently, it ought to be pronounced differently.

Practically, this guided Peterson's choices in a couple of key ways. For example, it was clear that orthographic *k* and *kh* represented different sounds (compare the city name *Vaes Dothrak* and the unrelated word *rakh*). Both Martin and American readers would accept that *kh* could represent a non-English sound, and so Peterson decided it would represent the sound [x]. Knowing the audience was English speakers led Peterson to treat *y* as [j] and j as [dʒ] – a choice which might have been quite different had the author and audience been speakers of German or Finnish. Following this line of thinking, though, Peterson elected to have *khaleesi* proncunced [ˈxa.le.e.si]. In this instance, the instincts of English speakers were too great, and the word was fairly consistently pronounced [kʰə.ˈli.si], even in Dothraki. No amount of contrary recordings or entreaties could persuade production to do anything different. In this instance, Peterson should have relented and respelled the word *khalisi*, which would have been a defensible compromise.

Step 3: Create the phonology. This involves figuring out which sounds are present in the language, based on the analysis done in Step 2, and which alternations are meaningful. It also involves figuring out where there might be gaps in the system, and determining if those gaps ought or ought not to be filled. It also involves determining what restrictions should be placed on syllables and segments in terms of their placement at the beginnings or ends of words. Finally, it involves detailing the stress or tone system, depending on which is present. With Dothraki, this resulted in a couple of specific choices:

- Leaning into Martin's unique initial clusters with *h*, resulting in consonant clusters like *hr* (from *hrakkar*), *rh* (from *rhan*), and *mh* (from *mhar*). These were extended to include other such clusters that logically could have existed, like *hl* and *nh*.
- Leaving out the vowel *u* [u] entirely. There is no evidence of the vowel, outside its use in *qu* clusters, which were respelled *kw* for the sake of consistency. This resulted in a four-vowel system of *a* [a], *e* [e], *i* [i], and *o* [o], which gave Dothraki a unique sound.
- Allowing for vowel hiatus. Martin's work features many instances of consecutive vowels, whether different (*vaes, shierak, ai*) or identical (*khaleen, khaleesi*). Peterson extended this to include any sequences of the original four vowels.
- The inclusion of geminate consonants. (Gemination uses doubled spelling to indicate a lengthened pronunciation.) Martin's original work allows for nearly any consonant to be geminated (*rhaggat, hrakkar, Jommo, hranna, Tolorro, jaqqa, Zollo*), so Peterson followed his example and made gemination a prominent feature of the language.

The stress system was Peterson's own invention but followed what he believed to be the natural stresses readers would have assigned to the words present.

Step 4: Analyse the phrases and sentences. Though phrases and sentences are separate entities, it pays to analyse them together, as phrase structure is often mirrored in sentence structure, and vice versa. This involves using whatever translations one can find, either directly in the text or implied, of the invented material in the work. At that point, it's simply a logic puzzle: If *a b c* means 'The dog is chasing a pigeon' and *d b* means 'The dog is sleeping', then the chances are that *b* means 'the dog', *a* means 'is chasing', *d* means 'is sleeping', *c* means 'a pigeon', and the word order is verb-subject-object. Provided there is enough material, it should be simple to figure out what the basic phrase structure is, and if there is any kind of inflection. Without going into too much detail, the main conclusions for Dothraki were as follows:

- There are two full sentences presented very near to each other in *A Game of Thrones*. The first is *Khalakka dothrae!* which is translated as 'The prince is riding!', and the second is *Khalakka dothrae mr'anha!* which is translated as 'A prince rides inside me!' In analysing material like this, Peterson elected to treat actual translations as completely faithful, to go with the simplest explanations rather than resort to convoluted explanations, and to keep with the spirit of the material. Based on those two sentences and their provided translations (plus the additional fact that *khal* is well established as the word for the leader of a Dothraki *khalasar*), Peterson determined that *khalakka* was 'prince', *dothrae* was 'rides', and *mr'anha* was 'inside me'. Furthermore, he determined that the language had no articles by the fact that *khalakka* is translated as 'a prince' and 'the prince'; the basic present or non-past tense lacked a progressive/non-progressive distinction; the basic word order was subject-verb-object; the language used prepositions, rather than postpositions; and the first-person pronoun was *anha*.
- The phrase *Rakh! Rakh! Rakh haj!* translated as 'A boy! A boy! A strong boy!' helped Peterson determine that adjectives followed the nouns they modified. Comparing this to other noun phrases yielded positive results, as city names like *Vaes Dothrak* and *Vaes Tolorro* likewise suggested a noun-adjective structure, as did more complex constructions like *khal rhae mhar* 'sore foot king'.
- A word like *khal* compared to *khalakka*, *khaleesi*, and *khaleen*, as well as the trio of words *dothrae*, *dothrak*, and *Dothraki* suggested the presence of suffixal inflection, so when further inflection was required, Peterson stuck with primarily suffixal inflection.

Step 5: Build the rest of the language. At this point, it's up to the conlanger to determine that they have successfully accounted for all the data, at which point they can fill in whatever gaps exist in the grammar, and continue building the language as they see fit, guided always by the original material.

Previously, it was mentioned that Martin's *Song of Ice and Fire* presented the best possible scenario for a conlanger. That's because the most important aspect of an adapted conlang is consistency. It is more important that a conlang be consistent than interesting. Martin's work with both Dothraki and Valyrian is entirely consistent. This isn't the case with a lot of other works – including the other works mentioned above. Where the author presents inconsistent material that ought to be consistent, the conlanger has three choices:

1. Decide on a consistent pattern and ignore the aberrant one.
2. Decide on a consistent pattern and treat the aberrant one as an exception.
3. Decide that the language is inconsistent and unworthy of serious explication.

Depending on the material present, one of the above solutions may seem more appropriate than the others. For example, in Leigh Bardugo's *Grisha* trilogy, there are two Ravkan language terms featuring *sol* 'sun' as a modifier: *Sol Koroleva* 'Sun Queen' and *Soldat Sol* 'Sun Soldiers'. There's no obvious reason why *sol* occurs before *koroleva* but after *soldat*. David Peterson happened to be personal friends with Bardugo and asked her about it. She said she didn't like the double *sol* sequence in *Sol Soldat*. For Peterson, this didn't seem like sufficient reason to displace the adjective, as such displacement wasn't supported by the rest of the material. Considering the options, Peterson felt it wouldn't be wise to ignore the switch, as both terms are well known in the series, and were both likely to be used on screen in the Netflix adaptation. Peterson also felt it didn't seem wise to treat all material as entirely inconsistent, as there were very few inexplicable inconsistencies throughout Bardugo's work. That left Peterson with the task of explaining the exception.

The solution here involved a lot of behind-the-scenes language building that ended up having far-reaching consequences for the Ravkan language as a whole. Peterson first decided that it was key that *sol* was, at base, a noun being used as a nominal modifier, rather than an adjective. In many languages, a genitive construction is often functionally equivalent to nominal modification – i.e. 'Sun Queen' and 'Queen of the Sun' or 'Sun Soldiers' and 'Soldiers of the Sun'. At this point, Peterson had already decided that the standard order of an adjective and noun would be adjective-noun. This meant that *Sol Koroleva* was already in the correct order, and its lack of adjective-noun agreement is explained by the fact that *sol* is a nominal, rather than adjectival, modifier (using English as an analogue, the term is Sun Queen not Solar Queen). This only left *Soldat Sol* in need of an explanation.

Here, Peterson leaned on the fact that Bardugo modelled the Ravkan language on Russian. Russian is a language with three grammatical genders: masculine, feminine, and neuter. Ravkan need not have any genders – or the same genders – but given Bardugo's inspiration, it wouldn't be odd if Ravkan did have the same three genders, and so Peterson retained them. Next came the construction. A basic possessive construction in Ravkan features a noun in the nominative followed by a noun in the partitive. Thus, 'Soldiers of the Sun' would be *soldat* 'soldiers' followed by *sol* 'sun' in the partitive. Gender membership is notoriously fickle, so *sol* 'sun' could very well be in any of the three genders, but their partitive singular forms helped decide the issue. Were *sol* masculine, the partitive singular would be *soli*; were it feminine, it would be *sola*; were it neuter, on the other hand, the partitive and nominative would be identical: *sol*. Thus, with minor grammatical support, both key terms could be preserved exactly as they appeared in the original text.

There are some works where the material is either so sparse or so inconsistent that it has to be abandoned almost entirely. For example, in Terry Brooks' *Shannara* series, there is little to tie together the various invented language bits. It's unclear if they come from a single language, and there's little to tie any of the terms together. Consequently, it made sense to Peterson to treat it as inconsistent, and only adapt the terms and names that fit with the language Peterson ended up building for the show *The Shannara Chronicles*.

Fortunately, outside of key terms and names and the overall sound of the language, a professional conlanger experiences few outside constraints on how they do what they do. That is, decisions about grammar and word shape are left entirely to the conlanger. Some studios have legal departments that may vet key terms to ensure they aren't close in sound to an offensive term in some natural language, but these are usually very large studios that are planning to release localised versions of the show or film in many different territories. In other words, unless the conlanger happens to be working on a Disney production, they're probably in the clear.

How is most of your time spent?

A professional conlanger spends the bulk of their time working on a television show or film in translation. Many conlangers think of the creation aspect of language creation as the important part, but on a major production all of that work is essentially background work – the work the production wants the conlanger to hurry up and finish so they can deliver the requisite translated dialogue.

As a direct consequence of the above, there is a hidden skill that is required of all professional conlangers: conlang fluency. For many conlangers (the authors of the present text definitely included), the joy of language creation and lexical expansion doesn't require actual fluency in the conlang itself. That is, the joy comes in creating new words, not memorising them. As a translator, though, the fewer times one has to reference the dictionary and grammar, the better. When designing a grammar, it might behoove the conlanger to create a grammar that fits their particular learning style, all else being equal. All languages will ultimately need to express any possible thought, but it pays for a language creator to reflect on what comes most easily to them. For example, is having a set number of cases with a wide variety of uses easier than remembering a list of adpositions and their specific uses? Is it easier to remember a large set of verb forms, or a large set of auxiliaries? The answers to these questions may surprise the conlanger, as it may in fact be different from the strategies employed by their own first language.

The next largest time commitment is recording. It's vital that every line of the series be recorded by someone who knows how the line is meant to be pronounced so that the actors can hear and repeat it. The way actors use the material they're given varies, but the majority of actors greatly appreciate being able to hear a line of a constructed language exactly as it's meant to be delivered. A conlanger's skill in pronouncing their own language effectively is often a selling point when it comes to future employment. If a conlanger's pronunciation is halting, inconsistent, and unclear, it won't inspire confidence in actors who have to deliver it while also doing everything else the scene requires of them (conveying emotion, performing a stunt, listening to and responding to other actors' performances, etc.).

In addition to this, there is a lot of office work that is likely common to any job: reading and responding to emails from various members of the production, and occasionally (often at the beginning of the season) phone or video conference meetings with production and, on occasion, actors. While they may not take up a lot of time, they are vital in building relationships with production staff and reinforcing the value of the hired conlanger.

What control do you have over performance?

A conlanger has almost no control at all over how their language will be pronounced on screen. There are a few key reasons for this, some of which have no solution, but some of which may, in future.

First, a production often employs one or more dialect coaches. A dialect coach is a person who helps an actor develop a particular accent or effectively pronounce a language that isn't their own. Dialect coaches rarely have any kind of qualifications for conlangs and are often handed the materials developed by a language creator and expected to help the actors pronounce this new language with which they have no experience. The results are usually uninspiring. In the experience of Peterson, there are few dialect coaches who are capable of pronouncing the languages accurately themselves, making it unsurprising that they aren't able to effectively teach actors to do it well. They are often satisfied with subpar performances, allowing actors to do something that, to their ear, is 'close enough.' rather than pronouncing it correctly. When there is a dialect coach on the production, the conlanger is rarely allowed access to any actor – and in fact, is rarely allowed access to the dialect coach. It's up to the conlanger to be satisfied that they've been paid to do work and accept that what they hear on screen will likely bear only a passing resemblance to the actual work they've done.

Second, with or without a dialect coach, the conlanger rarely gets access to the actors. When they do, it's rarely for enough time for adequate training, and almost never with the entire cast. On a television show, this is often a matter of course, as there will be an innumerable number of extras and day players who may have one or two lines, and may not actually be cast until the week of filming. Even on a film, production often won't go to the trouble of setting up coaching sessions between an actor and a conlanger unless the actor asks for it. And, of course, they don't go to the trouble of informing the actors that such a thing is even possible, so actors rarely ever ask. In our experience, asking to set up coaching sessions with the actors – even being on set while the actors are there – rarely yields successful results. This often comes down to cost: a language creator is seen as non-essential crew, and so the production won't foot the bill for their travel and lodging.

Third, even in situations where the actors are doing their best work and are working with the materials provided with full access to the conlanger on staff, and the conlangers have access to the 'dailies' (the instant, unedited footage) with the ability to give input on which takes were good and which weren't, conlang dialogue is still the lowest priority for the editor. The editor is the person who decides which takes end up on screen. Working on Syfy's *Defiance*, author David Peterson had all of the above. He gave feedback on dailies for every scene his dialogue was used in and had a direct line to all the main cast. Yet sometimes poor takes, with respect specifically to conlang dialogue, were the ones that made it to the screen. There were any number of reasons that this happened – for example, a boom mic was visible in the best conlang take; one actor was standing in front of another; there was a mistake in the English dialogue; one of the actors had a weird expression on their face; a candle wouldn't light; etc. In other words, when take one has great conlang dialogue but a mistake elsewhere, and take two has a mistake in the conlang dialogue but the rest is perfect, the editor without fail will choose take two. This can often be frustrating for the conlanger and the actor who made the mistake, because they'll know it was a mistake, and that might be the only take where they made that mistake. Ultimately every artisan involved in the production has to deal with this, though, so it comes with the territory of working on a major production with lots of moving parts.

As a final note, when actors struggle on the day of shooting, or if the director/producer isn't 'feeling' it, it is often in the power of the director to simply do all of the constructed language dialogue in English. Thus, a conlanger will have done all the work, and the actors will have tried their best, but despite all that, someone in a position of authority will decide to wash it all away. In fact, it may even go a step further, with all the conlang dialogue having been shot, when the editor decides to scrap the scenes, as happened with the Paramount film *Noah* from 2014.

Really, the only way for a conlanger to ensure that their dialogue comes off perfectly is to be the director, editor, and executive producer of the show or film. One day this may happen, but it hasn't happened yet.

Looking ahead

In some ways, working on a television show or film can be a frustrating experience for a conlanger. Many conlangers dream of their words being spoken on screen, so it can be devastating when they get that opportunity only to find that their words are spoken poorly, if at all. Even so, we see the present state as part of a greater trajectory. Films and television shows that feature a created language before *Avatar* number in the single digits. Now there are multiple shows and/or films every single year that feature one or more created languages. As the opportunities increase, industry familiarity with language creators will also increase, and just as the job is better now than it was in 2009, so shall the job in 2059 be even better than it is now, provided that conlangers with the opportunity to showcase their work continue to press for a greater role and better treatment whenever and wherever they're able to work.

CHAPTER 3

On the inner workings of language creation: using conlangs to drive reader engagement in fictional worlds

BenJamin Johnson, Anthony Gutierrez, and Nicolás Matías Campi

> In this chapter, Johnson, Gutierrez, and Campi share their personal experiences of language invention and design, considering what constitutes 'good conlanging' and offering their top tips for successful language creation. Drawing upon their collective experience as professional conlangers and commissioners, they discuss the intricacies of conlanging as a practice, presenting a detailed and unique insight into the pragmatic experience of language creation from the conlanger's side of the linguistic fence. Along the way, they consider the role conlangers play in shaping and defining readerly experience through language design, addressing the effects conlangs have on engagement and immersion.

Introduction

The language creator (*conlanger*) who creates languages (*conlangs*) for anything more than personal fulfilment has to strike several careful balances: good conlanging and good linguistics, being true to the language and the world it is being created for, and, perhaps most importantly, making it accessible to the casual reader who may not be interested in thumbing through a glossary in order to figure out what is going on in the novel they are trying to read. Conlanger and author must work together to leverage various alphabets, scripts, transliterations, orthographic conventions, and translations to maintain the balance between developing the richness and character a conlang provides and not distracting the reader with unnecessary technicalities. The presence of a conlang must add to the overall experience, not detract from it.

Why use a constructed language in writing?

The main reason for an author to consider using a constructed language is to add realism to a work of fiction. A large percentage of the world's fiction is written in English; still more in Spanish, German, and other common contemporary languages. Yet the characters in fiction, especially in science fiction and fantasy settings, are rarely representative of speakers of those language groups. Authors may use various shortcuts, like making reference to 'the Common Tongue' or 'Galactic Standard', which, more often than not, means English, though they may not say it overtly. For the discerning reader, however, this may not always be sufficient.

Ryan Long, of the Riddlesbrood Touring Theatre Company, describes his decision to use a constructed language, Brooding (curated by Benjamin Johnson: <linguifex.com/wiki/Brooding>) in Riddlesbrood's plays: 'Some people might say, well, why bother to use a constructed language in a show, and the reason is authenticity. And people, when they see a magical world, a world that doesn't exist, that they've never been to: it just bothers the mind to imagine that everybody speaks English!' (2015 interview with Ryan Long <vimeo.com/232731860>; bonus material from the movie *Conlanging, The Art Of Crafting Tongues* at <conlangingfilm.com>).

In addition to easing the suspension of disbelief that can be jarred by swallowing the assumption that everyone in the vast universe speaks English, a conlang can provide other cultural failsafes in a work of fiction. An author may be tempted to get around the 'English Problem' by choosing another existing language, but that could lead to a number of cultural missteps. Insisting that the great lovers speak French, or the great warlords speak Mongolian, or the characters from Some Really Cold Place speak Inuktitut could be controversial, offensive, or even ridiculous. Using a conlang provides a way to break out of this cultural minefield and create something truly unique for a fictional culture.

Conlangs are a way to enrich the material and world of a story, and only add to it if done properly. A constructed language itself can be great for world-building and has the capacity to intrigue the reader; however, if not handled correctly, a clumsily-wielded conlang can be a detriment to the overall experience. Inundating readers with words and terms with no means of divining their meanings from context alone causes confusion on the part of the reader and makes them focus on the wrong aspects of dialogue and the overall story. All of the most successful uses of conlangs in fantasy and sci-fi as part of their world-building and storytelling make the world feel alive and lived in. This sense of realism aids the reader's suspension of disbelief and can make them more engaged with the text.

What are the drawbacks of using a constructed language in fiction?

The main drawback of using a constructed language is that it is easy to go overboard. It can be difficult to gauge how much is too much. 'Less is more', as they say, but authors and conlangers alike can fall prey to the trap of thinking, 'If less is more, just think how much more "more" could be!' The ultimate goal in using a conlang should be to complement the work without detracting from it.

Statistically, maybe one reader in ten will want more information about a constructed language that appears in the fiction they are reading. Another one in ten will be annoyed at the very presence of a conlang, and there is not much that can be said to appease them. The rest will probably range from mild curiosity to indifference. An author may be tempted to include a lengthy appendix with pronunciation charts, verb tables, a dictionary, and any number of other guides to the technical aspects of the language – and, by all means, should be encouraged to do so! – but while that first reader should be able to seek out additional engagement with the language, 'additional engagement' should not be a requirement for appreciating the piece of writing as a whole.

In short: don't force your readers to learn your conlang.

Aside from blatant overuse, there are some other pitfalls to be avoided that we will be sharing later in this chapter, but before we get into the business of integrating a conlang into fiction without completely alienating that one aforementioned reader who doesn't like it, there are questions to be answered about whether an author needs a professional conlanger, where and how to locate one, and some of the more technical aspects of creating and using a conlang.

Working with a language creator

Is it necessary to hire a conlanger?

Many authors begin by attempting to create a conlang on their own, and some quite successfully. Some authors have become quite accomplished conlangers while creating language to include in their writing. Perhaps more common is the 'Tolkien model', in which conlangers, faced with indecision about what to do with their conlang once it has been created, turn to fiction and hope to write something compelling enough into which to incorporate their prized language!

However, the more technical aspects of linguistics and conlanging may not be your forté as an author. Many authors can feel so trapped by the pressure to create a conlang that captures the right aesthetic while holding up to scrutiny from readers that their writing can suffer or stagnate as a result.

We recommend that everyone try their hand at conlanging at some point, but don't be afraid to ask for help if the process is a hindrance or you feel that you are in over your head. If you do choose to work with a conlanger, you also need not start from scratch. You can work with them (and with the guidelines outlined later in this chapter) to preserve the work you have already done while taking care of the details that will help you bring the language to life on the page.

An author can certainly create a language on their own; however, to construct a fully-fledged language requires practice. Learning to create a language can take months if not years due to all the lingo and theory that one has to learn. Because of this, it is often best to hire a professional conlanger as it not only makes the process simpler, but they will likely have ideas or concerns about the language that the author may not have considered.

How to hire a conlanger

The easiest way to hire a conlanger is to discover that you have a friend who is a conlanger and enlist their services. As conlanging gains popularity as a hobby, many more people are trying their hand at it, and still more are becoming increasingly open about conlanging as a practice who may have previously been in 'the conlang closet'. However, be cautious when making use of the 'friend' model, and be sure that both of you take time to draft a strong, clear contract. All too often, friends and family members fall into the trap of thinking that a contract somehow suggests a lack of trust. Quite the opposite is true, however a contract ensures that all parties know exactly what is expected of them and eliminates any need for personal feelings to get involved.

If you do not know any conlangers, however, the best way to hire a skilled conlanger at present is to contact the Language Creation Society (LCS <jobs.conlang.org>), an organisation which hosts a Jobs Board to which member conlangers can apply. The LCS will work with you to create a job description that will detail your requirements in a way that will help you find the best match for your project.

Generally, job postings for conlangers will request language background and samples of a conlanger's work. How to judge those samples is very subjective; there are not many criteria for the layperson to judge a conlang, so ultimately it may just come down to which samples you find the most aesthetically pleasing or similar to the aesthetic you are looking for. But it is important to keep non-subjective factors in mind when choosing a conlanger to work with. For instance, you may or may not need a unique writing system for the language, which requires a very different set of skills than just creating a language, especially if you need a font, or vector graphics, or other technical work products that not all conlangers have the skills or the access to expensive software to create for you.

Are there benefits to hiring more than one conlanger?

You may wonder whether it is better to hire a single conlanger, or perhaps a team of linguists with complementary expertise. In almost all cases, a single conlanger is sufficient. Only in large world-building scenarios where you require several highly developed languages might it make sense to hire more than one conlanger. Even in those rare cases, it is best to start with one conlanger to be your main point of contact, and work with them to hire additional language artists as necessary.

When should a conlanger be brought into the writing process?

In order to get the most out of working with a language creator, it is best to bring a conlanger into the process as early as possible. Creating some names or a few words in advance might help a conlanger get a sense of the aesthetic that the author is trying to achieve, but creating too much in advance might unwittingly create constraints on the conlanger that will be difficult to get around later on.

Two of the very worst things an author can do before hiring a conlanger are:

1. Creating various lines of 'gibberish,' hoping that it can be back-formed into a conlang later; worse still if this gibberish is supposed to have a specific meaning!
2. Creating a unique alphabet based on the literal Latin alphabet – that is, the letters A to Z replaced by different symbols. This is fun for creating codes or ciphers, but it is not how writing systems work, and a conlanger will have a bad time accommodating these kinds of requests.

Both of these are very common situations, however; in fact, many authors get as far as inventing some gibberish and creating an alphabet long before they realise that they need the help of a professional but have already become invested in what they have created.

This may give a conlanger a bad time at first, but a skilled language creator might even find that these additional restrictions result in adding interesting nuances to a language that neither conlanger nor author would have conceived of otherwise.

Is a contract between author and conlanger necessary?

Absolutely! As mentioned earlier, a contract is not there because you do not trust each other; it is there so that everyone knows what to expect. That is true of all contracts, but particularly important in a situation like this where each party might have expertise or understanding about the subject matter that the other does not.

On the inner workings of language creation

There are myriad contract templates that can be downloaded from a number of sources, as generic or specific as you like. Most conlangers who have worked with other authors will have their own contract template ready to draft. The essential information a contract between author and conlanger must contain, however, is the following:

Confidentiality/non-disclosure
This is a section that lays out each party's expectations about what can be talked about and to whom. For example, the conlanger agrees not to tell anyone what the author is writing about before it gets published. This may or may not include talking about the language itself. The conlanger may want to carve out exceptions here, such as the right to use the conlang in portfolio samples.

Ownership/intellectual property
This spells out who owns the material generated in production of the language (e.g. dictionary, formal grammar, notes, and so on). Ownership of the actual language is a little more complicated, legally speaking (see the section on copyright, below), but ostensibly this outlines who 'owns' the language. Usually, ownership rests with the author, who is paying for the work, but a conlanger may want to retain some degree of control over the language, such as the right of first refusal to work with the author on future projects expanding the language.

Other useful inclusions
A conlanger may want to include a clause that requires that any work by the author credit them for the creation of the language.

An author may want a section that limits their obligation to include the conlang in their work; that is, even if the work is completed satisfactorily, they are not required to use it for the work in question and may change their mind about using the language at all.

Both parties often benefit from a section authorising collaboration between the conlanger and other contractors or vendors working with the author. For instance, this allows a conlanger to work with an artist or font creator to include the language in other work commissioned by the artist without violating the non-disclosure clause.

Scope of Work
The most essential part of the contract, however, should be the Scope of Work. This lays out exactly what the conlanger is required to do and exactly how much they are to be paid to do it. It may also spell out deadlines of when work products and payments are due, and any consequences for missing those deadlines. Both parties should pay particularly close attention to this section and make sure that everything you want to get out of this relationship is accounted for within it!

How much of an author's work should be shared with a conlanger?

Assuming you have a relatively comprehensive non-disclosure clause in your contract, there is no reason not to share the bulk of your story ideas and world-building with a conlanger. You never know what little details might give life to larger ideas that will enrich the language, or what details from the language may in turn enhance your storyline.

Maintaining a smooth author-conlanger collaboration

The most important factor is regular communication. In our own collaborations, the authors have found that it can be very helpful to arrange a weekly or bi-weekly short meeting to keep on the books. You do not have to actually meet every week, but at least you have to check in regularly to see whether you have anything to meet about. It may seem kind of redundant, but it is the best way to avoid getting into a bad situation where you are getting no feedback at all. It is actually fairly common that a conlanger will be faced with limited feedback, and that is okay – there are stages of language creation where there is not much to give feedback about. But it is good to build a mechanism into the system early where author comment can be requested. It would be terrible to complete months of work on a conlang only to be told that it is all wrong!

Building on another facet of communication, it is important for you to develop a common language to talk about your common language. Authors cannot be expected to know linguistics terminology, but you will need to be able to talk about various aspects of the language in a way that you both understand. Some authors may have unrealistic expectations about what can be done in a language, or even how the mechanisms of language work. Jamin was once asked to create 'a language that folds up so that it's impossible to tell lies'. These words mean nothing to a linguist, and he had to disappoint that author, who also wanted his language to be 'as round as possible'.

Conlanger and author should work together to determine exactly what is necessary for the language. Figure out what words you actually need created, not every word you may ever use. You can always create more later.

There are other areas where conlangers and authors alike can fall prey to misconceptions about conlangs. Recently there has been a very common belief that all conlangs need to be developed from a proto-language. This is certainly one tool of many that a conlanger can use to develop nuance in a conlang, but it is not always necessary, and more often than not it is probably the wrong direction to take the language, especially if all that is needed is a simple naming language or a basic grammar. There is also a persistent belief that all words need to be derived from some sort of elaborate metaphor, and this can be one of those 'dithering points' for personal conlangers who have the luxury of ruminating over individual words and phonemes over the course of years, but such luxury is rarely afforded to the conlanger creating a language for someone else. For instance, perhaps the word for 'hand' derived from a verb meaning 'to catch', and that in turn comes from a word for 'food' and that derives from the word for 'mouth'. While it is certainly possible, the word for 'hand' is probably a root word in nearly all languages. You can just create a word without an elaborate back-story.

A note for conlangers working with an author for the first time

For most conlangers, the process of creating a new language is a very personal one. But when creating a language for someone else – be it an author, a graphic novelist, a playwright, or any other kind of artist who is relying on the conlanger's skillset to enhance their own vision – conlangers may find themselves in unfamiliar territory, navigating deadlines, accommodating differing aesthetics, managing unfamiliar personalities, and not having the luxury of 'dithering' or 'fiddling' with a conlang to achieve the perfect phonaesthetic or grammatical nuance. The conlanger must strike a careful balance with each new client to make sure they are respecting their client's goals for the language while maintaining their own artistic vision.

For the language creator who has never worked with a client before, it can be a jarring experience to begin conlanging for someone else; the very process of creating a language for a client is very different to creating one for yourself.

First and foremost is a diminished sense of 'ownership' over the language being created. Most conlangs are very personal and their creators can be very protective over them and their development. This may be said about almost any type of art. But when that conlang is for a client, the conlanger must be less personally invested. This might be one of the major points of contention for conlangers everywhere looking to collaborate. The process of conlanging is so personal, it is very hard to find people compatible enough for collaborations to be a common sight. Unlike other types of art, in conlanging the fun and joy derive often from the nuts and bolts of the language but it is important to remember that you are working under someone else's aesthetic, and that aesthetic may not match your own. It is up to you to point out when certain features or nuances of the language you are creating might not make sense aesthetically, but ultimately your client has to be happy with the outcome – not you.

Once you get used to this new dynamic, though, it can also be quite liberating to work under the constraints of what in olden days might have been called a 'patron', as it were: it is just a matter of retraining one's creativity to flow in different directions. Particularly when there are time constraints, the freedom not to 'dither' is a benefit that many conlangers are not aware is possible until confronted with it. And what we mean by that is many conlangers, when creating a language for themselves, may spend years making up their minds about a single phoneme or pronoun or noun case. You will not have the option to change something later on (and it is important to keep track of what parts of the language become public so you know if you have some wiggle-room if you absolutely need to make a change later). Sometimes you are confronted with the horrible freedom of just making a decision and committing to it! This 'horrible freedom' can be a double-edged sword, however: you still have to think through the various processes and make sure you are not breaking a feature that has not been invented yet, or painting yourself into a corner by limiting options you may want back later. Restraints might also allow you to make decisions you wouldn't have considered before, or use features you still haven't tried but were hoping to find an excuse to do so.

What to know about constructed languages

Does the author (or conlanger) hold copyright over the conlang?
Bluntly, no; neither does.

That is not to say that an author does not have creative control over the development of a constructed language, or that a language creator cannot be credited for its creation: It means that the very concept of 'language' does not fit into any of the standard models of intellectual property law; that is, it does not fit neatly under Copyright, Patent, or Trademark.

A conlang is not likely to be granted a patent, as patents are reserved for processes, machines, articles of manufacture, or composition of matter (United States Code: inventions patentable 35 USC § 101 (1952)), and while it may be possible to trademark individual words or phrases, an entire language would not be feasible. Copyright is the most logical branch of intellectual property to address the question of language, but the very definition of language may fall short of what is able to be addressed by copyright. Or, to put it another way, copyright is a blunt instrument that was not designed to operate on something as nuanced as the very concept of language.

The view held by most legal scholars is that a language is a 'system' or an 'idea', and the legal concept of copyright specifically does not extend to systems, ideas, procedures, concepts, nor methods of operation.

There currently exist no laws (in the United States or elsewhere) that specifically address the intellectual property implications of languages – constructed or otherwise – and at the time of this writing, such rights have not been determined conclusively by a court. There are a few cases involving constructed languages which have been dismissed or otherwise settled without providing any sort of guidance as to how a constructed language might be treated under copyright law, including the long-time feud between Loglan (of The Loglan Institute) and Lojban (of the Logical Language Group) or the more recent action of *Paramount* v. *Axanar*, in which Paramount's claim of ownership of the Klingon language was later dropped from the suit.

The Language Creation Society (LCS), which filed an amicus brief on behalf of Axanar in the aforementioned case (<https://conlang.org/axanar>), has this to say about the copyright of language:

> We firmly believe that conlangers should receive credit for their work. Specific works describing a conlang, such as the *Klingon Dictionary*, *Living Language Dothraki*, or Ithkuil website are creative works in their own right, entitled to full legal protection. So are works that are in a conlang, such as Klingon *Hamlet*, Esperanto poetry, Ithkuil music, and Verdurian stories.
>
> However, a constructed language itself is not protected, and should not be. Copyright law is simply too blunt a tool for this.
>
> Allowing copyright claims to a language would create a monopoly on use extending far beyond what is needed to protect the original work or to claim credit for the language's creation. The potential threat of a lawsuit for merely using a conlang, or creating new works to make it more accessible, has a chilling effect; it makes conlangers, poets, authors, educators, scholars, and others less likely to build on and enjoy each other's work, to the detriment of conlanging in general.
>
> We believe that everyone has the right to use any language – including conlangs – without having to ask anyone's permission.

There was also a case in which speakers of *palawa kani* (<en.wikipedia.org/wiki/Palawa_kani>), a reconstructed Tasmanian language, have attempted to assert ownership over the language, and requested that information about it be removed from Wikipedia. The request was rejected by Wikipedia, and to date the issue remains undetermined.

None of this should discourage the very idea of using a constructed language in fiction, however. It is unlikely that anyone will try to 'steal' your conlang, but much more likely that it will draw additional engagement from readers who enjoy the language and may even want to try to learn it.

Is a 'complete' conlang necessary?
The real question here is: what is a 'complete' conlang? Or perhaps even more philosophically: when is a conlang 'finished'? Both of these questions are impossible to answer, as no language – natural or constructed – is ever done evolving as long as it is being used. However, there are a few benchmarks we can set that may help to determine which features are necessary, which can be avoided, and which can be set aside for further development.

Types of conlangs by 'completeness'
There are certainly other types of conlangs out there, and the following may be mixed and matched as necessary for the work in question, but here are some of our recommended points on a spectrum of completeness:

- *Naming Language*. The most basic conlang you may need is what is often referred to as a 'Naming Language'. This is usually a language that has a phonology and perhaps some basic phonotactics and orthography. Depending on how names are derived in your conlang, a naming language may also need to have some basic words that form elements of names (often words for plants, animals, natural phenomena, or descriptive adjectives such as colours). If your names are not derived in such a manner, even additional words may be unnecessary.

- *Conlang Sketch*. A sketch is the most basic form of functional conlang, consisting of a phonology, some core vocabulary (usually around fifty words), and a very basic grammar to be able to construct the simplest of sentences.

- *Basic Conlang*. A bit more than a sketch, a basic conlang has more vocabulary (at least a hundred words) and may describe more complex sentences, such as how to construct questions or commands. A basic conlang usually includes a short document in which the phonology, orthography, and some basic aspects of grammar are described, usually with a number of examples to illustrate the processes being described.

- *Advanced Conlang*. An advanced conlang is usually more than is needed for a work of fiction, at least in the beginning. This form of conlang usually includes a large lexicon (up to a thousand words or more), a complex grammar document describing many aspects of the language's grammar, and often also includes a unique writing system.

Should my conlang be derived from existing languages?
When speaking of languages' relationship to other languages (natural or constructed), the terms *a priori* and *a posteriori* are often used to describe another spectrum along which languages may be constructed (see also Peterson and Sams, this volume).

A posteriori conlangs are those which are derived – entirely or in part – from an existing language or languages. For example, the Braereth languages (Tenibvreth, Merineth, and Eomentesa), spoken in an upcoming Kindle Vella serial by C. J. Kavanaugh, are Romance languages that are designed to be similar enough to several existing languages such as French, Spanish, and Italian that readers who have passing familiarity with any of those languages should be able to understand many of their words with ease. *A posteriori* conlangs are relatively rare in fiction, however, since most science fiction and fantasy deals with extra-terrestrial worlds, or at least environments that are not based on the modern Earth, so it makes little sense for the characters inhabiting such an environment to speak an Earth-based language unless there is a clear back-story present that explains the presence of terrestrial languages.

There are also varying levels of hybrid languages which may borrow vocabulary or grammatical structures from existing languages, such as the International Auxiliary Language Esperanto, which consists of mainly Western European vocabulary in a unique 'logical' grammar structure, with some lexical gaps filled by invented words. This approach is not terribly useful for fiction writing, however, unless you happen to be writing in Esperanto, but a similar approach may be taken with historical or alternative history fiction in which a conlanger may take some elements of a known language or language family and fill in the gaps with invented structure and vocabulary.

A priori conlangs, at the opposite end of the spectrum, are by far the most frequently used in fiction, particularly in the areas of sci-fi and fantasy. These are languages where the vocabulary is completely unrelated to other existing Earth languages (though a family of *a priori* conlangs may be related to one another).

Determining where on this spectrum your conlang belongs is a conversation to have with your conlanger, though the latter (*a priori*) end is usually the logical choice.

Integrating a constructed language into writing

The goal in using a conlang in writing should be to bring colour and texture to your world-building through the language. A small percentage of readers may be enamoured with the language and want to learn more, flip through a dictionary of the language, study a pronunciation guide, or look up information about it online. Another small percentage of readers will not care at all about the language, or may be hostile to its presence. But the author must write for that third group: the middle crowd, who might not even notice the language or register that it is a conlang.

A conlang should add to the work and not distract from it. On the most basic level, this means that names of characters and places should be rendered in a format that is easily parsed by the reader through the lens of English (or the default language of your medium). The reader should not be distracted by thumbing through an appendix to figure out how to pronounce each new name they encounter. And, as English is also one of the worst languages to use as a medium to convey phonological information, as an author you may have to learn to be comfortable with the idea that a lot of readers are going to get the names wrong, and a lot of readers are just not going to care.

Any work that makes extensive use of a conlang ought to be able to have a guide or appendix of some sort where the interested reader can look up elements about which they may have questions, such as pronunciation rules, maybe a short guide of common phrases or a brief glossary, or read a little bit about the language. However, it needs to be optional. A reader who wants to know more should have the option to do so, and the reader who does not care should not miss out on any key context.

A constructed language in a piece of literature can operate on several other levels, though. The languages that Anthony and Jamin have developed for Aterra operate on the work in essentially five levels, and each level has a specific purpose. Not all of the languages of Aterra have all of these levels. Some do not have native scripts yet or may have native scripts that do not have a 'deep orthography' as does Modern Standard Imperial (called *Drikva Yakke* in that tongue), which is the primary language spoken on the planet. But most of them fit into at least a few of these categories for the purposes of storytelling.

Level 1: idioms, expressions, metaphors, (quasi-)literal translation

For example, the phrase *Ta kve pà yakke gvida* is how you would say 'We speak Modern Standard Imperial' in the Modern Standard Imperial language, but it would translate literally to something like 'We say the words of the Empire.' Adding this kind of a translation in a dialogue can be nice for a little flavour, and yet is not incomprehensible.

Characters may have a particular way of speaking like this that is reflective of their 'native' language, even though their dialogue is translated into English. In the Aterran world particularly, Anthony and Jamin have worked out various 'accents' that Northern or Imperial or Ashian speakers may have in English, and they use this type of dialogue to indicate a non-native parlance, and there are turns of phrase and idioms in each of the languages spoken by the cultures of Aterra.

This is a great way to dip a toe into acknowledging that the characters are speaking languages other than English, but this first level needs to be used thoughtfully and in moderation. Too much, and it can sound stilted or gimmicky. There is a similar trick used in old-timey propaganda language, so you want to make sure your use of culturally specific idioms and turns of phrase are adding nuance and not making your reader feel as if they are being indoctrinated!

Level 2: 'Anglicisation'

Level 2 is Anglicisation, and we use Anglicisation here particularly in contrast to the terms Romanisation and Transliteration (below). The main purpose of the Anglicisation level is to give the reader a quick-and-easy way to pronounce a word or name or short phrase as closely as possible without annoying them and sending them to the appendix. In the case of names, a rough transcription will usually do; in some cases, a close English name or word may be adopted, for example, the character whose name in Modern Standard Imperial is geidʒ/Geidʒ/Geidlh may be called 'Gauge', and we are not going to browbeat our readers into understanding that the coda should be 'lateralised' and what that entails. Because they don't care. Some conlangs will have a phonology that lends itself well to conversion into English; others less so. Sometimes several variations need to be presented in hopes that one feels 'right', or at least close.

Level 3: Romanisation

Romanisation is a level that is not used broadly in the actual work. This is basically the next step up from Anglicisation, but it tries to preserve all of the detail of the actual pronunciation in a way that is still accessible to the anglophone audience, without being as technical as Transliteration. There is no 'deep orthography' here – it is as phonetic as possible to the English-speaking ear. For example, /ʃ/ and /θ/ are written out as *sh* and *th* At this level we are not trying to make anybody learn any new symbols they're not comfortable with. For the most part, though, unless there's a longer piece of text in the conlang, like an incantation or poem, or something that needs to be read in the language, this really isn't a level that is used much in anything 'reader-facing'. One brief caveat here, though: use apostrophes and the letter *h* judiciously. It can be tempting to overuse them to detrimental effect.

Level 4: Transliteration

Transliteration is a very technical level that Jamin uses mostly for his own benefit while he does the 'background work' of documenting the language. This is a one-to-one transcription of the native script presented in Roman letters. It maintains the native script's 'deep orthography'. For example, a double-*t* in Imperial is pronounced like a /ts/. In Romanisation it would be written out as *ts*, but in true transliteration, it would be written as *tt*. Transliteration is never used in a reader-facing environment.

Level 5: native script

Here the language is presented unfiltered, in its native script. The casual reader is probably not going to try to learn the script or look up the letters or try to sound it out. Here, the purpose is entirely visual, used on signs, for example, or to add detail to the artwork where we might find writing in our everyday lives.

A conlang may not use all of these levels, or you may find use for more, but you should have a strategy in place for making the language accessible on more than one level.

Should a conlang's grammar and/or lexicon be made public?

A great way to spark additional reader engagement is to offer your readers a website or interface where they can learn more about the language. Sites such as Linguifex, FrathWiki, and Lingufacture are dedicated to sharing information about conlangs. You may also want to develop your own website or wiki to host a dictionary or other information about your language.

Many authors are hesitant to share anything about the language before their work is published, for fear that someone may 'steal' it, but we recommend that you put it out there as soon as possible. Most websites have features built in that can easily demonstrate when a page was created or modified, so if there is any question about the origins of your language, putting it out there early is going to guarantee that it is out there first, and you control how it is introduced.

So, yes, make your language public for the reasons stated above. It helps with reader engagement and makes them want to spend more time in the world and even add to it like the languages present in *The Lord of the Rings* and *Star Trek*.

Conclusion

Don't annoy your readers.

CHAPTER 4

Dialects in constructed languages

Harry Cook

For fictional languages to appear authentic and naturalistic, they cannot be too neat or simple. Natural languages are almost always characterised by variation because they are curated by different communities of speakers across history. Most obviously, dialects of a language can encode social and historical variation and change. In this chapter, Harry Cook draws on his own experience as a conlanger to suggest ways in which fictional dialects of a fictional language could be imagined. He creates an island with different dialects arising from historical changes and cultural differences, drawing on genuine principles of linguistic differentiation in our world's languages. While fictional dialects add richness to the world-building, they also bring a naturalistic effect of authenticity.

Naturalism and richness

The practice of constructing languages has been gaining popularity as an element of wider world-building projects ever since Tolkien published his legendarium (see Tolkien 2016). With the advent of the internet and easy international dialogue, creating languages has become a community endeavour, ranging from private hobbyists to professionals working for large multinational film and television production companies. Though Tolkien incorporated dialectal variation in some of his imagined languages, for the most part the vast majority of conlangs in existence are presented as if in a single standard form.

The paradox underlying this monolithic view of languages is that many conlangs are imagined in order to appear naturalistic, and yet almost no naturally occurring human language has persisted with only one dialectal form. This has been the case throughout history even in those many circumstances in which authoritarian rulers and governments have tried to standardise one prestigious dialect for national identity, while stigmatising or indeed actively suppressing any other 'non-standard' dialectal forms (see Lippi-Green 2012). In fact, dialects are a persistent and integral part of any language, and can vary according to the gender, class, ethnicity, politics, education, and of course geographical location of their speakers. This complex of social, cultural, and geographical factors tends towards linguistic complexity and irregularity over time, as different groups alter their speech at different rates and for different purposes.

For a conlang to appear naturalistic, then, it too should contain irregular dialectal variations. In its own right, this variation will have the effect of complicating and enriching the imagined fictional world; at the same time, the language creator will have to imagine the social and cultural settings that have caused the dialectal variation itself. A virtuous feedback loop can be created between languages and fictional world, so that both a naturalistic appearance and a rich setting can be integrated.

Traditionally, the field of dialectology drew the boundaries of dialects in terms of mutual intelligibility (see Cramer 2016): if the speakers of two dialects could more or less understand each other, then they were speaking variants of the same language, rather than different languages. However, the fact that language boundaries often coincided with the sharp borders between one country and another suggested that this was a highly idealised definition of dialect. For example, across the Scandinavian North Germanic language area, speakers might claim to be speaking distinctly Norwegian, Swedish or Danish within their own countries, but in fact people in villages close to the borders are highly likely to understand each other. Furthermore, speakers within one country but distant from each other might have dialects that are so divergent that they are not in fact mutually intelligible. The Scandinavian languages are in a *dialect continuum* (Chambers and Trudgill 2012).

It is more accurate to recognise that speakers' own sense of their own language usage, tied up with their own identities, has a significant impact on how they regard their own dialect. This is *perceptual dialectology*, defined by Cramer (2016: 1) as

> the study of how nonlinguists understand dialectal variation. This field of inquiry seeks to include what nonlinguists think about linguistic practices, including where they think variation comes from, where they think it exists, and why they think it happens, in holistic examinations of variation that incorporate aspects of both linguistic production and perception.

Put plainly, in perceptual dialectology, the line between a dialect and a language is established by asking the speakers where they think the line is. Clearly, in an imagined world and its invented language users, this is the responsibility of the conlang creator, who must devise the landscape, people, culture, society, and language altogether as an integrated whole.

Conlanging an illustrative language

I have been conlanging as a hobby since I was thirteen or fourteen years old. In this time I have made over a dozen conlangs, of which about half a dozen are decent and are finished to some kind of degree. For the past few years all of the conlangs I have made have been part of a larger world-building project. I have created two continents and have been steadily populating them with languages belonging to a few different language families.

The main family I have worked on so far is the Tarikhic language family. The name 'Tarikhic' comes from *tarikh* meaning 'common' in Tanol. Tanol is my most developed conlang, with a thoroughly worked-out grammar, and a lexicon approaching one thousand words. Crucially for my argument in this chapter, Tanol is comprised of several dialects, and possesses established principles of pragmatics, a set of idioms, and even some folk stories.

Within the context of my fictional world, the Ruhem (the speakers of Tanol) have recently started exploring linguistic matters and have begun to link languages together into language families. The family most salient to them is dubbed *rémzuléré tharikh tivernav*, meaning 'the family of (the) common languages'. The word for 'common' here is *tharikh*. In my integration of morphological and phonological rules, the /t/ of *tarikh* undergoes a soft mutation to /θ/ as a result of the prior genitive ending -*éré* on *rémzúl* (family, related group). Here, I have been concerned to align linguistic and social matters, for example.

To show how I go about creating dialects for my conlangs, in this chapter I am going to create a basic conlang with five different dialects to demonstrate some of the most important features of what we might call *conlects* (constructed dialects). For this simple illustration, the dialects will be determined by geography, since linguistic variation based on social factors would require a lot more work on the culture of the people who speak this language. In constructing them, I will draw for comparison on patterns and principles that already exist in some other languages in our actual world. We will call the language *Âliya*. To create this name, we could take a verb like *ûli* (to be native, local) and add a suffix -*ya* (forming abstracts). So we get, through vowel gradation, *Âliya*, meaning something like 'the native method, idea, language'.

The general phonology of our illustrative language will be fairly modest, with mostly head-marking morphology. This means that – unlike English and many European languages – the head of phrases will take most of the grammatical marking. In a phrase like 'the gift is with him', the head of the prepositional phrase is *with*, but *him* receives the marking (we don't say 'the gift is with-im he' or something like this). This means English is mostly dependent marking: in a given phrase, the dependent of the head will take the marking. Languages with head marking, such as the northwest Caucasian language Abkhaz, will mark the adposition for what it is describing, i.e. a noun. For example, in Abkhaz, the phrase 'Sáb jeq'ne' ('at my father's place') is constructed as follows:

1.   S - *áb*   *jə* - *q'nə́*
    1SG.POSS father 3SG.POSS at
    'At my father's place'

The notation here denotes 1st person singular possessive (1SG.POSS) and 3rd person singular possessive (3SG.POSS). In Abkhaz, the postposition (a preposition that comes after the noun) -*q'nə́* receives marking for the noun, in this case the gender agreement *jə-* (Chirikba 2003).

In terms of verbal marking, this means that the verb in head-marking languages takes far more marking than in dependent-marking languages like English, German, Russian, etc. Often verbs in head-marking languages receive marking for both the subject and the object, rather than just the subject (as is the case for most European languages). This is the case in Classical Nahuatl, a central American language, as demonstrated below:

2.   *Ti* - *nĕch* - *itta*
    2SG - 1SG - see
    'You see me'

Here in Nahuatl, we see the verb *tinēchitta* taking marking for both the subject 'You' and the object 'me', as is the standard for all Classical Nahuatl transitive verbs (Andrews 2003).

We can also have a simple gender system in nouns, where nouns are classed as animate or inanimate. This classification will affect the marking on nominal modifiers as well as putting certain restraints on the marking nouns can take. It is often the case in the world's languages that inanimate nouns receive far less marking than animate nouns, and this is the case in English as well, to a certain extent:

3.   'The knife cut the branches'

is technically grammatical, but sounds a little bit strange. Perhaps with a more animate subject, the sentence might sound better.

4.   'The man cut the branches with the knife'

There are certain languages like the North American Blackfoot where the subject of a clause cannot be inanimate (Frantz 2009). Therefore, a sentence like (3) would be realised in Blackfoot as follows:

Dialects in constructed languages

5. | Om | a | isttoán | a | iiht | sikahksinii | 'p | i |
    |---|---|---|---|---|---|---|---|
    | DEM | 3PROX.AN | knife | 3PROX.AN | INST | cut.TI | X:IN | IN.PL |

ann	istsi	ikkstsíksi	istsi
DEM	IN.PL	branch	IN.PL

    'By means of the knife (someone) cut the branches'

Here, the demonstrative (DEM) and proximal animate (3PROX.AN) mark the knife which is instrumental (INST); the word for 'cut' is transitive (TI); there are several plural (PL) markers contained (IN) by the remaining grammatical places. This is an impersonal construction: there is no actual subject within the clause, but the way the clause is structured and its constituents marked means that there must be an animate subject in this clause.

Something else that is very common cross-linguistically for inanimates is that they cannot take plural marking, or at least if they can this marking may be optional. This is the case in the South Asian language, Tamil (Schiffman 1999).

6. | Oru | manaivi | marrum | rendu | manaivi | - | nga |
    |---|---|---|---|---|---|---|
    | One | wife | and | two | wife | | PL |

    'One wife and two wives'

7. | Oru | mēse | marrum | rendu | mēse |
    |---|---|---|---|---|
    | One | table | and | two | table |

    'One table and two tables'

In (6), the plural suffix -nga can be applied to the word for 'wife'; in (7), a plural marking could have been applied, but it is very uncommon to do so, especially before a numeral.

These sorts of subtle cultural variations can make for variant dialectal forms, and recognising the wide range of linguistic possibilities across the actual world's languages allows us to range freely ourselves when we create new imagined languages and dialects. In creating dialects of Âliya, I have kept these sorts of principles and patterns in mind.

Âliya and its dialects

Âliya is a mini-conlang constructed for the purposes of this chapter. We can imagine that it has five main dialect centres spread from north to south. The country where Âliya is spoken is called *Elke-Saga*, literally 'our land' (see Graphic 4.1). The city of *Yumin* will be the centre of the northernmost dialect, then going further south the centres are *Pitona, Atala, Tlagan*, and finally the south-eastern tip and the island are the area where the *Kanson* dialect is spoken.

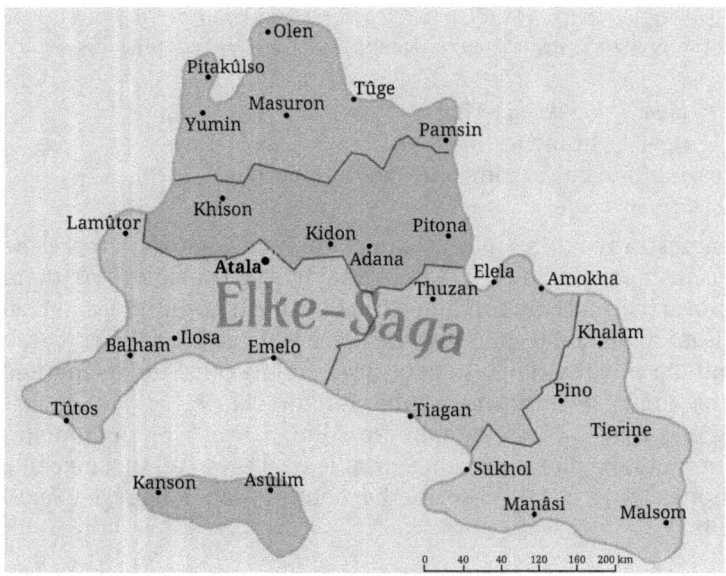

Graphic 4.1 A map of Elke-Saga, the area where Âliya is spoken

These dialects are named after the main cities, suggesting a strong local standardisation process has occurred historically, with each area identifying with its main urban area. The dialect of *Atala*, being the capital of Elke-Saga, is considered the standard, and has the most speakers. Because of this, much of the scholarly discourse, dictionaries and canonical, prestigious texts in Âliya are generally written in the *Atala* dialect.

Phonology
The phonology of Âliya is shown in Graphics 4.2 and 4.3, where stress is mostly penultimate and only medial clusters of a sonorant followed by an obstruent or two sonorants are permitted. Front unrounded vowels are contrasted by length, and vowel hiatus is disallowed (that is, in effect, all vowels are pronounced).

There is a lot of potential for variation in this inventory: the voiced stops could spirantise to voiced fricatives; /ŋ/ (especially as it is allowed in initial

Consonants		Labial	Alveolar		Palatal	Velar
			Central	Lateral		
Nasal		m	n			ŋ (ng)
Stop	Voiceless	p	t	t͡ɬ (tl)		k
	Voiced	b	d	d͡ɮ (dl)		g
Fricative			s	ɬ (lh)		x (kh)
Approximant			l		j (y)	w

Graphic 4.2 The consonants of Âliya

Dialects in constructed languages   53

Vowels	Front		Back
	Unrounded	Rounded	
High	i, iː (ī)	yː (û)	u
Mid	e, eː (ē)		o
Low	a, aː (ā)		ɑː (â)

Graphic 4.3 The vowels of Âliya

position) could be realised as an alveolar nasal or a voiced velar stop. The lateral affricates could also simplify to another kind of affricate, or turn into full fricatives, or merge into each other. In terms of vowels, /aː/ could merge with /ɑː/; /yː/ could merge with either /uː/ or /iː/; and length could be lost altogether. Nasal vowels could evolve from the loss of coda nasals, and unstressed vowels may lose some of their quality. These represent a set of possible variants that could be exploited for the conlecter.

Let us say that voiced consonantal spirantisation happens in the Tlagan dialect before migration south to the island. We could also say that [oː] doesn't become [ɑː] like it did in the more northern dialects and instead keeps its mid-height. These changes are shown in (8).

8. Proto-language:
   /qiŋ/ - lake + /oj/ - diminutive → /ˈqi.ŋoj/ - pond, puddle

9. Old form before sound shifts:
   /ˈku.goː/ - pond, puddle

10. Atala dialect:
    /ˈku.gɑː/ - pond, puddle

11. Tlagan dialect:
    /ˈku.ɣoː/ - pond, puddle

A further change could happen in the island dialect as shown below in (12), where these voiced spirants are then lost, as in the transition from Latin to Old French (/vita/ → /viðɛ/ → /via/, modern French *vie*, /vi/).

12. Kanson dialect:
    /ˈku.ɣoː/ > /ˈku.oː/ - pond, puddle
    /ˈsa.ðin/ > /ˈsa.in/ - fruit
    /ˈŋe.βon/ > /ˈŋe.on/ - to sow

A final change that could be applied to the Tlagan and Kanson dialects is the unrounding of /y/ in all environments (a similar change happened in Middle

English). As a change after this, the Tlagan dialect could lose /j/ when it is followed by /i/.

13. Atala dialect:
    /ˈjyː.ke/ - man

14. Tlagan dialect:
    /ˈiː.ke/ - man

15. Kanson dialect:
    /ˈjiː.ke/ - man

In the north, we might imagine there could be changes regarding coda nasals (at the end of words). Coda nasals are often lost in a coda position cross-linguistically, invariably resulting in nasalisation (and sometimes lengthening) of the preceding vowel. Nasal vowels normally lose their quality in some way: in this case, high nasal vowels could lose their height and merge with mid-nasal vowels, as shown in (16) to (19).

16. Atala dialect:
    /ˈtin.su/ - fire

17. Yumin dialect:
    /ˈtĩ.su/ > /ˈtẽ.su/ - fire

18. Atala dialect:
    /ˈtem.su/ - wine

19. Yumin dialect:
    /ˈtẽ.su/ - wine

Furthermore, after this loss of nasals, /s/ could voice to /z/ intervocalically, giving an even more divergent sound to one of the dialect/accent forms.

Northern dialects of Âliya could also be conservative in some areas where the other dialects had these changes. For example, a change from the proto-language where the velar nasal becomes a voiced velar stop between vowels might never have taken place in Yumin, meaning that, in the north, /ˈku.gɑː/ is pronounced /ˈku.ŋɑː/.

Another simple example of northern conservatism could be that the change where /uː/ became /yː/ in other dialects never occurred north of Atala.

20. Pitona and Yumin dialects:
    /ˈjuː.ke/ - man

Dialects in constructed languages 55

Let us imagine that the lateral obstruents are likely to change too: rare and complex sounds such as /d͡ɮ/ tend to be extremely unstable. In many dialects of English, dental fricatives have been lost in various ways such as fronting to labiodentals or becoming some kind of coronal stop (Blevins 2004).

In Yumin, the lateral affricates could have evolved into non-lateral phonemes, such as retroflex affricates. Similarly, in the Kanson, a similar change could have happened independently, but instead of shifting into retroflex affricates they lose their laterality and become plain coronal affricates.

21. Atala dialect:
    /t͡ɬɑː/ - in (inanimate form)

22. Yumin dialect:
    /t͡ʂɑː/ - in (inanimate form)

23. Kanson dialect:
    /t͡soː/ - in (inanimate form)

For the sake of simplicity, I will give all morphosyntactic and lexical variation in the standard phonology until the final comparison.

Morphology

Verbs exist in one of two stems: present and past. In the proto-form of Âliya, the past was marked with an -*i* suffix on the verb, which subsequently had an influence on the vowels in the root and then was mostly lost or merged with the stem.

24. **kūno* to love → *gûno* - to love
    *kūno - to love + -*i* → **kūnoi* → *gûne* - to have loved
    *sel - to notice, realise → *sal* - to see, watch
    *sel - to notice, realise + -*i* → *sali* → *sel* - to have seen, watched
    *halēng - to inscribe, mark, scratch → *lhēnɡ* - to write
    *halēng - to inscribe, mark, scratch + -*i* → *lhīgi* - to have written

More morphological marking can be appended to these stems to create more verbal meaning. There is an irrealis prefix *d(a)-* which when applied to the non-past stem creates the future tense, but when applied to the past stem creates the irrealis mode.

25. *Da - gûno*
    IRR - love.PRES
    'He/she will love'

26. *Da - gûne*
    IRR - love.PST
    'He/she would/could/might love'

However, let us imagine that in recent history, many speakers, especially in the north, started to reduplicate the onset and nucleus of the stressed syllable of the stem in place of the future tense, which took over as the more productive morphological strategy. So now between the dialects there is a discontinuity between which morphology is used for each verb. Northern speakers would use constructions like (27) and (28), whereas other speakers would stick to the more conservative constructions like (29) and (30).

27. *Lhē ~ lhēng*
    write.PRES ~ IRR
    'He/she will write'

28. *Lhī ~ lhīgi*
    write.PST ~ IRR
    'He/she would/could/might write'

29. *Da - lhēng*
    IRR - write.PRES
    'He/she will write'

30. *Da - lhīgi*
    IRR - write.PST
    'He/she would/could/might write'

Another element of variation could arise from a result of interrogative morphology interacting with this irrealis verb form. Let's say that a *yes-no question* particle evolves from a word such as *lhân* (meaning 'whether' or 'if'), from two older words meaning 'on doubt'. When this word is in a clause, the verb must be in its irrealis form, and speakers may also choose to front the verb to be next to this word, meaning that the standard OV structure of the language becomes VO.

31. *Ensi   yûke   ekh -   no -   gûno*
    DEF.AN   man   2SG   3SG   love.PRES
    'You love the man'

32. *Lhân   ekh -   no -   da -   gûne   ensi   yûke*
    if   2SG –   3SG -   IRR -   love.PST DEF.AN   man
    'Do you love the man?'

Dialects in constructed languages 57

Some speakers may start to see this *lhân* particle as unnecessary and redundant, and the new position of the verb and irrealis form is enough to form the interrogative and so omit the *lhân* particle:

33. Ensi   yûke   ekh -   no -   gûno
    DEF.AN   man   2SG   3SG   love.PRES
    'You love the man'

34. Ekh - no - da -   gûne   ensi   yûke
    2SG   3SG   IRR   love.PST   DEF.AN   man
    'Do you love the man?'

In this way the irrealis verb form will also serve as an interrogative verb form. It would be possible for other speakers to innovate a new way of asking questions, especially if they are seeking a particular response. Something similar to the Mandarin *A-not-A* construction could arise (where a question offers two polar opposite possible replies), depending on whether the speakers are seeking an affirmative or negative answer. Let's say they use a construction something like 'you see the man or see' to mean 'you see the man, right?' (seeking an affirmative answer), and 'you see the man not-or see' to mean 'you don't see the man, do you?' (seeking a negative answer). Due to its semantic implications, the second part of the construction would likely be placed in the irrealis.

35. Ensi   yûke   ekh -   no -   sal   ne   da -   sel
    DEF.AN   man   2SG   3S   see.PRES   or   IRR   see.PST
    'You see the man, right?' (affirmative answer)

36. Ensi   yûke   ekh -   no -   sal   enke   da –   sel
    DEF.AN   man   2SG   3SG   see.PRES   not.or   IRR   see.PST
    'You don't see the man, do you?' (negative answer)

It is likely this *A-n/or-A* construction would evolve in our island dialect, isolated from the main two forms of asking *yes-no* questions (with the irrealis and verb-fronting along with *lhân*). It might have evolved a bit earlier on too, so the mainland question constructions became completely lost on the Kanson island and peninsula.

Negation

On the topic of negation, we could take some inspiration from colloquial forms of French negation, where the two-part negation strategy of *ne...pas* is often reduced to just one part, *pas*. Etymologically this is very interesting, because *pas* comes from Latin *passum* meaning 'a step', so the *ne...pas* construction originally meant something like 'I don't see him one step'; it is similar in pattern to the English 'I didn't eat one bit of it'. So the original negative particle, *ne*, is lost. (This is called Jespersen's cycle, after Jespersen 1917.)

We could say originally a construction similar to this in Âliya became the standard form of negation, but in many dialects the original negative particle was lost, yet perhaps was retained in our island Kanson dialect.

So in the proto-language (shown here with the * to indicate an historical estimate!) there was a kind of emphatic negation as in (37).

37. *Qe   ngel   k'a   non   kūno -   i
    not   piece   1SG   3SG   see   PST
    'I didn't love him' (literally 'I didn't love him one bit')

Later on, this could have evolved into the standard negation before migration to the island:

38. Ko   nge -   n   <k>   o - gūne
    not   NEG   <1SG>   3SG   love.PST
    'I didn't love him'

(In *o-gūne* we see metathesis resulting in the infixation of the 1st person singular verb marker due to the following resonant). The proto-form results in the modern mainland negation shown in (39) and the modern island negation shown in (40):

39. Nge -   n   <k>   o - gûne
    NEG   <1SG>   2SG   love.PST
    'I didn't love him'

40. Ko   nge -   n   <k>   o - gûne
    not   NEG   <1SG>   3SG   love.PST
    'I didn't love him'

Relativisation

As a final example of variation within our invented language, we can take a look at how subordinate clauses might be handled. Cross-linguistically in our actual world, we see lots of different methods of subordination such as the use of interrogative pronouns (like in many Indo-European languages), particles like 'that' in English or a possessive marker like 的 (de) in Mandarin.

There are also strategies like pronoun retention, where the pronoun is reintroduced in the relative clause, especially in positions where accessibility is low. In English pronoun strategy, this would be like saying 'the woman

I saw her yesterday', instead of 'the woman who(m)/that I saw yesterday'. In many languages (such as English), the two clauses can just be placed adjacent to each other: 'the woman I saw yesterday', for example, where there is no relativising element.

In Âliya, the standard strategy might be to use the article to introduce the relative clause, with the article depending on the animacy of the antecedent. *Ensi* could be used for animate antecedents and *emlâ* for inanimate antecedents.

41. Yûke   ensi   nge -   l <k>   ēm
    man   DEF.AN   NEG   <1SG>   know.PRES
    'A man who doesn't know me'

42. Sum   emlâ   ken
    house   DEF.INAN   be.old.PRES
    'A house which is old'

In (41) and (42), we see the antecedent is in the most accessible position – according to Keenan and Comrie (1977) – the subject. In many languages, if the antecedent is in a less accessible position, like direct or indirect object, then a resumptive pronoun is introduced. This could be the same in Âliya: if the antecedent is in any position besides the subject of the relative clause, it must be reintroduced by way of a resumptive pronoun (historically formed by combining *ma, an old demonstrative, with the relevant pronoun).

43. Ensi   yûke   ensi   mon   nge -   l <k>   ēm
    DEF.AN   man   DEF.AN   3SG.RESUM   NEG   <1SG>   know.PRES
    'The man who(m) I don't know'

44. Emlâ   sum   emlâ   ma   nigon   ka -   sel
    DEF.INAN   house   DEF.INAN   3.INAN.RESUM   yesterday   1SG   see.PST
    'The house which I saw yesterday'

In terms of dialectal variation, it would be highly likely that our different dialects would disagree on how inaccessible a position would have to be for the resumptive pronoun to be introduced. In some (let's say in Yumin and Pitoma) it may be as in (43) and (44), where anything past the subject must be reintroduced, but others (let's say the Atala and Tlagan dialects) may regard the object and possibly even the indirect object as accessible for the antecedent.

It is also possible that the southern dialect of Kanson could leave out the relativising element altogether (the definite article), using a null element instead. These two different strategies and the combination of them are demonstrated from (45) through to (49).

45. *Yûke   nge   - l <k>   ēm*
    man   NEG   <1SG>   know.PRES
    'A man (that) doesn't know me'

45. *Sum   ken*
    house   be.old.PRES
    'A house (that) is old'

47. *Ensi   yûke   nge -   l <k>   ēm*
    DEF.AN   man   NEG   <1SG>   know.PRES
    'The man (who(m)) I don't know'

48. *Emlâ   sum   nigon   ka -   sel*
    DEF.INAN   house   yesterday   1SG   see.PST
    'The house (which) I saw yesterday'

49. *Ensi   edwā   ge   ensi   wâ   mon   ek - suse*
    DEF.AN dog   be.PST DEF.AN   on.AN   3SG.RESUM   1SG - talk.PST
    'That was the dog I was talking about'

It is very likely that this system, whereby the resumptive pronoun is only introduced relatively low down in the accessibility hierarchy, was the original in the language, and over time what some speakers have internalised as inaccessible has been expanded to everything aside from the subject, probably due to analogy. All in all then, the dialects of Âliya can be imagined to exhibit quite a lot of variation in grammatical relativisation, with a conservative form and newer variants that are spreading and becoming more popular. As in many of our actual world's languages, we can imagine the newer forms in Âliya's dialects being popular with younger speakers.

Lexical variation

Lexical variation is perhaps the most noticeable feature of dialectal differences, for non-specialists. It would be easy for us to imagine different, perhaps etymologically cognate synonyms for the same idea in different dialects. For example, instead of using *yûke* for 'man', a new word may arise in one dialect from a verb meaning 'to be free' with an agent suffix on it, something with the meaning of a 'freeman', or one not under the control of a lord. This innovation would indicate a social change, of course. If one of the other dialect areas were more misogynistic in social outlook, then perhaps the very same word might come to be used to refer to unmarried women in general, and even pejorate in meaning to become a word for a prostitute.

Different foreign languages might also influence different dialects. For example, if a new group migrates into one of our mainland dialect areas and starts trading with them, then it is highly likely that there will be an exchange of vocabulary – especially for trade goods and terms for money or transactions. A similar thing may happen in the island dialect if there was already a small enclave of foreigners in residence.

Lexical variation is fairly simple even for non-linguists to understand. Often vocabulary differences are a major source of amusement for non-linguists to compare across dialects, possibly only secondary in salience to pronunciation. For language creators, lexical differences are a very easy way to make dialectal variation, and indeed this is often one of the key steps in creating larger language families. One can coin new words in dialects or languages, or have old ones survive, borrow from other languages, have words retain older meanings, or take on new ones.

Full comparison of the dialects of Âliya

Putting all these morphosyntactic and lexical ideas together with our ideas for phonological changes we will have our full dialects. The following three sentences of increasing complexity show examples of our five dialects of Âliya:

'Will the dog stand up in the house?'
Yumin: *Khu ~ khusi ensi edwā tlâ emlâ sum?*
Pitona: *Khu ~ khusi ensi edwā tlâ emlâ sum?*
Atala: *Lhân da-khusi ensi edwā tlâ emlâ sum?*
Tlagan: *Da-khusi ensi edwā tlâ emlâ sum?*
Kanson: *Ensi edwā tlâ emlâ sum da-khusi ne da-khusi?*

'She isn't the woman that I knew'
Yumin: *Ensi sādim nge-ge mon k-ālhīm*
Pitona: *Ensi sādim nge-ge mon k-ālhīm*
Atala: *Ensi sādim nge-ge ensi mon k-ālhīm*
Tlagan: *Ensi sādim nge-ge k-ālhīm*
Kanson: *Ensi sādim ko nge-ge k-ālhīm*

'I don't see the house which I used to live in'
Yumin: *Emlâ sum nge-ka-sal tlâ ma ka-lo ~ long*
Pitona: *Emlâ sum nge-ka-sal tlâ ma ka-lo ~ long*
Atala: *Emlâ sum nge-ka-sal emlâ tlâ ma ka-leng*
Tlagan: *Emlâ sum nge-ka-sal tlâ ma ka-leng*
Kanson: *Emlâ sum ko nge-ka-sal emlâ tlâ ma ka-leng*

What I have done here is very much just a very short example of a few days' worth of simple conlanging to create what is quite a rich dialect continuum. With several months of work, these systems can gain incredible depth and complexity, beyond just the surface-level differences. Decisions made for linguistic reasons might lead to creative decisions about the society, culture, and history of the lands and peoples of Elke-Saga. This is why I find the lack of dialectal variation among artlangs somewhat disappointing, since even with a small amount of effort, a conlang can be greatly enriched if it is an element of a larger project.

Conlanging involves finding the line between scholarly discipline and artistic creativity, which can sometimes feel paradoxical, an artificial version of a uniquely natural human phenomenon. However, like a composer trying to replicate the sounds of waves on the shore or wind through the trees, many conlangers try to replicate what is found in natural languages to put into their own creations. In the process, the outcome is enriched. Perhaps adding dialects can help to fill in some of the depth, undertones, and resonance of an imagined, composed language.

References

Andrews, R. J. (2003) *Workbook for Introduction to Classical Nahuatl*. Norman: University of Oklahoma Press.
Blevins, J. (2004) *Evolutionary Phonology: The Emergence of Sound Patterns*. Cambridge: Cambridge University Press.
Chambers, J. K. and Trudgill, P. (2012) *Dialectology* (2nd edn). Cambridge: Cambridge University Press.
Chirikba, V. A. (2003) *Abkhaz*. Munich: LINCOM.
Cramer, J. (2016) *Perceptual Dialectology*. New York: Oxford University Press.
Frantz, D. G. (2009) *Blackfoot Grammar*. Toronto: University of Toronto Press.
Jespersen, O. (1917) *Negation in English and Other Languages*. Copenhagen: AF Høst.
Keenan, E. L. and Comrie, B. (1977) 'Noun phrase accessibility and universal grammar', *Linguistic Inquiry* 8 (1): 63–99.
Lippi-Green, R. (2012) *English with an Accent: Language, Ideology and Discrimination in the United States* (2nd edn). New York: Routledge.
Schiffman, H. F. (1999) *A Reference Grammar of Spoken Tamil*. Cambridge: Cambridge University Press.
Tolkien, J. R. R. (2016) *A Secret Vice* (eds D. Fimi and A. Higgins). London: HarperCollins.

CHAPTER 5

Alien typographies in sf and the influence of Asian languages

Victor Fernandes Andrade and Sebastião Alves Teixeira Lopes

> Looking to the creation of extra-terrestrial languages, Andrade and Lopes present a comparative account of alien typographies in science fiction. Drawing upon the theory of Orientalism, they examine the exotification of real-world East Asian languages and the exotifying function of conlangs themselves. Taking into account a variety of fictional languages, from Aurebesh to Futhork, the authors consider the ways in which Asian languages undergo processes of exotification to inspire alien language design. They place particular focus on the design and aesthetics of alien writing systems, analysing the ways in which Asian characters are manipulated for visual impact in literature and on-screen.

Introduction

In constructing fantasy languages for works of fiction, some writers and filmmakers also decide to create a writing system to represent them. Often, the goal is for the language to look foreign, to which purpose the creators utilise graphic design features present in Asian languages. This apparently places fictional aliens in the same otherness position occupied by the Asian alien, to a Western audience.

This comparative study aims to demonstrate, utilising methods and nomenclature stemming from the field of typographical analysis, the visual similarities that take place between these fictional languages and real-world Asian languages, and to discuss, drawing on the theory of Orientalism expanded by authors such as Minear (1980), Dirlik (1996) and Yoon (2017), any connections that might be uncovered between real and fictional processes of this 'exotification'.

We will demonstrate that authors and language creators seem to explore the Western consumer's pre-existing conceptions of alterity to confer this sense of exoticism onto their fictional languages. This invariably involves mimicking core typographic characteristics from different Asian writing systems and, as we argue, could be reinforcing and perpetuating stereotypes.

The exotifying function of conlangs

Early enquiries into the study of conlangs usually discussed the functions or roles of fictional languages in sf texts (Stockwell 2006, Cheyne 2008). Stockwell mostly uses the term *neographies* to refer to written conlangs and assigns them three possible functions in fiction: *elaborative, indexical,* and *emblematic.* Whereas the elaborative function describes the characterisation feature of conlangs and the emblematic function the embodiment of ideas, the indexical function is present in our assessment of their speakers – and the imaginary world they inhabit – as a foreign entity. The indexical feature works as an interface between the reader and the new, unfamiliar worlds and people they encounter during the readerly experience, and it is thus the most appropriate to describe the polarising factor of encounters such as human and alien, coloniser and colonised, West and East.

Cheyne (2008) suggests four goals of created languages in fiction, while describing four levels of communication that the glossopoeic narrative can contain. According to her, on the first level, every created language expresses difference. It is not irrelevant that Cheyne chooses to posit the notion of difference as the very first level on the hierarchy of glossopoeic communication, as she writes:

> While the alien utterance may also signify at a number of other levels, this one is universal. Within the meta-text (i.e., all previous sf texts) that defines the conventions of the genre, the utterance in a created language signifies that 'This is alien.'
>
> (Cheyne 2008: 392)

While Cheyne discusses sf only, Stockwell draws on at least one example from outside the genre by referencing *Tintin*, but this does not detract from the understanding of both theories as close interpretations of glossopoeic functions. More recently, Noletto and Lopes produced a series of articles in which they formally address language creation as glossopoesis and focus mainly on discussing the secondary narrative framework potential of conlangs (Noletto and Lopes 2019), demonstrating how, through the use of created languages, authors can convey information about characters, settings, or plot that serve to enrich the narrative experience (Noletto, Lopes and Costa 2017).

Ultimately, the readings presented above build upon the fundamental notion of difference expressed through the poetics of science fiction, specifically through the creation of fictional languages. As a textual artifice, glossopoesis has the main appeal of establishing such a difference in a way that the reader can experience first-hand, playing on the notion of the dialogue between sf and the real world as Delany discusses in *The American Shore*:

> The s-f text speaks inward, of course, as do the texts of mundane fiction, to create a subject (characters, plot, theme . . .). It also speaks outward to create a world, a world in dialogue with the real. And, of course, the real world speaks inward to construct its dialogue with both.
>
> (Delany 2014: 48)

Taking Delany's trivalency into consideration, it is possible to understand that glossopoesis widens the gap between our world and the fictional world. Stockwell's indexical function as well as Cheyne's alien encounter both serve as a method of accessing that perceived difference, and both authors emblematic functions illustrate the cultural artefacts that separate alien cultures from our own. Noletto and Lopes' (2019) understanding of glossopoesis as a secondary narrative framework also builds on the idea that conlangs can act by allowing the reader access to a fundamentally distinct part of a created world, aiding the perception of themes that would differentiate real and fictional worlds.

This means that when used in fiction, glossopoesis may further the perceptual difference between our experience of reality and the experience of those worlds, and while it does so in the specific ways described accurately by the functions earlier mentioned, the main effect is exoticising their speakers – just how much and in which ways is what varies.

Perspectives on Orientalism

The 'Orient' as an amalgam of exotic cultures was, for a long time, the image of an extremely unspecific area of studies long called 'Orientalism' (Said 2003). This discipline outlived the colonialist system that created it and went on to act in favour of imperialism in the twentieth century (da Silva 2016). In 1978, Edward Said published the book *Orientalism*, where he details the long process of characterisation of the Orient and the Oriental in the European and, consequently, Western popular imagination, throughout centuries of colonialism, exploitation, and relations marked by prejudice. *Orientalism* itself initiates a critique of the Orientalist discipline.

Despite its focus on the Arab world, the concept of Orientalism and the creation of the 'other' is not a phenomenon restricted to the relations between the West and the Middle East or the Islamic world. Far Eastern countries also suffer similar Manichean Orientalist characterisation, and several authors have expanded upon Said's original interpretation, adding in their own research to adapt it to the specific realities of the exoticisation experienced by the cultures studied by them (Minear 1980, Dirlik 1996, Yoon 2017).

It is understood, then, that there are specific relations of different nations and cultures towards Orientalism. While one cannot understand the process of exoticisation of various Oriental countries in a way that encompasses the diversity of these historical relations, there are elements in common that allow dialogue between those different relations of alterity and oppression.

Fiction and sf in particular were never strangers to discourses of othering: in many cases, it is one of the mechanics of estrangement employed by sf writers, as discussed by Cheyne (2008) when talking about fictional languages and the expression of difference. Many sf works, however, draw inspiration from specific cultures and ethnic groups when doing worldbuilding for certain species, and the result is a process of othering heavily anchored on pre-existing real-world social mechanics. A look at this othering phenomenon reveals a history of exoticisation: what Holborn (1991) calls *Japonisme* was a tendency to import visual and narrative themes, aesthetic elements and design tropes from Japan.

> The dialogue between Japan and the West is frequently described in terms of Japan's absorption of the West. The pattern of imitation, absorption and finally reinterpretation of Western ideas is explicit [...] In contrast, the West's absorption of Japan is inconclusive and rarely described. *Japonisme* was the first stage in the imitation of a Japanese aesthetic. It was primarily decorative and involved the borrowing of Japanese motifs and design elements. Oriental views provided the West with spectacle.
>
> (Holborn 1991: 18)

Even though *Japonisme* is often seen as a phenomenon from the past, the influence of Japan and other Asian cultures on the West's imagination has been active ever since and can be seen in Lucas' and Herbert's admitted inspiration from Japanese and Arabic cultures respectively in designing their *Star Wars* and *Dune* sf universes. In fact, mimicry of the colonialised (or decolonialised) other is present in sf just as much as in real life: two contrasting instances of that can be found in the fetishisation of inhabiting a (literally) colonised body and 'going native' in James Cameron's *Avatar* (2009) and the social critique sleeved in the metaphor of stealing the black body in Jordan Peele's *Get Out* (2017).

It is interesting to perceive how mimicry, a phenomenon originally described by Bhabha (1984: 126) as 'the sign of a double articulation; a complex strategy of reform, regulation, and discipline, which "appropriates" the Other as it visualises power', tends to be employed by the coloniser in sf dynamics. This happens not only in-universe, but also at an extratextual level when the inspiration for a certain culture, species, or even the imaginary universe's aesthetics is taken from another real-world 'otherised' people. It is possible, thus, that sf mimicry of the decolonialised other is a form of preserving hegemonical relations in the realm of fiction, positioning their fictional characters in alterity positions analogous to those occupied by certain earthly cultures.

The exoticisation of Oriental languages

If language is directly related to both society and culture, it makes sense that one would view the language of a civilisation through the same network of signifiers they use to read the people of that civilisation. It is not surprising, then, that several Asian writing systems are shrouded by mystique in the eyes of the Western viewer. Chinese hanzi (colloquially known in the west as 'ideograms', alternatively 'sinographs'), to cite the most popular and contextually relevant example due to its influence on the history of writing amongst many countries in east Asia, are seen as refractory and poetic (Fenollosa et al. 2009), and oftentimes impossibly complicated (Moser 1991). Therefore, when the West uses Asian languages in its visual representations, it is almost invariably for exotification purposes. This can happen in large scale, such as in the fashion industry:

> Another example Chinese netizens still use to highlight the inappropriate use of Chinese characters, is the 2017 Spring Summer Collection from Designer Han Kjobenhavn. The Chinese print on the shoe reads: 回旋踢和麵烤面包. In English: 'Roundhouse kick and bakes white bread.' This isn't some cultural idiom – and according to Chinese netizens, the phrase makes as little sense in Chinese as it does in English. On the official website of the brand, it said the design is 'to pay tribute to Eastern culture with Chinese character embroidery'.
>
> (Zheng 2018: n.p.)

And it also happens in the personal lives of several Westerners, one example being the popular singer Ariana Grande, who tattooed the word 七輪 (*shichirin*) on her hand. Though it is not possible to ascertain why the singer chose to write the word in Japanese (presumably aesthetic preference), what can be ascertained is that *shichirin* is, in fact, a type of grill. She went on record (AFP 2019) explaining that the characters つの指 that should have been written between 七 and 輪 were cut off from the design because she 'wouldn't have lasted one more symbol' for the pain. Grande is not an isolated case, and many others are showcased in 'Hanzi Smatter', a nearly two-decade-old blog dedicated to chronicling such misuses of Chinese and Japanese orthography in these pseudo-Asian tattoos (Tian 2021).

The modern literary and media canons are not exempt from this Orientalist view of Asian languages either. During the glossopoeic development of *Dune*'s (1965) languages, Frank Herbert – and later John Quijada in the *The Dune Encyclopedia* (McNelly 1984) – tried to approximate the languages created to earthly counterparts, since the universe of *Dune* is supposed to be a far-future version of our own universe. This resulted in its Fremen language looking like slightly modified Arabic, but such a similarity was intentional. There was a literary objective in approximating the desert nomads of the planet Arrakis with Arabic people, which furthers the argument that Western storytelling often employs the artifice of mimicking Asian cultures to characterise its exotic aliens. More strictly on the subject of written language, the cinematic classic *The Matrix* (1999) imprinted into the popular imagination the idea of computer code as strings of text descending in cascades of mysterious characters, decipherable only by the most skilled of hackers. The characters used by the filmmakers to visually compose that code are nothing more than assorted Japanese katakana alongside regular numbers. Another example of prejudiced views from the West towards the East can be found in an asemic interpretation of Chinese in an early Hergé comic, *Tintin au Pays des Soviets* (1929). While Hergé had access to literature and Chinese individuals to help him at least be accurate while writing 'Chinese' – which, later in life, he in fact did with *Le Lotus Bleu* (1934), aided and informed by Chinese artist Zhang Chongren – his first venture into writing did not worry as much about that as it did in utilising stereotypes for comedic purposes.

Typographical analyses

The next subsections will go over the typographical analyses of each fictional alphabet used in this study, detailing anatomical traits of the characters (width, height, stroke thickness, etc.) that will be used so as to demonstrate the visual similarity between these created languages and certain Asian writing systems from the real world.

Aurebesh and Futhork (*Star Wars*)

To create the galaxy of *Star Wars*, George Lucas notoriously drew inspiration from a very specific piece of Japanese culture. The aesthetics, aura, and sound in his fictional universe bear a strong influence from the filmography of Japanese director Akira Kurosawa, the most obvious example being the Jedi: diplomatic emissaries of the ruling government who are also highly skilled in martial combat, have strong philosophical beliefs, and whose iconic weapon is a sword – all of those are also accurate descriptors of the samurai who inhabited most of Kurosawa's works. This influence has been previously noted in discussions of Lucas' works (Shedd 2016) and by the director himself (Lucas 2014, Barber 2016). The idiomatic connection was first expressed through characters' names: Obi-Wan Kenobi, Qui-Gon Jinn, Yoda, Anakin – all syllabic sequences that sound, to the unfamiliar Western ear, vaguely Asian, even if ultimately only in *apophenia* (the perceptual tendency to make connections between random elements).

Despite this onomastic display of glossopoesis, *Star Wars* does not really employ a conlang as the language of the Jedi, nor as the main language of the galaxy. The principal characters, with few exceptions such as Jabba the Hutt (who speaks a created language apparently inspired by Quechua) (Burrt 2001) and Chewbacca (whose language is composed of growls and moans), all speak diverse dialectal variations of English. So, to convey through language the 'foreignness' and mystique that had to also apply to the main cast, and to the aesthetic of the galaxy as a whole, the filmmakers turned to written language. There already existed a template for an alphabet native to the *Star Wars* galaxy: a collection of characters displayed on a computer screen in the first minutes of *Star Wars: Return of the Jedi* (1983).

Stephen Crane, involved in the creation of the miniature role-playing game *Star Wars Miniatures Battles*, adapted those characters into a full-fledged alphabet, Aurebesh, published for the first time in the *Star Wars Miniatures Battles Companion* (1994).

When the prequel trilogy came into being with *Star Wars: The Phantom Menace* (1999), sixteen years after the last movie release, a slightly modified version of Crane's Aurebesh could be seen in the display of a ship flown by Anakin, one of the protagonists. Several other scripts were used in the film, each one semiotically related to the core ideas meant to be represented by the characters who used them – one example being the two languages used by the people of the planet Naboo.

In the galaxy of *Star Wars*, Naboo is home to a civilisation with a special affinity to arts and culture (Barr et al. 2021), and its urban layout and royal setting has previously been noted to resemble the European Renaissance and its ornamented castles (Svozil 2006). The people who lived in its cities, also called the Naboo, are neighbours to another species that live right below them – quite literally, in underwater settlements – called Gungans. Not only do the Gungans speak in some kind of pidgin, but they also seem very childish compared to the elegant, cultured Naboo, even shaking their heads, pouting, and spitting when annoyed. The whole characterisation of the Naboo, aesthetic and contextual, helps depict them in the same light Eurocentric texts depicted Europe throughout history: a classic place of wondrous culture and refined architecture that happens to share the world with neighbours who dress in tatters and fight with slingshots and sticks.

It is no surprise, then, that the two alphabets associated with Naboo (no written language is ever associated with Gungans) have their names – Futhark and Futhork – derived from an ancient form of writing associated with Scandinavian and Germanic peoples, the Futhork runes. Since Futhark is derived from Old Italic script, it is safe to say the runes have deep roots in European cultural history. It is not only the names of the two Naboo scripts that are echoic of European culture; the shapes of the characters in the Futhork alphabet, used by the commoners of Naboo, are also very reminiscent of our own Latin script – the whole set of letters, numbers, and associated glyphs used primarily to write most Italic and Germanic languages.

Though Futhork appears slightly more angular than the Latin script, it also features round shapes and curves, and some of its characters are reminiscent of our own alphabet:

⌠, ⌡5, ⌡4, ⌡⌡, Ш, ⌐, U, ⌐, and ⌐

Although it might seem like it because of the fixed height of all Futhork characters, the similarities are not exclusive to the majuscule variant of the Latin alphabet. There is inversion, mirroring, and extension when we compare multiple characters:

⌐-⌐, ⌐-⌐, ⌐-⌐, ⌐-⌐, ⌐-⌐, ⌐-(⌐)

All of these creative design choices may be inspired by a layman's perspective on the visual similarity between the Latin character pairs **p** - **q** (mirrorring), **b** - **d** (mirrorring), **b** - **p** (inversion), **m** - **n** (extension), or **i** - **j** (extension).

The case of Naboo only corroborates the argument about Aurebesh, which quickly grew through media and fandom to become the cultural marker of the galaxy as a whole, being inspired by a particular script of Asian origin.

If one considers the previously discussed Eastern influence on *Star Wars* and analyses the typographical traits of Aurebesh, it becomes all the easier to identify the similarities that exist between Aurebesh and Katakana, one of the three scripts that work together to create the Japanese writing system. Not only are some shapes strikingly similar, but characteristics such as a generally narrow aperture size – what is usually described when talking of katakana as 'sharp angles' – and unconnected strokes are common traits between both of those scripts:

Aurebesh	ヲ	フ	ヷ	≡	⊐	√	ᴅ	≠	⩘	∆	▢	ⅎ	⌇⊐	⼑
Katakana	ヨ	フ	ウ	ミ	コ	レ	リ	ヒ	ル	ム	ロ	ヨ	ユ	カ

Though it is not possible to state categorically that the graphemes constituting the Aurebesh script were consciously inspired by Katakana, it seems likely that while designing the characters later adapted by Crane into Aurebesh, Lucas tapped once more into the semiotic field of Japanese culture, the result being the typographical similarities discussed above.

Galach and Fremen (*Dune*)

While language plays a mainly exoticising function in the background of *Star Wars*, in *Dune* it is ever-present and emblematic of the socio-political

Alien typographies in sf and the influence of Asian languages 71

connections Frank Herbert aimed to create between his oeuvre and the real world. Though in a very distant timeframe from the present time, the characters of *Dune* are linked to Earth by their far-removed ancestors and carry with them a certain lexical baggage. Realistically, of course, no easily recognisable traces of language would remain after 20,000 years, when the story is set, but suspension of disbelief should work well enough to conceal this technicality from anyone but those close to the study of languages. Two of the many forms Herbert thought of are especially relevant here for their connection to real-world languages: Galach and Fremen.

Galach is, as the name implies, spoken throughout the galaxy as a *lingua franca*. It is said to be a 'hybrid Inglo-Slavic' (Herbert 1965), and probably reflects the author's projection of his time's geopolitics into the far future – *Dune* was written in the 1960s, when the United States and the Soviet Union were intertwined in ideological conflict and proxy wars as the world's most powerful imperialist states. Perhaps the biggest marker of a perceived-Russian aesthetic choice would be in the character of Baron Vladimir Harkonnen. 'The Russian sound was clearly meant to engage our prejudices – which, it must be remembered, were much stronger when Dune was written in the early sixties than they are now' (O'Reilly 1981).

Galach would see a few written iterations: glyphs on the background of the menus in *Emperor: Battle for Dune*, a 2001 strategy game for PC; some decorative writing on David Lynch's 1984 movie adaptation; and a script created by the art department of Denis Villeneuve's 2021 movie adaptation. However, it is not possible to deduce with reasonable certainty that either of the first two are Galach, which makes Villeneuve's Galach the most fitting for analysis since it has been used in texts that were read diegetically.

All glyphs that could be identified by freezing the frame in the movie can be compared to both the Latin alphabet and the Cyrillic alphabet. Our key finding is that many of the characters seem to have been designed through a process of rotating, splitting and mirroring across body width, back-to-back duplication and mirroring, combining or simply making minor structural changes to Latin and Cyrillic graphemes.

Galach	Ʃ	H	∩	Ʊ	A	⅄	Þ	ԛ	V
Latin	E, Œ	H	n, U	G	A	Y, T	p, b	P, q	A, V
Cyrillic	Е	Н	П		А	У, Т	р, Ь	Р	А

Galach	Ǝ	⊥	Ʒ	Ф	ɧ	४	Ω	Л
Latin	E	F	Z		h, n		T, c	
Cyrillic	Е			Ф	Г	Ю	Т, с	Л

In designing the language, Villeneuve's art department seem to have aimed for characters which shared a likeness in both the Latin and Cyrillic alphabets, perhaps to stress the conceptual idea that Galach is, as stated in *Dune*, a hybrid Inglo-Slavic language. The comparison above shows identical or nearly identical design in both the Latin and the Cyrillic alphabets.

Although Galach is the language of the galaxy, the setting of *Dune* is mostly on Arrakis, the desert planet on which the protagonist Paul Atreides spends most of his time, so it makes sense that the reader would be exposed to much more Fremen than Galach. Fremen is the language of the homonymous desert-dwellers of Arrakis, and it shares a surprising amount of its lexicon with Arabic. In tandem with the ideas discussed here connecting glossopoeic exoticising and the real-world phenomenon of Orientalism, Csicsery-Ronay (2012: 41) affirms that Herbert uses 'foreign neologisms to create exotic effects'.

The first created script to come out of *Dune* was a written version of Fremen developed by John Quijada, who would later be acknowledged in the conlanging community as the creator of the highly complex Ithkuil language. Quijada's Fremen script was created to feature in *The Dune Encyclopedia*, and as such its canonicity is usually dismissed when taken into the context of the larger *Dune* mythos. However, its contents were approved by Frank Herbert in the *Encyclopedia*'s introduction, and though certain narratives and back-stories were contradicted in later instalments in the series, no further iterations of written Fremen were developed (David J. Peterson's Chakobsa is the language spoken by the Fremen in the 2021 movie adaptation, but it is not Fremen in the literary canon, where Fremen evolved from Chakobsa). Being so, it is the closest example at hand of a script that stayed true to Herbert's vision of associating the Fremen people with Arabs (Herbert 1969).

Quijada's Fremen is not very far from the abjad used to write the Arabic language. Many characters read as graphical simplifications of Arabic ones. We have constructed the following table to show probable corresponding Arabic counterparts to each Fremen character, based on the associated Arabic phoneme, the Latin correspondent as stated in *The Dune Encyclopedia* (McNelly 1984: 329), and overall graphic similarity.

Quijada's Fremen	ا	ب	د	س	)	ف	ع	غ	و	ا	ح	ک	د	ل
Arabic letter	ا	ب	د	ض		ف	ع	غ			ج	ك	ذ	ل
Latin correspondent	a	b	d	dh	e	f	g	gh	h	i	j	k	kh	l

Quijada's Fremen	م	ں	ه	ك	)	ں	س	ط	۷	٩	و	ى	ظ	
Arabic letter	م	ن		ق	ر	س	ش	ط		و	و	ي	ظ	
Latin correspondent	m	n	o	q	r	s	sh	t	th	u	w	y	z	

Alien typographies in sf and the influence of Asian languages 73

The most distinguishing difference is the addition of vowels as graphemes and not as diacritics – while in Arabic the vowels are usually denoted by paraorthographical signage, in Fremen there are dedicated characters for each vowel, coincidentally matching the English morphological vowels a, e, i, o, u. The fact that Quijada added vowels as fully-fledged graphemes and that those vowels scanned perfectly into the Latin alphabetical vowel roster, as opposed to Arabic's short and long vowels, perhaps makes his Fremen – apparently intended to look like Arabic given the amount of overlap – more accessible to the Western reader.

Conclusion

Earlier in this chapter we revised the exotifying function of created languages and observed cases in literature and media where Asian languages such as Japanese and Chinese were used by writers and movie directors principally for visual impact. Additionally, through comparison with the phenomenon of pseudo-Asian tattoos and the use of hanzi, kanji, and kana in Western clothing, we explored how Western artists and writers sometimes use real languages they do not understand – usually of Asian origin – to create a sense of the mysterious and exotic. This supports the argument that there is a parallel between the ways a Western reader perceives Asian languages and fictional sf languages.

After employing typographical analysis as a method of studying the writing systems created to represent the language of alien universes and people in sf, we were able to determine perceived visual similarity between Aurebesh, from *Star Wars*, and Katakana, one of the Japanese writing systems; Futhork, from *Star Wars*, and the Latin script; Galach, from *Dune*, and both the Cyrillic and Latin scripts; and Fremen, from *The Dune Encyclopedia*, and the Arabic script. Through this method, it was possible to demonstrate a way in which, through typography and glossopoesis, Western authors of literature and media can employ postcolonial mimicry of otherised subjects such as Japanese, Arabic, and Russian people so as to situate their universes and characters in alterity positions occupied in the Western reader's mind by those mimicked people. This process relies on an exoticisation of Asian languages in the Occident that mirrors the exoticisation function of glossopoesis used by sf authors to express difference between their human protagonists and their fictional marginalised others.

References

AFP (2019) 'Ariana Grande mocked for Japanese tattoo typo: "Leave me and my grill alone"', *The Guardian*, 13 January <https://www.theguardian.com/music/2019/jan/31/ariana-grande-mocked-for-japanese-tattoo-typo-leave-me-and-my-grill-alone>

Avatar (2009) J. Cameron (director). 20th Century Fox.
Barber, N. (2016) 'The film Star Wars stole from', *BBC*, 4th January <https://www.bbc.com/culture/article/20160104-the-film-star-wars-stole-from>
Barr, T., Bray, A. and Horton, C. (2021) Star Wars: *The Visual Encyclopedia*. London: Dorling Kindersley.
Bhabha, H. (1984) 'Of mimicry and man: the ambivalence of colonial discourse', *October* 28: 125–33.
Burrt, B. (2001) *Galaxy Phrase Book and Travel Guide*. London: Dorling Kindersley.
Cheyne, R. (2008) 'Created languages in science fiction', *Science Fiction Studies* 35 (3): 386–403.
Crane, S. (1994) *Star Wars Miniatures Battles Companion*. New York: West End Games.
Csicsery-Ronay, I. (2012) *The Seven Beauties of Science Fiction*. Middleton: Wesleyan University Press.
Delany, S. R. (2014) *The American Shore: Meditations on a Tale of Science Fiction by Thomas M. Disch – 'Angouleme'*. Middletown: Wesleyan University Press.
Dirlik, A. (1996) 'Chinese history and the question of orientalism', *History and Theory* 35 (4): 96–118.
Dune (2021) D. Villeneuve (director). Warner Brothers.
Fenollosa, E., Pound, E., Stalling, J. and Klein, L. (2009) *The Chinese Written Character as a Medium for Poetry*. New York: Fordham University Press.
Get Out (2017) J. Peele (director). Universal Pictures.
Herbert, F. (1965) *Dune*. Boston: Chilton Books.
Herbert, F. (1969) *Interview with Frank Herbert by Dr. McNelly* [Interview, 3 February]. Paulina June and George Pollak Library; California State University, Fullerton. <https://californiarevealed.org/islandora/object/cavpp%3A14674>
Hergé (1929) *Tintin au Pays des Soviets*. Brussels: Le Petit Vingtième.
Hergé (1934) *Le Lotus Bleu*. Brussels: Le Petit Vingtième.
Holborn, M. (1991) *Beyond Japan: A Photo Theatre*. London: Jonathan Cape.
Lucas, G. (2014) 'George Lucas on Akira Kurosawa', *Criterion*, 19 March 2014 <https://www.criterion.com/current/posts/3102-george-lucas-on-akira-kurosawa>
McNelly, W. E. D. (1984) *The Dune Encyclopedia*. New York: Putnam.
Minear, R. H. (1980) 'Orientalism and the study of Japan', *The Journal of Asian Studies* 39 (3): 507–17.
Moser, D. (1991) 'Why Chinese is so damn hard', *Sino-Platonic Papers* 27: 59–70 <http://sino-platonic.org/complete/spp027_john_defrancis.pdf>
Noletto, I. A. C. and Lopes, S. A. T. (2019) 'Language and ideology: glossopoesis as a secondary narrative framework in Le Guin's *The Dispossessed*', *Acta Scientiarum Language and Culture* 41 (2): e43961.
Noletto, I. A. C., Lopes, S. A. T. and Costa, M. T. de A. (2017) 'Satire in Swift's own words: considerations on glossopoesis in *Gulliver's Travels*', *Journal of English Language and Literature* 7 (2): 519–24.
O'Reilly, T. (1981) *Frank Herbert*. New York: Frederick Ungar.
Said, E. W. (2003) *Orientalism*. London: Penguin.
Shedd, W. T. (2016) *Tracing the Evolving Nexus of Race, Species, and 'Otherness' in the* Star Wars *Film Franchise*. Washington: Georgetown University.
da Silva, L. L. S. (2016) 'O embate entre Edward Said e Bernard Lewis no contexto da ressignificação do Orientalismo', *Antropolítica – Revista Contemporânea de Antropologia* 40: 280–306.
Star Wars (1977) G. Lucas (director). Lucasfilm.

Star Wars: The Phantom Menace (1999) (G. Lucas, director). Lucasfilm.
Stockwell, P. (2006) 'Invented language in literature', in K. Brown (ed.) *Encyclopedia of Language and Linguistics* (2nd edn). Amsterdam: Elsevier, pp. 3–10.
Svozil, K. (2006) *Aesthetics and Scarcity: A Physics Perspective on Ornament*. Vienna: University of Technology Vienna Press.
The Matrix (1999) The Wachowskis (directors). Warner Brothers.
The Phantom Menace (1999) G. Lucas (director). Lucasfilm.
The Return of the Jedi (1983) R. Marquand (director). Lucasfilm.
Tian, T. (2021) *Hanzi Smatter* <http://hanzismatter.blogspot.com/>
Yoon, J.-p. (2017) 'Reconfiguring orientalism: Japan and Korea as depicted by early twentieth-century French orientalist literature', *Interventions* 19 (8): 1132–52.
Zheng, R. (2018) 'Chinese characters in fashion design: cultural appropriation or appreciation?', *Jing Daily*, 5 June <https://jingdaily.com/chinese-characters-fashion-design/>

CHAPTER 6

Design intentions and actual perception of fictional languages: Quenya, Sindarin, and Na'vi

Bettina Beinhoff

This chapter presents an empirical account of fictional language creation, through a comparative analysis of three popular conlangs. Taking a mixed quantitative and qualitative approach, Beinhoff investigates audience perceptions of J. R. R. Tolkien's Elvish languages, Quenya and Sindarin, and Paul Frommer's Na'vi, designed for James Cameron's (2009) blockbuster movie *Avatar*. Beinhoff's findings offer new insights into the phonaesthetics of fictional languages, highlighting the ways in which real readers and listeners respond to invented languages, and charting the correlation between language design and language effects.

Introduction

Fictional languages are typically designed to suit a specific character or group of characters, but they are also often created with a certain type of audience in mind. Because of film and television, such languages are often not read – as the title of this volume suggests – but rather heard. In Tolkien's works, for example, his fictional languages were initially in print only (although early recordings do exist in which Tolkien himself speaks these languages). More recently, fictional languages increasingly form part of the dialogue and soundtrack of films and TV series. Since the hugely successful movie productions of *The Lord of the Rings* and *The Hobbit* by director Peter Jackson over the past twenty-one years, new generations of Tolkien fans are likely to have heard his languages before seeing them in print, especially the Elvish languages Quenya and Sindarin. Other fictional languages have also been developed primarily for film productions, such as the language Na'vi which was created for the film *Avatar*, directed by James Cameron and released in 2009. Na'vi was designed as a language that cinemagoers would hear, rather than read, appropriately since Na'vi is part of an oral culture that does not rely on writing.

This chapter will explore the design aims underlying the creation process of these languages – Quenya, Sindarin, and Na'vi – and how these languages are perceived outside of their fictional contexts. The aim of the study is not to detect any potential design 'flaws', but rather to find out to what extent the perception and evaluation of these languages rely on the fictional context or whether they are in themselves a vehicle for certain traits. The key question is: Are the language creators' aims reflected in listeners' evaluations? The study on which this chapter is based is part of a larger research project into constructed languages (of which fictional languages are a subset). For the purpose of this chapter, I will report on the three languages Quenya, Sindarin, and Na'vi, and the responses of southern English participants in the UK to explore the relation of design aims and perception of fictional languages in depth.

In the following section, I focus on the design aims and how they are reflected in the fictional languages. This will be followed by a section on how the fictional languages are perceived by participants when they hear them outside of their fictional context. The chapter will close with a discussion of whether the design aims match the participants' perceptions and evaluations.

Designing languages: aims and intentions

Designing a fictional language is a very complex endeavour in which the language creator has to consider and develop each aspect of the language, from the sound system through morphology and syntax (grammar) to semantics (meaning relations) and pragmatics (contextual meaning). Arguably, the first of these domains that someone would encounter who hears the language for the first time, is the sound system. And indeed, for many language creators this is the main focus and often the starting point for a new language (Beinhoff 2015). Apart from a personal sense of aesthetics, many language creators use sound symbolism to inform the sound structure and patterns of their languages. Sound symbolism is the 'hypothesized systematic relationship between sound and meaning' (Ohala 1997: 98; see also Hinton et al. 1994, Ohala 1994), that is, the idea that certain sounds convey certain meanings (see also Mooshammer et al., Chapter 7 in this volume). However, as many language creators strive for a naturalistic and realistic-sounding language, they might often use elements of sound symbolism (such as the idea that certain sounds may sound 'harsh' or 'soft') in combination with other patterns that can be found in natural languages (Beinhoff 2015).

Surprisingly little research has been done so far on these languages themselves and most of these studies have focused on the function of fictional languages as stylistic or literary devices (see for example the chapter on *Phantasiesprachen* [imagined languages] in Helmich 2016). Closely related to fictional languages is the creation of character names, which are also supposed to reveal some of the attributes of the character. Here, the use of speech sounds is considered crucial to expressing such attributes as they fulfil specific functions within the fictional setting (see Elsen 2008). Accordingly, authors tend to make prolific use of sound symbolism (Black and Wilcox 2011). Thus, fictional names – and by extension fictional languages – can function as identity markers for the fictional characters they are associated with. For example, Galadriel from Tolkien's *Lord of the Rings* is a royal Elf whose name consists of voiced consonants and open vowels and front vowels which should make the name sound pleasant and perhaps more elevated and regal. Conversely, the name of one of the Orc captains from the same novel, Grishnákh, contains consonants that make the name sound less pleasant and rather rough: it begins with the consonant combination /gr/ that is reminiscent of a growl and contains the voiceless consonants /ʃ/ and /k/.

There is very little research on fictional languages from a linguistic perspective (this volume being one notable exception), but fortunately Tolkien's languages are relatively well-researched and also well-documented by himself and his contemporaries. This is not the case for the language Na'vi, from *Avatar*. While it is possible to rely on primary and secondary sources when examining the design aims for Tolkien's languages, the key source of information on Na'vi is the language creator himself, Paul Frommer. He kindly agreed to answer an extensive number of questions about Na'vi, its design aims, process, and intentions and I would like to thank him again for all his time and patience. In the following, I will discuss the design process and the aims for each of the three languages, Quenya, Sindarin, and Na'vi. These three languages were selected as they have been created for very different characters and, as such, they are structurally quite different, as will be discussed in more depth below.

Quenya and Sindarin

Tolkien's main work of literary fiction, the three-part novel *The Lord of the Rings*, is set within a fantasy world populated by a number of fictitious life forms, such as the humanoid Hobbits, Dwarfs, and Elves. Even though the main character of the novel is a Hobbit, the Elves are central characters in the story and their culture a key part of the fictitious world. In the case of Tolkien's Elvish languages Quenya and Sindarin, the creation process drew heavily on other – mostly European – languages and the creator's own sense of aesthetics (Weiner and Marshall 2011). Quenya is the High Elven language, and Sindarin is the Grey Elven language of a somewhat lower status (Weiner and Marshall 2011). For Tolkien, these languages were the centre of attention while the actual character and characteristics of the Elves were developed alongside, if not after, the languages themselves. Tolkien's aim was for both languages to sound 'aesthetically pleasing' and he designed Quenya to sound 'especially pleasant' (in one of his letters to Naomi Mitchison, letter 144 in Carpenter 1981; see also Fimi and Higgins 2016). Sindarin was supposed to sound 'harsher and heavier, more consonantal' than Quenya (Weiner and Marshall 2011: 82), which implies that in Tolkien's view a greater number of consonants would make a language sound harsher.

Both Sindarin and Quenya have a number of consonants that are not present in Tolkien's first language English, such as the velar fricative /x/ and the aspirated approximant /ʍ/. The consonant /r/ is pronounced as a tap [ɾ] or trill [r], never as an approximant, adding to the Celtic feel of the languages which Tolkien found attractive and that he thought was fitting for the '"Celtic" type of legends and stories told of its speakers' (letter 144 in Carpenter 1981). Sindarin and Quenya also have long vs. short consonants: in Sindarin sirion vs. o**ss**iriand and **M**ordor vs. ra**mm**as, which was inspired by Finnish. As Quenya was supposed to sound more fluid and softer (Weiner and Marshall 2011: 82), Tolkien made it 'less consonantal' than Sindarin and also less than the three languages that served as its main inspiration: Latin, Finnish, and Greek (letter 144 in Carpenter 1981).

The vowel systems of Quenya and Sindarin contain vowels that also exist in British English; Tolkien described them as being 'of normal kind' (Tolkien 1955: 490), presumably in relation to the language his work was written in. The short vowels written as i, e, a, o, and u are the same as in English 'mach**i**ne, w**e**re, f**a**ther, f**o**r, br**u**te' (Tolkien 1955: 490; my emphasis). Sindarin has long vowels which are pronounced similarly to the short ones, only with more length. Quenya has two long vowels which are pronounced 'tenser' than the short vowels (Tolkien 1955: 490). The only vowel that may strike speakers of British English as somewhat unusual is the rounded front vowel /y/ which appears in Sindarin only.

Na'vi

The background to the development of Na'vi is very different to that of Sindarin and Quenya. Na'vi is the language of the people inhabiting the fictional moon Pandora in the movie *Avatar*, which means that the fictional world already existed when the language was created. Thus, the language had to align with the pre-existing fictional culture. In the narrative of the movie, a human protagonist learns the language and a small part of the storyline is devoted to his language learning efforts. The Na'vi language and culture are presented as central elements in the movie.

The director, James Cameron, approached the linguist Paul Frommer with a request to create a new language for the movie. Cameron's main concerns were that the language should sound appealing, but also complicated (Frommer, July 2019, personal communication). Further considerations were that the language had to be producible by human actors and that it would be interesting and intricate enough for fans of the movie to further explore Na'vi. Thus, the language design had to balance some degree of simplicity with complexity. At the same time, the aim was for the language to sound interesting in some way, a bit exotic and pleasant – at least to Western listeners. To achieve this, Frommer made use of a number of strategies across all linguistic domains; however, I will focus on its phonology here. Na'vi contains a number of sounds that are unusual for Western/European languages, such as ejectives, a strongly trilled /r/, and phonemic glottal stop /ʔ/. It does not contain some familiar sounds, such as voiced oral stops and it has unusual consonant clusters, like /fŋ/ in initial position. The phonology of Na'vi also allows for relatively long vowel sequences to achieve a softer and gentle sound. The vowels of Na'vi have corresponding sounds or very close approximations in the English vowel inventory (a detailed account of the Na'vi phonology can be found at the *Learn Na'vi* website).

Over the years, an enthusiastic and thriving community of Na'vi speakers has developed. While many of these Na'vi learners and speakers certainly started learning the language because they liked the movie, many seem to have been drawn to Na'vi because of its successful design and the culture it reflects (see Schreyer 2015).

Perceiving fictional languages: evaluations and interpretations

To date, there has been very little research on how fictional languages are perceived (but see Mooshammer et al., Chapter 7 this volume). There have been some studies that have explored the effects of fictional names (such as Elsen 2008, Croft 2009; see also discussion in Wilcox et al. 2018), but so far no study has investigated whether the design aims of the language creators are actually reflected in how their languages are perceived, especially outside of the fictional environment in which they are typically embedded. This is important as it would show to what extent the design strategies employed in the creation process are actually effective. It would also reveal if and how listeners make use of sound symbolism as a strategy to make sense of an unknown language. This could provide useful feedback for future language creation projects. Thus, the key specific question of this study is: are Tolkien's and Frommer's aims reflected in listeners' evaluations of Quenya, Sindarin, and Na'vi?

Methodology

The research design for this study made use of two research methods: an online survey and structured interviews. In the online survey, participants rated audio recordings of Quenya, Sindarin, and Na'vi as to how 'pleasant', 'friendly', 'natural', 'strange', 'educated', 'peaceful', 'familiar', 'artificial', and 'aggressive' they sounded. The responses were recorded on a 7-point Likert scale for each of these traits, from [1] 'very pleasant' to [7] 'not pleasant', and so on (see below). The list of attitudinal traits is derived from well-established sociolinguistic studies that elicited perceptions towards natural languages and accents (see Garrett 2010, Giles 1970, Lambert et al. 1968; see also Beinhoff 2013) and they were refined by consulting Tolkien's writing and secondary writings on his languages. In the case of Na'vi, I asked Paul Frommer for relevant traits that reflect his language design aims. Taken together, this resulted in the following list of traits.

very pleasant	not pleasant
very friendly	not friendly
very natural	not natural
very strange	not strange
very educated	not educated
very peaceful	not peaceful
very familiar	not familiar
very artificial	not artificial
very aggressive	not aggressive

As part of an online survey, each language was played on a separate screen, followed by the Likert scales, one for each trait. After listening to the recording, participants clicked the relevant box on each scale, depending on their impression of the language. Once they had completed one language, they clicked a button which brought up the next language. The audio recordings were between 22 and 30 seconds long. Participants did not know what languages they were listening to and no further context was provided. As participants were listening to the recordings in succession, it was inevitable that they might unintentionally compare the recordings. To address this, the recordings were presented in two different randomisation patterns (through two different survey links, where half of the participants received one link and the other half the other) and the results checked for effects of the sequence in which the recordings were heard, but no such effects were detected.

The recordings for Sindarin and Quenya were taken from a well-known website dedicated to Tolkien's languages with kind permission of the web hosts (Tolkien's Linguistic cellar: <https://glaemscrafu.jrrvf.com/english/index.html>). The Na'vi recording was kindly made available by Paul Frommer with permission to use for this study. All recordings were in a neutral and calm tone of voice. The Sindarin and Quenya recordings were spoken by the web hosts, those of Na'vi was spoken by Paul Frommer. All three recordings had male voices. To make the task easier for those who provided the recordings, no specific texts were requested, which means that the recordings were of different texts. In the interviews, participants commented that they did not notice this. In both the survey and the interview, participants could hear each recording only once before responding.

Participants accessed the survey through a link that was distributed through mailing lists and social networks. Participants from a number of language backgrounds took part in this survey, but for the purpose of this chapter, I will report on the results of the twenty people from southern England with English as their first language to align these with the participants in the interviews.

The interviews were conducted online using Zoom with ten southern British English participants (from Cambridgeshire, Norfolk, Essex, and East Sussex), all of whom had English as their first language and had only limited knowledge of other languages (up to secondary school level in, for example, Spanish or French). Participants were initially recruited on campus in Cambridge and then recruited 'friends of friends' (i.e. using the snowball principle). Ultimately, of all interviewees, half were engaged in linguistic study (two in linguistics and three in language teaching) and the other half studied or had studied other subjects. They reported to take part in this study out of interest in science fiction and fantasy. The interviews were semi-structured and questions aimed at eliciting information that could add further depth to the findings from the surveys. Each participant listened to one language (the same recordings as for the survey were used; again, no information on the languages was given), followed by a set of questions. Examples of these questions are 'describe the language in your own words', 'who might speak this language?' and 'where might this language be spoken?'. Once each question had been answered, the next language was played and the procedure was repeated. The interviews lasted typically around 50 minutes. As with the survey, the language recordings were played in succession and in two different randomisation patterns in the interviews. While participants made remarks that implied they compared the recordings, they still considered each recording in its own right and used ways to describe and evaluate that were independent from those of previous recordings. Those few comparative statements that were made were used as an aid to describe the languages. In the following section, I will report the results for each of the languages.

Results for Quenya

Before analysing the ratings for Quenya, it is useful to summarise the design aims of Tolkien for this language as it will make it easier to compare intention against the actual perception and evaluation of Quenya. As mentioned earlier in this chapter, Quenya was designed to sound 'aesthetically pleasing' and 'especially pleasant' (letter 144 in Carpenter 1981). Based on Tolkien's writing and his letters, especially his comment that the language should be 'of a European kind in style and structure' (letter 144 in Carpenter 1981), it is evident that he also wanted this language to sound natural and not artificial. We can infer from this that the language was not supposed to sound strange in the sense of 'odd' or 'outlandish', though it will likely

Design intentions and actual perception of fictional languages

be perceived as strange in the sense of 'unknown', which was part of the design. From his letters and essays – and from his depiction of the speakers of Quenya – it is also apparent that the language is not supposed to sound aggressive and that it is associated with a higher level of education as the High Elven language (see also Fimi and Higgins 2016). This is also indirectly supported by Tolkien's comment that the languages which inspired him in the creation of Quenya, namely Finnish and Greek, give him '"phonaesthetic" pleasure' (letter 144 in Carpenter 1981). There is no specific information on the traits *friendly*, *peaceful*, and *familiar*, which are also used in this study, though from the depiction of the Elvish culture in Tolkien's novels it is likely that Quenya would be associated with friendliness and peacefulness. However, since there is no specific information on these traits available from Tolkien himself, I did not indicate the intended aims for these traits in the below graph (see Graphic 6.1).

When interpreting this graph, it is important to keep in mind that we are looking at mean values, averaged for twenty participants. For this reason, the evaluations can only ever be trends as participants rarely ever completely agree. With this in mind, mean ratings below the middle category of 4 are considered to lean towards the 'very' category and those over 4 as leaning towards the 'not' category. In this way, a 'low' bar for example for *pleasant* is interpreted as reflecting a general tendency to perceive the language as relatively pleasant. Note also that participants are likely to use the middle category of 4 to express uncertainty, which is visible in the trait *familiar*. This uncertainty could be explained by the combination of familiar and unfamiliar structures in Quenya; it contains patterns and sounds

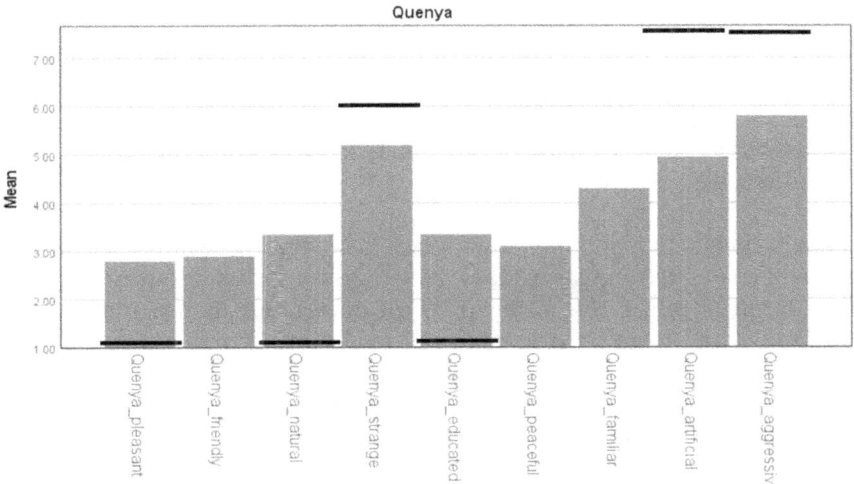

Graphic 6.1 Mean ratings for Quenya on all traits (where 1 = very pleasant, friendly, etc., and 7 = not pleasant, friendly, etc.). The black lines across the bars indicate the language design intentions

that the participants will have been familiar with (through the presence of sounds that also exist in British English) while also containing sounds and structures that are not typically present in the participants' environments.

Graphic 6.1 shows Tolkien's design intentions marked with black lines, while the ratings from the online survey are depicted in grey bars. From this graph it is quite clear that our participants rated Quenya as sounding quite *pleasant* and fairly *natural* and *educated*. The language was rated as sounding relatively strange. Participants also rated Quenya as not very artificial, and they certainly did not think it sounded aggressive. These results align reasonably well with Tolkien's stated design intentions, although perhaps the ratings for *artificial* are not as much towards the 'not artificial' side of the scale as expected and intended.

The interviews provide more in-depth information on why Quenya may have been evaluated in this way. When asked to describe the language in their own words, many participants mentioned specific sounds, such as 'rolled r', but also commented on the absence of 'rough sounds'. One participant mentioned that 'it ended with lots of o's and a's'. According to the participants, all of this made the language 'flow nicely', made it sound 'comforting' and 'nice'. So, overall, the sound structure makes Quenya sound very pleasant to the interviewees. Participants also commented on the rhythm of the language which one described as 'bouncy', and which was perceived as contributing to the pleasantness of the language. As with all three languages in this study, participants found it difficult to place the language. When asked where this language might be spoken or who might speak it, all participants expressed uncertainty. Most participants did in fact list several locations, for example:

> I was getting a mix of, I got a mix of the old English because it sounded like a mixture of English words and Dutch at first and the kind and then I thought maybe south Asia, so towards India then maybe middle east but I also heard maybe mm ... maybe southern Europe so Italian influence.... (Participant E10)

Most participants mentioned a Romance language, though one participant thought it sounded similar to Slavic languages and another thought it might be a Bantu language. This may explain the uncertainty in the survey ratings for *familiar*, as Romance languages will sound quite familiar to our participants, but there remain elements in Quenya that made it hard to locate. This will also have contributed to the rating for the trait *strange* in the sense of 'unknown' or 'difficult to identify'.

Results for Sindarin

As with Quenya, we have to rely on Tolkien's writing when determining his design aims for Sindarin. As mentioned earlier in this chapter,

Design intentions and actual perception of fictional languages 85

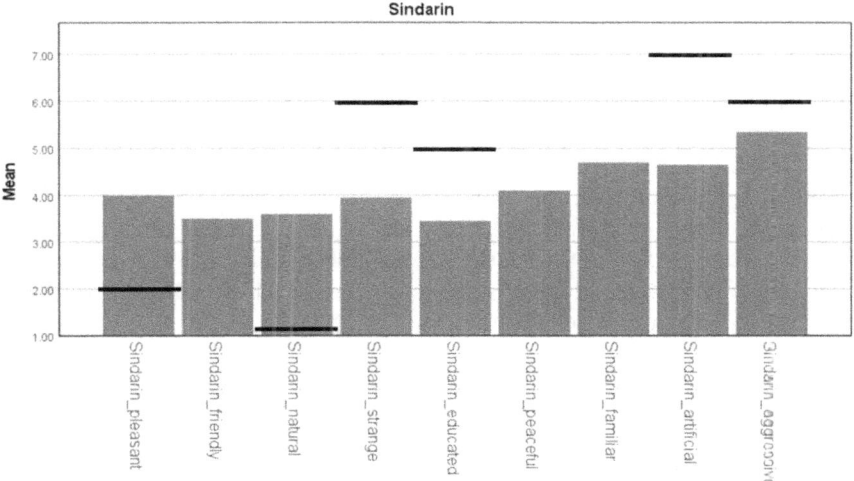

Graphic 6.2 Mean ratings for Sindarin on all traits (where 1 = very pleasant, friendly, etc., and 7 = not pleasant, friendly, etc.). The black lines across the bars indicate the language design intentions

Quenya and Sindarin are related and the aims for Sindarin are similar to those for Quenya. However, as Sindarin is supposed to sound 'harsher and heavier' than Quenya (Weiner and Marshall 2011: 82), and given that within the fictional context it is used for more mundane purposes than Quenya, it is likely to be supposed to sound a little less *pleasant* than Quenya and perhaps not as *educated*. The aims for *natural* and *artificial* are the same for Sindarin and Quenya as Tolkien aimed for naturalness across both languages. However, seeing that Sindarin is a language that is also used in conflict and battle, and given the aim for it to sound 'harsher and heavier', there is probably some leeway for it to sound slightly more aggressive than Quenya, though explicit aggressiveness is still not part of the design. As for Quenya, there is no specific information on the traits *friendly*, *peaceful*, and *familiar*, which results in the following interpretation of aims for the language as indicated by the black lines in Graphic 6.2.

As Quenya and Sindarin are related languages, it makes sense to begin with a comparison of how they have been rated. Graphic 6.2 indicates that Sindarin was indeed rated as less *pleasant* than Quenya. The biggest difference in the average ratings for these two languages is on this particular trait, where the mean ratings differ by more than one point. Sindarin was rated slightly less *natural* and slightly more *artificial* than Quenya, but this is a very minor difference. Similarly, Sindarin was evaluated as sounding slightly more *strange* and a little more *aggressive* than Quenya, but again these are only minor differences.

One of Tolkien's aims was for Sindarin to sound harsher and therefore presumably less *pleasant* then Quenya and this is reflected in the ratings. Sindarin was indeed rated as less pleasant than Quenya, though within the scope of the rating scale used, it has been placed within the middle category – meaning that it was also not an unpleasant language to listen to. The evaluations for *natural* and *strange* are just below the middle point and while this does not meet the intended aims, it still shows that Sindarin did not sound expressly unnatural and it also did not sound very strange, which may well be because of the relatively familiar sounds in the language (this will be explored more in the interview data below). Ironically, these sounds may also have contributed to the rating for *artificial*, which was placed just slightly above the middle point. To our participants, Sindarin still sounded quite *educated* and not particularly *aggressive*, but – as mentioned above – it was evaluated as sounding a bit different to Quenya on these traits, and these differences were as intended.

The interviews suggest that participants were indeed reminded of languages with which they are vaguely familiar. For example, the presence of 'harsh' sounds, such as /x/, made them think of Dutch or German. The combination of the sound structure and intonation made one participant think that this could be a Celtic language and more specifically Welsh, which was indeed part of Tolkien's aims for the Elvish languages in general. Welsh was one of the languages that he drew inspiration from in the design of Sindarin. One participant commented, 'I got quite a fantasy vibe from it and an Elvish vibe from it', and this is the only instance where one of the languages in this study was correctly identified. However, overall, participants placed this language in a number of different locations, such as 'southern Mediterranean', 'Europe or European-esque areas of Canada and the US' and 'south or central America', though most located this language in Western Europe, perhaps explaining the slightly higher rating on the trait *familiar*. Participants generally described this language in positive terms, for example as 'tuneful, melodic', 'quite smooth', and 'it was quite familiar'. Negative comments such as 'There was no nice rhythm to it, it was very bare' were rare but show that participants by no means always agree in their evaluations and descriptions of these languages.

Results for Na'vi

Unlike for Quenya and Sindarin, the design aims for Na'vi do not have to be inferred from the literature. Rather, the creator of the language, Paul Frommer, kindly made the information about the language's design and the design intentions available to me. He also indicated the design intentions and aims for each of the traits used in this study. This is different from how the intended traits were inferred from Tolkien's writing but offers a more precise and complete account of what Na'vi was planned to sound like. As there is less writing and research on Na'vi as compared to Sindarin and

Design intentions and actual perception of fictional languages 87

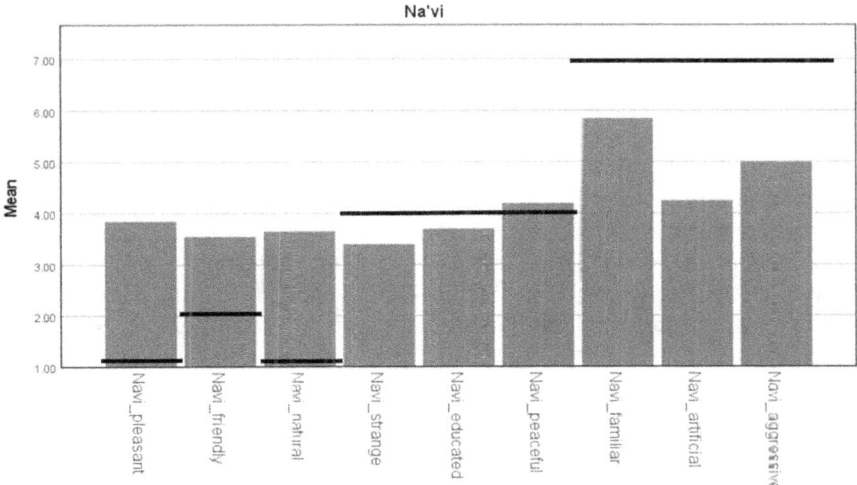

Graphic 6.3 Mean ratings for Na'vi on all traits (where 1 = very pleasant, friendly, etc., and 7 = not pleasant, friendly, etc.). The black lines across the bars indicate the language design intentions

Quenya, the language creator himself is the richest source of information on the language. This means that at times, in comparison, the information for Sindarin and Quenya could be ambiguous for some traits but is considered in the analysis and discussion of the data. Accordingly, Na'vi has a full set of design intentions, as indicated by the black bars on Graphic 6.3. These show that Na'vi is supposed to sound very *pleasant*, perhaps in line with the intention that fans of the movie might find it pleasant and interesting enough to want to learn it. Na'vi is also meant to sound fairly *friendly*, though the design aim was not to make it sound particularly *educated* or *peaceful*, which is in keeping with the fictional culture that the language represents. Within the fictional realm, the Na'vi people are not 'educated' as understood through a typical Western/colonial lens and much of the movie deals with their fight against intruders from Earth. Yet, the language itself is not intended to sound aggressive as such. Na'vi is supposed to sound moderately strange and very unfamiliar as it is spoken by an alien people in a different star system. Like the other two fictional languages in this study, Na'vi should sound very natural and not artificial, like a natural language.

For Na'vi, the ratings for many of the traits are clustered around the middle category with most being slightly below 4 (see Graphic 6.3). Na'vi was rated as very unfamiliar – in fact the least familiar out of all three languages reported here – which could explain the level of uncertainty that is often expressed with ratings near the middle category on unevennumbered scales, such as the one used here. This means that the ratings for *pleasant, friendly, natural,* and *artificial* do not reflect the language creator's intentions, but the ratings for *strange, educated,* and *peaceful* are very close to the intended score. Na'vi was supposed to sound unfamiliar, and this is visible in the participants' ratings, while the rating for *aggressive* is leaning more towards 'not aggressive' with a mean score of 5.

The interviews are very helpful in making sense of these survey results. All interviewees commented on some of the sounds when describing Na'vi. As with Quenya and Sindarin, participants mentioned sounds that do not occur in their variety of English (southern British), in particular the trill or 'rolled' /r/ and the ejective sounds. The latter were described in various ways: some interviewees described them as 'popping sounds' while others used the words 'plosives' and 'glottal stops' to describe them. This is interesting because plosives and glottal stops are very common features of the interviewees' variety of English; what they picked up on here is that the ejective sounds of Na'vi are more forceful versions of some of these plosives and that glottal stops are used in different positions and more frequently in Na'vi. It also shows that some of the participants were quite well-informed on linguistic terminology. These ejectives and glottal stops, together with the other design features employed to make this language sound unfamiliar and alien, will have given rise to the impression that it sounds 'a bit harsher' to my interviewees and that there were 'not many familiar sounds'. Of course, Na'vi does have a number of sounds that also occur in English, but the unfamiliar sounds may have distracted from them. Apart from commenting on specific sounds, participants also described the language as 'exotic', which aligned with Frommer's design intentions.

Participants had difficulties locating Na'vi. Some tried to locate it by using specific sounds as guidance, such as 'hearing that roll or that trill kind of made me think Middle Eastern, Farsi but also from the sound of his voice it could be maybe afric/ some part of Africa'. Again, this comment shows that Na'vi was indeed perceived as sounding 'exotic', but it also shows how some participants 'exoticised' other cultures. Some thought that Na'vi sounded a bit like Arabic due to the unfamiliar sounds. Other interviewees located Na'vi as generally 'non-European' without being able to narrow it down any further. Interestingly, others saw Na'vi as potentially a language of 'one of those smaller European countries'. Altogether, this indicates a great deal of uncertainty about the language itself. Clearly, participants were not sure how to contextualise Na'vi within their own frame of reference and unfamiliar sounds were the main reason for that.

Discussion

The results indicate that all three languages were perceived as intended by the language creators for at least some of the traits used in the survey. For example, Quenya was supposed to sound 'specially pleasant' by Tolkien (from his letters to Naomi Mitchison, letter 144 in Carpenter 1981) and it was indeed rated as very pleasant by my research participants. In fact, it was by far the language rated as sounding most *pleasant* out of all three languages discussed in this chapter. This was further supported by the interview data where Quenya was described as, for example, sounding 'comforting' and 'nice'. In the interviews, participants linked these positive evaluations to the absence of what they perceived as 'rough' sounds, which likely reflects Tolkien's strategy of making it 'less consonantal'. The rhythm of the language also seemed to have contributed to the positive evaluation of Quenya as interviewees commented on this in particular; for example, by calling it a 'bouncy' language.

It is interesting to compare the results of Quenya to those of Sindarin. The aim for Sindarin was for it to sound 'aesthetically pleasing', though less so than Quenya (from Tolkien's letters to Naomi Mitchison, letter 144 in Carpenter 1981, Fimi and Higgins 2016). The language was supposed to sound 'harsher and heavier, more consonantal' than Quenya (Weiner and Marshall 2011: 82), which was realised by including more consonants in Sindarin words. The results from the survey indicate that Sindarin was indeed perceived as less pleasant than Quenya. This seems to have been due to the presence of certain consonants: for example, participants in the interviews commented on the sound /x/ in this language which they thought sounded 'harsh'. The language structure – in particular, the combination of the sound structure and intonation – reminded participants of Celtic languages, in particular Welsh, which is in line with the intentions of Tolkien who aimed for a Celtic feel in both Quenya and Sindarin.

Similarly, Na'vi was intended to sound unusual and exotic; the survey results indicate that this has indeed been achieved as it was rated as very *unfamiliar* (the least familiar-sounding language out of all three languages included in this chapter) and as very *strange*. The interview data suggests that this was due to the unusual sounds and sound patterns of the language. Participants commented especially on the trill /r/, ejective sounds, and glottal stops. Na'vi was also rated as fairly *peaceful*, which was also intended by the language creator, though the interview participants made no specific comments on this. Rather, they focused on the unfamiliar sounds, which also contributed to evaluations that were not intended for this language. For example, Na'vi was rated as less *pleasant* and less *friendly* than intended, which is likely due to the presence of a lot of unfamiliar sounds which may have caused some uncertainty and made participants seek out the middle category of the rating scale as a way to express their indecision. This became more evident in the interviews where participants imitated some of these unfamiliar sounds and commented that the language sounded 'a bit harsher'. This is in line with findings by Mooshammer et al. (Chapter 7 this volume) who found that 'alien sounds' received more negative ratings in their study.

In a similar way, both Quenya and Sindarin also had some ratings that were not as intended, especially for the traits *artificial* and *natural*, where both languages were rated as more artificial and less natural than intended. This is important because Tolkien drew a lot of inspiration from a number of natural languages to make Quenya and Sindarin sound as natural as possible. Interestingly, neither artificiality nor naturalness were mentioned in the interviews, which might indicate that these traits were not especially salient for the participants. It is therefore likely that the ratings for artificial and natural reflect a level of uncertainty (as we have seen for Na'vi for *pleasant and friendly*), or it is due to the relative unfamiliarity of some of the sounds mentioned in the interviews. Regardless, it is important to observe that the design strategies implemented by the language creators worked for some of the traits, but not for others. This also reveals that the fictional setting within which the languages are placed, the characters speaking these languages, and the languages themselves work in unison in creating a specific atmosphere and eliciting a specific set of attitudes.

A further important finding of this study is that sound symbolism does indeed play a major role in how these fictional languages were perceived and thus confirms the important role of this concept in language design (Beinhoff 2015). Participants explicitly mentioned specific sounds during the interviews and connected these sounds with certain perceptions, for example, /x/ sounds 'harsh'. Only sounds were mentioned that were not part of the sound inventory of the participants' first language, southern British English (e.g. the trill /r/, the sound /x/, and ejectives). It is possible that other sounds may have contributed to the evaluations as well, but participants were not aware of how familiar sounds may influence how they think about these languages. This point of investigation is beyond the scope of this study but would be an interesting one to follow up in future research. Another interesting observation is that participants only mentioned consonants in their description of the languages and not vowels. This may be because almost all of the vowels in the languages discussed here are relatively familiar to the participants. Mooshammer et al. (this volume) found that vowels contribute to the perceived pleasantness of a language, but given that vowels were not mentioned as a positive attribute of the languages it may also be that vowels were less salient as compared to consonants for the participants.

Conclusion

In summary, the study shows that all three languages were perceived as intended on some traits, such as *pleasant*. However, on other traits, the languages were evaluated differently compared to the design aims. This is not a flaw in the design of the languages; rather, it shows how important it is for the fictional context and the characters to align with the fictional language in constructing a holistic and convincing fictional setting. The languages are also successful outside of this fictional setting as all three languages have enthusiastic fans who learn these languages and communicate in them. For Na'vi, this has been found to be the case even for people who are not fans of the movie *Avatar*, but who were attracted to Na'vi by its interesting design and welcoming community (Schreyer 2015). Thus, even if these languages were evaluated negatively on some traits when heard in isolation, the cultural context they are part of seems to moderate this.

The choice of specific sounds (especially of consonants) is particularly effective in achieving design intentions; for example, the use of certain sounds makes Quenya sound pleasant and makes Na'vi sound exotic and unfamiliar. This suggests that the use and importance of sound symbolism in character names, as described by Elsen (2008) and Black and Wilcox (2011), can be extended to entire fictional languages. It is noteworthy, however, that our participants represented one particular language background, the main variety of which, English, they shared with the language creators. It is important to include participants from a variety of different language backgrounds in this research to find out whether these evaluations and strategies operate across languages or are specific to English-speaking participants. Research is currently underway to address this by including participants with other first languages and from other cultures in this study, though it would be equally important to include fictional languages that were designed by language creators with different first languages.

References

Adams, M. (ed.) (2011) *From Elvish to Klingon. Exploring Invented Languages*. Oxford: Oxford University Press.
Avatar (2009) J. Cameron (director). 20th Century Fox.
Beinhoff, B. (2013) *Perceiving Identity through Accent: Attitudes towards Non-Native Speakers and their Accents in English*. Bern: Peter Lang.
Beinhoff, B. (2015) 'Why are alien languages inherently human?', *Foundation: The International Review of Science Fiction* 122: 5–19.
Black, S. and Wilcox, B. (2011) 'Sense and serendipity: some ways fiction writers choose character names', *Names* 59 (3): 152–63.
Carpenter, H. (1981) *The Letters of JRR Tolkien*. Boston: Houghton Mifflin.
Croft, J. B. (2009) 'Naming the evil one: onomastic strategies in Tolkien and Rowling', *Mythlore* 28: 149–63.
Elsen, H. (2008) *Phantastische Namen*. Tuebingen: Gunter Narr Verlag.
Fimi, D. and Higgins, A. (eds) (2016) *J. R. R. Tolkien: A Secret Vice. Tolkien on Invented Languages*. London: HarperCollins.
Garrett, P. (2010) *Attitudes to Language*. Cambridge: Cambridge University Press.
Giles, H. (1970) 'Evaluative reactions to accents', *Educational Review* 22 (3): 211–27.
Helmich, W. (2016) *Ästhetik der Mehrsprachigkeit*. Heidelberg: Universitätsverlag Winter.
Hinton, L., Nichols, J. and Ohala, J. J. (eds) (1994) *Sound Symbolism*. Cambridge: Cambridge University Press.

Lambert, W. E., Gardner, R. C., Olton, R. and Tunstall, K. (1968) 'A study of the roles of attitudes and motivation in second-language learning', in J. Fishman (ed.) *Readings in the Sociology of Language*. New York: Mouton Publishers, pp. 473–91.

Learn Na'vi website: <https://learnnavi.org/navi-phonetics/>

Ohala, J. J. (1994) 'The frequency code underlies the sound-symbolic use of voice pitch', in J. Hinton, J. Nichols and J. J. Ohala (eds) *Sound Symbolism*. Cambridge: Cambridge University Press, pp. 325–47.

Ohala, J. J. (1997) 'Sound symbolism', *Proceedings of the 4th Seoul International Conference on Linguistics [SICOL]*, 11–15 August 1997, pp. 98–103.

Schreyer, C. (2015) 'The digital fandom of Na'vi speakers', *Performance and Performativity in Fandom. Transformative Works and Cultures* 18. <https://journal.transformativeworks.org/index.php/twc/article/download/610/512?inline=1>

Tolkien, J. R. R. (1955) *The Return of the King. The Lord of the Rings Part 3*. London: HarperCollins.

Weiner, E. S. C. and Marshall, J. (2011) 'Tolkien's invented languages', in M. Adams (ed.) *From Elvish to Klingon. Exploring Invented Languages*. Oxford: Oxford University Press, pp. 75–109.

Wilcox, B., Brown, B. L., Baker-Smemoe, W. and Morrison, T. G. (2018) 'Tolkien's phonoprint in character names throughout his invented languages', *Names* 66 (3): 135–43.

CHAPTER 7

The phonaesthetics of constructed languages: results from an online rating experiment

*Christine Mooshammer, Dominique Bobeck,
Henrik Hornecker, Kierán Meinhardt, Olga Olina,
Marie Christin Walch, and Qiang Xia*

> This chapter returns to the question of phonaesthetics addressed in Chapter 6. Here, the authors present an alternate empirical account of the issue which examines whether the symbolic effects of fictional languages are detectable by the everyday listener. Like Beinhoff, they concern themselves with listener response to fictional languages, measuring both positive and negative reactions to fourteen conlangs. These range from perhaps the most famous Klingon through to the lesser-known original creations Horn and ʕUiʕuid invented by Dominique Bobeck, one of the co-authors of this chapter. Working with native speakers of both English and German, the researchers take into account the ways in which a listener's L1, linguistic knowledge, and familiarity with a fictional language may impact upon their aesthetic and emotional judgements and their ability to identify a particular conlang out of context, without the impact of visual input or plot connection.

Introduction

Phonaesthetics, a compound deriving from Ancient Greek φωνή 'sound, voice' and αἰσθητική 'aesthetics', presupposes that phones and their combinations have an intrinsic property of being perceived as delightful or displeasing by human beings (Bloomfield 1909). Although several authors prior to J. R. R. Tolkien theorised about whether, and if so how, sound and meaning are related (Plato 1997, Locke 2004, Leibniz 1981, de Saussure 1916), it was the creator of Middle-earth who made use of these observations for the first time when conceiving his fantasy universe and its dwellers. For instance, the phonology of Quenya, the language of the graceful Elves, is supposedly based on that of the Finnish language, which Tolkien regarded as aesthetically highly pleasing (in one of his letters, Tolkien writes that coming across a Finnish grammar was like 'discovering a complete wine-cellar filled with bottles of an amazing wine of a kind and flavour never tasted before' [Tolkien 1981: 228]). Such features as the frequent use of long vowels or Quenya's tendency to open syllables are borrowed from Finnish (see Tolkien 2016: xvii). On the other hand, in Black Speech, a language spoken in the dark realm of Mordor by the evil and primitive Orcs, guttural sounds and complex consonant clusters are very frequent (see for example Podhorodecka 2007, Flieger 2017).

How did Tolkien come across the idea that Quenya fits better to the Elves and Black Speech to the Orcs? Specific sounds seem to possess certain properties making a language sound more, or less, pleasant. A major question arises whether these phonaesthetic properties are universal, i.e. they produce similar reactions in listeners regardless of their linguistic background, or if the impressions vary depending on the listeners' native tongue. Tolkien argued for the latter, so he used Old English as rendering of the language of the Rohirrim to construct a setting of an old civilisation related to his own, contemporary culture (Tolkien 2021). Likewise, Tolkien's goal was to achieve a euphonious sound for his Elvish languages and the translations from the Common Speech, at least in the perception of the English-speaking audience (Tolkien 2005: 752).

The effect of phonaesthetics in the perception of natural languages was investigated by Reiterer et al. (2020) and Kogan and Reiterer (2021). Both studies rely on results from a rating experiment, in which sixteen European languages were originally rated on twenty-two different scales. The number of scales was subsequently reduced to five via Principal Component Analysis. The resulting components were termed *beauty*, *status*, *eroticism*, *softness*, and *orderliness* based on the factor loadings of the original scales. The ratings given by forty-five participants with diverse native languages (mostly Slovene and German) seem to be affected mainly by two kinds of characteristics: firstly, the inherent properties of a language, such as its phonetics and phonology; and, secondly, external factors such as the first language of the participants and their familiarity with the presented languages. Regarding the language inherent properties, several factors play a role. The higher the sonority, the vocalic share, and the faster the speech rate accompanied by flatter intonation, the more pleasantly the languages are perceived. High sonority goes hand in hand with a higher share of vowels, liquids, and to a lesser degree also nasals. In contrast, low sonority means a higher frequency of (voiceless) stops, affricates, and fricatives (Vennemann 1988). Thus, based on Reiterer et al. (2020) and Kogan and Reiterer (2021), the lower the sonority, the slower the speech rate, and the wider the ranges in intonation, the more negative are the ratings.

The second important correlation in language assessment concerns the participants' L2 knowledge. Languages with higher recognition rate were rated better (except German despite its 100 per cent recognition rate in the above study). Even lower scores in sonority and related properties could be cancelled out by recognition rates: for example, English has an average sonority value but was always identified as English, possibly leading to its more positive rating. Interestingly, genetic proximity between the respective language and the native language of a participant did not play an important role.

The impact of phonetic and phonological characteristics on perception was not only subject of research dealing with natural languages. For instance, Köhler (1947) conducted an experiment with two pseudowords *maluma* and *takete*, which were shown to participants in random order along with two drawings: one with round contours resembled a cloud, while the other was spiky and shaped like a star. The participants were asked to match the pseudowords with the drawings. Interestingly, most of the participants associated the round shape with *maluma* and the spiky one with *takete*.

Over fifty years later, Ramachandran and Hubbard (2001) replicated and improved the experiment by using more controlled stimuli, namely *kiki* for the spiky shape and *bouba* for the one resembling a cloud. Furthermore, the *kiki-bouba* experiment could be replicated for several typologically unrelated languages (Lockwood and Dingemanse 2015), yielding similar results regardless of the participants' cultural background and knowledge of writing systems (Ćwiek et al. 2022). Further studies have demonstrated that the human capacity to associate various sounds of natural languages with particular phenomena is not limited to shapes but extends to other sensory experiences. For instance, front vowels are more likely to be perceived as denoting brightness, sharpness, and quickness, whereas back vowels tend to be associated with darkness, rounding, and slowness. Also colours and even tastes can be connected to front or back vowels (for an overview see Lockwood and Dingemanse 2015).

The question remains whether sound symbolic effects in constructed languages are detectable, resulting in more positive or negative assessments, and if they apply equally for speakers of different languages, such as German and English. Albeit these two Germanic languages have much in common, they also exhibit important differences – to name just a few: a slightly weaker sonority for German (see Reiterer et al. 2020), the presence of certain sounds such as the allophonic variants of the dorsal fricative [ç, x, χ] as well as the rhotics [ʁ, r] in German (Kohler 1990), and the dental fricatives /θ, ð/ in English. Considering the minor impact of the respective first language (L1) on the assessment of a foreign language (Reiterer et al. 2020), it is especially interesting to examine the similarities and differences in ratings between the two groups of participants when assessing constructed languages.

Aims

The aim of the current study is twofold. According to one of the findings from our previous research (Mooshammer et al. 2021), listeners rate constructed languages as pleasant or unpleasant even if these are pronounced in a neutral way, i.e. without any emotional involvement of the speaker, presence of special sound effects or visual input, such as costumes and special make-up. Building on this assumption, we conducted a follow-up experiment investigating, firstly, whether there is any difference in ratings of the presented stimuli, and thus in the general perception of the language aesthetics, between native speakers of English and native speakers of German.

Secondly, we examine whether familiarity with a specific constructed language affects the rating results. Reiterer et al. (2020) found that language knowledge – a main factor in their study – generally influenced the ratings of natural languages in a positive direction, with the exception of German which was always recognised correctly but still received negative ratings. However, in their study, the investigated languages were partly the native languages of the participants and, therefore, there might be a confound between L1 and knowledge of languages. For constructed languages, this potential confound can be excluded since, obviously, native speakers do not exist. In the current study, we investigate the effect of correct identification of a conlang on the ratings and expect more positive ratings for conlangs that are recognised correctly.

Experiment

Materials

To investigate our questions, we designed an online experiment, which was hosted on the browser-based Percy platform (Draxler 2011). Utterances used in the experiment were collected from fantasy and science fiction books, screenplays, fan forums, and other online sources. We compiled material in the following fourteen conlangs: Adûnaic, (Neo-)Khuzdul, Quenya, and Sindarin from the Middle-earth universe designed by J. R. R. Tolkien and featured in his work *The Lord of the Rings* (see Tolkien 2021) as well as Neo-Orkish created by David Salo for the film adaptation (in the following text as Orkish) and based on the Orkish material from the novel; Atlantean constructed for the movie *Atlantis: The Lost Empire (2001)* and Klingon from the *Star Trek* universe, both conceived by Marc Okrand (Okrand 1992, 1996); Golic Vulcan, another conlang from the Star Trek universe (Gardner and The Vulcan Language Institute, 1980–2004); Dothraki created by David Peterson for the *Game of Thrones* series (Peterson 2015); Na'vi by Paul Frommer for the movie *Avatar*; Fjerdan by David Peterson and Christian Thalmann for Netflix's series *Shadow and Bone*; Kesh from Ursula K. Le Guin's novel

Always Coming Home (Le Guin 2016); Horn and ʃUiʃuid invented by Dominique Bobeck, one of the co-authors of this chapter. According to the designers' intention, Na'vi, Quenya, and Sindarin are supposed to sound pleasant or elegant, while Dothraki, Klingon, Orkish, and Horn should sound aggressive, harsh, and evil (see Tolkien 2021, Okrand 1996, Peterson 2015, Beinhoff, Chapter 6 this volume, Bobeck p.c.). For each of the fourteen conlangs, we selected three sentences avoiding well-known, and thus easily recognisable, buzzwords, such as *Khaleesi* in Dothraki. Each of the selected utterances consists of at least ten syllables, having a duration of 4–6 seconds when spoken. All stimuli were recorded by two speakers (m/f) in a quiet room at a 44100 Hz sampling rate and downsampled to 22050 Hz for better presentation online.

Procedure

At the beginning of the experiment, the following participant metadata were collected: gender, age, education, native language, languages spoken by parents, and background in linguistics. Participants were asked to rate the sentences on three 7-point Likert-scales: *pleasantness* (pleasant vs. unpleasant), *goodness* (good vs evil), and *peacefulness* (peaceful vs. aggressive). Participants were instructed to base the ratings on their personal impression of the stimulus that was being played. The order of the stimuli and the order of the scales were randomised for each participant. The fictionality of the languages was highlighted and participants could see the title of the experiment 'Assess fantasy languages' throughout the entire experiment. Each stimulus could maximally be played twice, and participants were not timed while rating. During the experiment, one optional break was offered after the twenty-eighth stimulus. In the second part of the experiment, the participants had the option to listen to one additional stimulus for each conlang and guess which language was played. The entire experiment lasted about twenty minutes. In sum, fifty-six stimuli (fourteen languages × two sentences × two speakers) were rated and fourteen additional stimuli (one for each language) were used in the optional language-guessing part.

Participants

In total, fifty-one English and eighty-six German speaking participants completed the experiment in English and in German respectively. Three participants in the English experiment and one in the German experiment were excluded because they did not vary in their ratings. Graphic 7.1 shows gender, age, native language, and background in linguistics of the remaining participants. Regarding 'Background in linguistics', we provided three categories: 'degree' for those who have already achieved at least one academic degree in linguistics, 'undergraduate' for those currently enrolled in linguistics classes, and 'no degree' for laypeople and those with little or no

		English	German
		48	85
Gender	- female	15	60
	- male	27	21
	- non-binary/other	6	4
Age	- mean	36.42	32.80
	- standard deviation	15.47	12.44
	- range	19-71	18-67
Background in linguistics	- degree	9	6
	- undergraduate	17	19
	- no degree	22	60
Native language	- ENG or GER	37	84
	- other	11	1

Graphic 7.1 Metadata of participants analysed in the study

previous knowledge in linguistics. In the English experiment thirty-seven participants were native speakers and in the German experiment eighty-four (see Graphic 7.1).

Analysis

The three rating scales were re-scaled by subtracting the midpoint 4 and then multiplying by -1, so that the positive ratings remained positive in the analysis. Since the results from the three scales were often similar, the three scales were sometimes averaged.

For addressing the first aim (comparing the ratings from English and German speaking participants), we excluded data of eleven participants from the English experiment and one participant from the German experiment because they were not native speakers of English or German. However, their answers were included in the optional guessing section since we expect language knowledge to influence the rating results regardless of the L1.

In order to address the second aim of this study, we categorised the participants' replies as given in the guessing part of the experiment. Guesses for natural languages were summarised in a single group 'Natlang'. Some imprecise guesses, such as 'Elvish' and 'Tolkien' for Sindarin and Quenya, were accepted as correct guesses.

Results

Ratings of conlangs

The first aim of this study is to compare the ratings of the fourteen conlangs for English and German native speakers. Graphic 7.2 shows the mean

The phonaesthetics of constructed languages 99

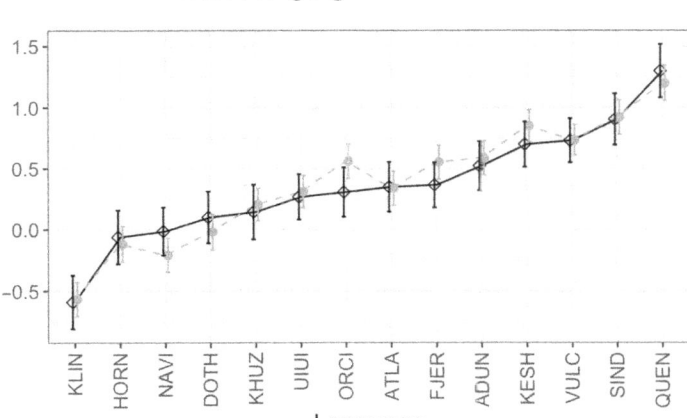

Graphic 7.2 Mean ratings with standard errors sorted by mean, native speakers only

ratings on all scales with standard errors sorted by mean. It is evident that the two groups of participants gave different ratings to different conlangs, confirming previous results of ours (Mooshammer et al. 2021). Compared to each other, the responses of the German- and English-speaking participants have yielded strikingly similar results. Interestingly, both groups rated Klingon as the most negative and Quenya as the most positive conlang, resulting in very similar mean scores for both groups. But with extremes set aside, slight differences in the order of the mean ratings can be observed. For example, Horn has been rated more negatively than Na'vi by the native speakers of English, while the order is reversed for the German-speaking participants. Although differences in the scores can be observed for Na'vi, Dothraki, Orkish, Fjerdan, and Kesh, their mean results differ only by maximally 0.25 rating points (in the case of Orkish).

The results on all three rating scales (pleasantness, goodness, peacefulness) are compared for English and German native speakers in Graphic 7.3. Although the mean ratings on all three scales show a similar picture with little deviation between the two groups of participants, differences can be observed for some conlangs. For example, Orkish and Fjerdan are rated more positively on the goodness scale by the German-speaking participants compared to the native speakers of English. In general, the German-speaking participants tend to give more positive ratings on the goodness and peacefulness scales, whereas the English-speaking participants usually rated the conlangs in our experiment as more pleasant. However, with the exception of Na'vi, which is rated as far more pleasant by English speakers than by the speakers of German, the ratings of English- and German-speaking participants never deviate by more than 0.35 rating points.

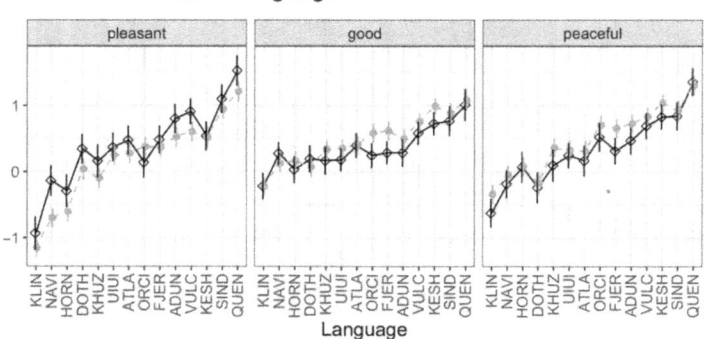

Graphic 7.3 Mean ratings with standard deviations for all three scales

Generally, the participants used the negative part of the scales less frequently than the positive. On the goodness scale, only Klingon received negative mean ratings; on the peacefulness scale, Klingon, Na'vi, and Dothraki are negative; and on the pleasantness scale Klingon, Na'vi, Horn, and Khuzdul are negative (the latter only for the German-speaking participants). Also, the ratings on the goodness scale show less extreme values compared to the other two scales.

Another noticeable difference between the rating results of the English- and German-speaking participants concerns the ratings given to the stimuli uttered by the female versus the male speaker. As shown in Graphic 7.4, the female speaker was on average rated better by the speakers of German,

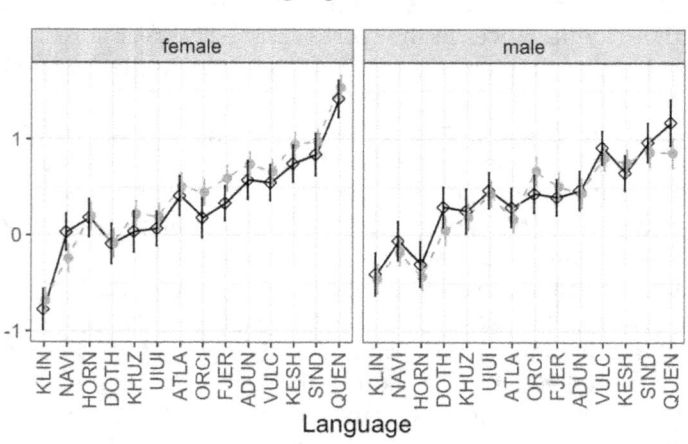

Graphic 7.4 Mean ratings with standard errors, shown for the female and the male speaker

The phonaesthetics of constructed languages 101

whereas the male speaker received higher scores from the English-speaking participants. The differences between the ratings given by the two groups of participants are less significant for the male than for the female speaker.

Identification of conlangs

The second aim of the current study is to investigate whether familiarity with a conlang results in its more positive assessment. To test this assumption, we presented the participants with additional stimuli for each conlang asking them to name the conlang in the provided text field (see Methods section above).

Graphic 7.5 lists which of the conlangs used in the experiment could be identified and how often these were identified correctly (the latter shaded grey). As shown in the last line of Graphic 7.5, most participants did not enter any information in the provided text field. Khuzdul, Adunaic, Fjerdan, Kesh, ʃUiʃuid, and Horn were never named by the participants, thus, they do not appear in the table. This was expected for ʃUiʃuid and Horn that were invented by Dominique Bobeck, a co-author, and have not been published yet. The conlangs that were identified correctly most often include Sindarin and Klingon (29 and 30), followed by Quenya (12), Orkish (9), and Na'vi (7). Dothraki was recognised three times, Vulcan and Atlantean were identified correctly only once. Even though throughout the entire experiment the participants were reminded of the fictionality of the languages by a sign 'Assess fantasy languages', the conlangs were sometimes mistaken

	ORCI	SIND	QUEN	KHUZ	ADUN	KLIN	VULC	DOTH	NAVI	ATLA	FJER	KESH	UIUI	HORN
Orkish	9	0	0	0	0	0	0	0	1	0	0	0	0	0
Elvish	0	16	8	1	2	0	0	0	0	0	0	0	0	0
Tolkien	0	2	0	0	0	0	0	0	0	0	0	0	0	0
Sindarin	0	11	3	0	1	0	0	0	0	0	1	0	0	0
Quenya	0	4	4	0	0	0	0	0	0	0	0	0	0	0
Klingon	0	0	0	0	0	30	1	0	2	0	0	0	0	6
Vulcan	0	0	0	0	0	0	1	0	0	0	0	0	0	0
Dothraki	0	0	0	1	0	0	0	3	0	0	0	0	1	2
Navi	1	0	0	0	0	0	1	0	7	0	0	1	0	1
Atlantean	0	0	0	0	0	0	0	0	0	1	0	0	0	0
Valyrian	0	0	1	0	1	0	0	0	0	0	0	0	0	0
Divine	0	0	0	0	1	0	0	0	0	0	0	0	0	0
Martian	0	0	0	0	0	0	0	0	0	0	0	0	1	0
Kelen	0	0	0	1	0	0	0	0	0	0	0	0	0	0
Natlang	3	4	2	10	0	2	3	2	4	3	2	4	6	
No reply	88	64	83	88	96	69	95	95	89	96	97	98	96	86

Graphic 7.5 Identification of conlangs: conlangs used in the experiment (Orkish–Atlantean, correct answers shaded grey), other fictional languages (Valyrian–Kelen), natural languages, number of empty entries

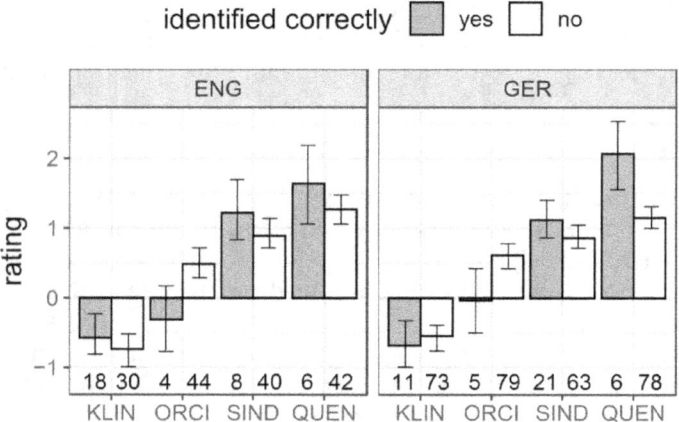

Graphic 7.6 Mean ratings with standard errors for Klingon, Orkish, Sindarin, and Quenya, depending on correct identification. Number of participants per condition is given at the bottom

for natural languages. The most frequently named natural language was Arabic (18 times), followed by Farsi (6), Hebrew (5), Finnish (3), and Swedish (2). The following languages were named once: Armenian, German, Hindi, Hungarian, Icelandic, Irish, Khoekhoe, Russian, Scandinavian, Serbian, Spanish, Swahili, Turkish, Welsh, and Xhosa. In general, except for Klingon and Sindarin only very few participants recognised the presented stimuli correctly.

Based on the results by Reiterer et al. (2020), we expect that participants rate a language more positively if they are familiar with it. Therefore, we compared the rating results for the conlangs that were most frequently recognised correctly. Graphic 7.6 shows the ratings, averaged across scales, and standard errors for the correctly identified conlangs in grey as well as the ratings of the participants who did not recognise the conlangs in white. The numbers for both are given at the bottom of the figure. Note, that for some languages, such as Orkish, the means are based on very few ratings and, therefore, the standard errors are quite large and should be interpreted with caution.

It becomes clear that knowing a language influences the rating results, but only partly in the direction predicted by Reiterer et al. (2020). The clearest counter-example is Orkish, which received more negative ratings if recognised and more positive ratings if unidentified. On the contrary, Sindarin and Quenya were rated more positively if identified correctly. However, this result is only reliable for the ratings of Quenya given by the German-speaking participants because the difference between the standard error ranges of the ratings with correct and with incorrect/without identification is only in that case large enough. For Klingon the correct identification does not seem to influence the ratings. There is a tendency for German-speaking participants who recognised Klingon to rate it slightly more negatively, and for English-speaking participants to rate it slightly more positively, but the differences are insignificant.

Discussion

To summarise, the current study demonstrates that conlangs are rated differently even if the sentences are uttered in a neutral voice devoid of any special sound effects or visual input, confirming the results of our previous experiment (see Mooshammer et al. 2021). The impressions conlangs evoke on listeners correspond mostly to the intentions of their creators. For instance, Quenya was rated most positively on all three scales, whereas Klingon received the most negative ratings. Nevertheless, two of the conlangs in our study were perceived differently from their creators' original intentions: Orkish was conceived by Tolkien as 'menacing, powerful, harsh as stone' (Tolkien 2021: 254), yet the ratings it received are moderate. Secondly, Na'vi was rated negatively by both groups of participants, despite it being designed to sound very pleasant and friendly (Beinhoff, Chapter 6 this volume).

The first aim of this study was to compare the ratings given by native speakers of German and English. For most conlangs, no major differences could be observed between the two groups of participants. German-speaking participants tended to give more positive ratings on the goodness and peacefulness scale, whereas English-speaking participants rated the conlangs slightly better on the pleasantness scale. Interestingly, the ratings given by the English-speaking participants were more positive for Na'vi and more negative for Orkish compared to the native speakers of German, which corresponds better to the creators' intentions. A possible explanation for this is that these conlangs were primarily designed for an English-speaking audience. Languages with familiar sound inventories tend to be assessed more positively (Reiterer et al. 2020). For example, the uvular fricative /χ/, which occurs in Orkish, is part of the phoneme inventory of the German language (Kohler 1990), however, it is absent in English. Seemingly, if a conlang has phonetical and phonological resemblances to the listeners' native tongue, it will be assessed more positively; on the contrary, more frequent deviations will result in a more negative assessment. To further investigate this assumption, we will analyse the relationship between the phonetic and phonological properties of the conlangs and the ratings by German- and English-speaking participants in a follow-up study.

Another difference between the ratings of English- and German-speaking participants was found for the two speakers of the stimuli. The female speaker received better ratings from the German-speaking participants and the male speaker slightly more positive ratings from the English-speaking participants. In Reiterer et al. (2020) the voice, and especially the gender of the speaker, had a significant influence on the ratings: female voices were rated significantly more positively than male voices independent of the language. However, in Reiterer et al. (2020) each sample from the sixteen European languages was produced by different speakers. In our study, this confound was avoided because each of the two speakers produced the stimuli from all conlangs. So, the impact of the factor voice was better controlled, but the factor gender remained. However, it should be emphasised that we do not know whether the differences in the rating of the female and the male speaker are really related to their gender since we had only one model speaker of each gender, and therefore we cannot generalise this to a gender effect on perception. The differences may also be caused by individual traits of the two speakers that are not (only) related to their gender. To examine the impact of gender, samples with more speakers per gender are needed.

The second aim of our study was to investigate whether familiarity with a certain conlang would influence the rating results. We observed that knowing a language does play a role in how it is assessed by a listener. This has also been confirmed by other studies. For instance, Reiterer et al. (2020) showed that a well-known prestigious language like English is perceived more positively than a well-known language like German that has the reputation of sounding harsh. We observed that the two Elvish languages Quenya and Sindarin received slightly better ratings if they were recognised, while Orkish, a language of evil and malicious people, is usually rated worse in this case. For Klingon the differences are too small to be conclusive.

In some instances, the participants erroneously assumed they had recognised the language correctly. This includes participants who indicated that one of the conlangs was in fact a natural language, despite being previously informed of the fictional nature of the languages in the experiment. This could explain why less extreme ratings were given on the goodness scale compared to the pleasantness scale. From informal feedback in a previous experiment (Mooshammer et al. 2021), we know that some people find it difficult to rate a language as good or evil due to concerns over bigotry or racism. In order to ease these concerns, we informed our participants that we used conlangs exclusively in our present experiments. However, because apparently some participants forgot or ignored this, they still might have been reluctant to rate a conlang as good or evil. Another explanation is that our participants found it more natural to rate a language as being more pleasant or unpleasant than providing ratings on the goodness and peacefulness scales and were therefore reluctant to rate a language as such.

What do our results imply for the design of a conlang? As we have previously shown, languages that are sonorous with many vowels and sonorants and with a large percentage of voicing are rated more pleasantly than other languages (see Mooshammer et al. 2021). Furthermore, we found in the case of Orkish that familiarity with the sounds of a language (resulting from their own L1) seems to have an impact of a language's assessment since Orkish was rated less pleasant by native speakers of English compared to native speakers of German. English lacks the velar and uvular fricatives occurring in Orkish and German. If conlangers want to exploit this aspect and extend it to listeners from a wider variety of native languages, they should include universally rare non-sonorous sounds, such as ejectives, for unpleasant sounding languages, keeping in mind that the notion of universality is often biased towards the better-known Western languages. It should be noted that typological distribution should not be confused with the loaded term *markedness*, which *can* include the sense of rarity in the world but has many more meanings, such as articulatory/conceptual complexity (Haspelmath 2006). These different concepts of markedness and universals are for example not kept apart by Reiterer et al. (2020: 169), who state that 'languages that display more universal patterns might be perceived as more "convenient" and therefore likable'. This is highly problematic since our data demonstrate that typologically rare sounds are present in the stimuli of languages with very positive ratings. Such a language is, for instance, Sindarin, which has the second most positive ratings. From the vantage point of language universals, a more negative assessment would be expected due to the presence of typologically rare sounds as voiceless velar/uvular fricatives, voiceless sonorants, and dental non-sibilant fricatives as, for example, the latter only occurs in about 7.58 per cent of natural languages (Maddieson 2013a) – this is less than the number of languages possessing uvular stops, i.e. around 15.17 per cent of natural languages (Maddieson 2013b). Therefore, it is not 'markedness' nor typological frequency that affects the likability of a foreign language but familiarity along with other factors such as sonority or the phonaesthetic character of certain sounds.

Beyond familiarity with certain sounds and sound patterns, the ratings can depend on the correct identification, as was found here for Orkish. For correct identification, however, the conlang needs to be widely known from popular culture, like Klingon. Whether familiarity with certain phonemes plays a role for the ratings will be tested in further experiments with participants with native languages that include ejectives or other rare non-sonorous sounds in their inventory, such as Georgian.

In conclusion, both German- and English-speaking participants rated most conlangs according to the assumed intentions of their creators, except for Na'vi and Orkish. For Na'vi more positive ratings were expected, for Orkish more negative. For the latter, two factors affected the ratings towards the intended negative direction: English participants generally rated Orkish more negatively than German participants, and participants who recognised it rated Orkish more in line with the expectations. Thus, our results indicate that familiarity seems to influence the perception, not just of natural languages, but also of conlangs, and that recognising a conlang can trigger biases and therefore affect the ratings.

Appendix: fully glossed stimuli

The stimuli used in this study are glossed following the Leipzig Glossing Rules (see Comrie et al. 2008). Additionally, EMPH stands for emphatic, VBLZ for verbaliser.

(Neo-)Orkish

1. Gû kîb-um kelk-um-ishi, burz-um-ishi. Akha gûm-ishi ashi gur-um.
   [gu: 'ki:bum 'kɛlkumiʃi 'buʀzumiʃi 'aχa 'gu:miʃi 'aʃi 'guʀum]
   No alive-NMLZ cold-NMLZ-LOC dark-NMLZ-LOC here void-LOC only dead-NMLZ
   'No life in coldness, in darkness. Here in void, only death.'

2. Makha n(a)-ash goi nazg ghar golug-shu?
   ['maχa naʃ gɔi̯ nazg ɣaʀ 'gɔlugʃu]
   Where be-3SG two ring other Elf-GEN
   'Where are the other two Elf rings?'

Quenya

3. Laurië lanta-r lassi súri-nen.
   [laurie lantar lassi su:rinen]
   Goldenly fall-PL leaf.PL wind-INS
   'Like gold fall the leaves in the wind.'

4. Yén-i ve lintë yulda-r avánier
   [je:ni ve linte juldar ava:nier]
   year-PL like swift draught-PL PASS.PRF.PL
   'The years have passed like swift draughts.'

Sindarin

5. Naur an edraith am-men! Naur dan i ngaur-hoth!
   [nau̯r an 'edraiθ 'am:ɛn nau̯r dan i 'ŋau̯rhɔθ]
   Fire for saving for-1PL fire against DEF werewolf-host
   'Fire be for saving of us! Fire against the werewolf-host!'

6. Ón-en i-estel edain, ú-cheb-in estel anim.
   ['ɔ:nen i'estel 'edai̯n 'u:xebin 'estel 'anim]
   give.PST-1SG DEF-hope human\PL NEG-keep-1SG hope for-1SG.EMPH
   'I gave hope to the Dúnedain, I have kept no hope for myself.'

(Neo-)Khuzdul

7. Kemeth-mâ ins buzrâ ins bazarî.
   [kɛˈmɛtʰma: ʔɪns ˈbʊzʁa: ʔɪns ˈbazaʁi:]
   sing\PRF-1PL as deep as deep\PL
   'We sing as deep as the deeps.'

8. Haram-mâ   ins   zudrâ   ins   bakanî.
   [ha'ʁamːa: ʔɪns 'zʊdʁa: ʔɪns: 'bakaniː]
   praise\PRF-1PL as   high   as   ray.of.light\PL
   'We praise as high as the rays of light.'

Adûnaic

9. Ar-Pharazôn-un   azagar   Avalôiy-ada.
   [ʔarfara'zoːnun   a'zagːara   ʔawa'loːijada]
   Ar-Pharazôn-NOM   wage.war\PST   Valar-ALL
   'Ar-Pharazôn was waging war against [the] Valar.'

10. Balîk   hazad   an-Nimruzîr   azûl-ada.
    [ba'liːk 'hazad   an'nimruzi ɪ   a'zuːlada]
    ship\PL   seven   GEN-Elendil   east-ALL
    'Seven ships of Elendil [went] eastward.'

Klingon

11. bI-jatlh-Ha'-chugh   qa-HoH!   yaj-'a'?
    [bɪdʒatɬxaʔtʃuɣ   qʰɑːox   jadʒʔaʔ]
    2SG-say-wrongly-COND   1SG>2SG-kill   understand-Q
    'If you say the wrong thing, I will kill you! Clear?'

12. bor-taS   bIr   jab-lu'-DI'   reH   QaQ-qu'   nay'.
    [bortʰɑʂ   bɪr   dʒɑbluʔɖɪʔ   rɛx   q͡χɑq͡χqʰuʔ   najʔ]
    Revenge   be.cold   serve-INDF-when   always   be.good-EMPH   dish
    'Revenge is a dish best served cold.'

Vulcan

13. Telv-tor   nash-veh   ripakhaik   dunap-lar.
    [telv.tɔr   naʃ.ve   riːpa.kʰaɪk   dʊ.na.plar]
    reading-VBLZ   DEM-one   irregular   book-PL
    'I read banned books.'

14. Ri   vun-sahrafel   du   hassu.
    [ri   vun.za.ra.fel   du   has.su]
    NEG   must-trust   2SG   doctor
    'You must not trust the doctor.'

Atlantean

15. Neshing-en-tem   gebr-in   de   pen-yoh.   Leb   es-e-neh   dup   duweren-top
    [nɛʃiŋɡɛnʰɛm   gɛbrin   dɛ   pʰɛnjɔx   lɛb   ʔɛsɛnɛx   dupʰ   duwɛrɛnʰɔpʰ]
    weapon-PL-ACC   2PL-GEN   down   put-IMP.PL   who   be-PRS-2PL Q.EMPH stranger-PL-VOC
    'Who are you strangers? And where are you from?
    (Lay down your weapons! Who on earth are you, strangers?)'

16. Moh   tamar   gwis-in   panneb-le-nen,   Kida-top.
    [mɔx   tʰamar gwisin   pʰanːɛblɛnɛn   kʰidatʰɔpʰ]
    2SG   law   1PL-GEN   know-PRS.PRF-2SG   Kida-VOC
    'You know the law, Kida. (You know our law, Kida.)'

Dothraki

17. Anha   zal-ak   asshekh-qoy-i   vezhven-a   yer-aan!
    [ˈanha zaˈlak   ˈaʃːɛxqoi   ˈvɛʒvɛna   jeraˈan]
    1SG   wish-1SG   day-blood.GEN   great-OBL   2SG.ALL
    'I wish you a happy birthday! (I wish you a happy blood-day!)'

18. Jin   hake   nem   nes-a   k'-anni.   Me   ray   risse   san   jahak-i.
    [d͡ʒin   ˈhake   nem   ˈnesa   ˈkanːi   me   rei   ˈrisːe   san   ˈd͡ʒahaki]
    DEM.PROX   name   PASS   know-3SG   of-1SG.GEN   3SG   have   cut-PST many   braid-PL
    'That name is known to me. He has cut many braids.'

Na'vi

19. Kaltxì.   Ngaru   lu   fpom   srak?
    [kalˈtʼɪ ŋaru   lu   fpom   srak]
    hello   you-DAT   be   well-being   Q
    'Hello. How are you?'

20. F-ay-vrrtep   fì-tsenge   lu   kxanì.
    [faj.ˈvrː.tɛp   fɪˈtseŋɛ   lu   ˈkʼanɪ]
    this-PL-demon   this-place-SG   be   forbidden
    'These demons are forbidden here.'

Kesh

21. Sinshan-z-an   ge-hóv-z-es   hai   ohn.
    [sɪn.ʃan.zan   gɛ.hoːv.zɛs   haɪ   ɔxn]
    Sinshan-EM-LOC   PRS-dwell-EM-2SG   now   Q
    'Are you living in Sinshan (a town) now?'

22. Húí-she-v   we-wey   tu-sheíye   rru   ge-stanai.
    [huːˈiː.ʃev   wɛwɛɪ   tʼə.ʃɛ.iː.jɛ drə   gɛ.sta.naɪ]
    2-legged-being-person-POSS   ADJ-all   SBJ-work   DEM   PRS-do-skilfully
    'The whole business of man is this: doing arts.'

Note: Kesh has two special grammatical modes, the 'Earth Mode' and the 'Sky Mode'. The 'Earth Mode' is used on verbs and nouns 'when speaking to and of living persons and local places, in one of the present tenses or with the auxiliaries meaning "can," "be able," "must," in every day informal conversation' (Le Guin 2016: 499). It is expressed by the suffix [z] and indicated with an *em* in glossing. The 'Sky Mode' is used otherwise and is expressed with a zero morpheme that we omit in our glossing.

ʃUiʃuid

23. Dumaa-r paul jo nemʰit= dir ɣurje garax-oo-r vuaʕ-e.
    [du'ma:r 'pʰaɲl jo 'nɛɹhɪ dɪr 'ɣʊrje gəra'xo:r 'vuə̯ʕe]
    sit.PRS.PL-3 king and ret.nue= 3SG.GEN upon horse-PL-GEN splendour-ADV
    'The king and his retinue are sitting splendidly on horses.'

24. Fagii-am daug-ug-a ɣa poriis-e jaok-e.
    [fa'gi:am daŋ'gu:ga ɣa pʰo'ri:se jaokʰe]
    destroy.PRS.PL-2 building-PL-ACC in island\PL-ADV wrath-ADV
    'You (pl.) are destroying the buildings on the islands out of wrath.'

Horn

25. Hoan t'ux kaax qa-paar-luq-ut šuuf-u um iš ᵃlʀak
    [ˈhoa̯n t'uχ 'kʰa:χ 'qʰapʰarˌluqʰutʰ 'ʃu:ɸu ʔum ʔiʃ əl'ʀak']
    people.I DEM.IIIA stone.IIIA 3.I.IPFV-love-drink-3.III water-REL.III fresh and cool
    'Of course, the people would like to drink cool and fresh water.'

26. Fiz'-uk'-uʀ qranš-ʟ-fl akᵊr p'a xa-lanq-ač
    [fi'ts'uk'uʀ 'qʰranʃuɬ ʔakʰər p'a χa'laɴqʰatʃʰ]
    be.sharp-CAUS-3.III mind-REL.III-2.POSS way.III NEG 3.III.IPFV-be.safe-NEG
    'Watch out! The way is not safe.'

Fjerdan

27. Per ver drüsje end jer ve drüs-kelle. Ver jer perjenger.
    [peʀ vu: dru:.ʒe ɛnt jea vi: dru:ʃ.kɛla vu: jeʀ peʀ.jeŋ.gə]
    2SG be.2SG witch and 1SG be.1SG witch-hunter be.2SG 1SG.POSS prisoner
    'You are a witch and I am a witch-hunter. You are my prisoner.'

28. Jer molle pe ccnet Enel mörd je nej afva trohem verret-n.
    [jeʀ molə peʀ u(/y:).net e:.nel mu:rt je nɛːʃ afa veʀet tro.hem]
    I exist.1SG you.ACC protect.INF only death 1SG.ACC NEG from break/keep.3SG.FUT oath-DEF
    'I was made to protect you. Only death will break me from this oath.'

References

Bloomfield, L. (1909) *A Semasiological Differentiation in Germanic Secondary Ablaut*. Chicago: University of Chicago Press.

Comrie, B., Haspelmath, M. and Bickel, B. (2008) 'The Leipzig Glossing Rules: conventions for interlinear morpheme-by-morpheme glosses'. <http://www.eva.mpg.de/lingua/resources/glossing-rules.php>

Ćwiek, A., Fuchs, S., Draxler, C., Asu, E. L., Dediu, D., Hiovain, K. and Winter, B. (2022) 'The bouba/kiki effect is robust across cultures and writing systems', *Philosophical Transactions of the Royal Society B* 377 (1841): 20200390.

Draxler, C. (2011) 'Percy – an HTML5 framework for media rich web experiments on mobile devices', *Proceedings of the Twelfth Annual Conference of the International Speech Communication Association*. Red Hook: Curran Associates, pp. 3346–7.

Flieger, V. (2017) 'The Orcs and the others: familiarity as estrangement in *The Lord of the Rings*', in C. Vaccaro and Y. Kisor (eds) *Tolkien and Alterity. The New Middle Ages*. Basingstoke: Palgrave Macmillan, pp. 205–22.

Gardner, M. R. and The Vulcan Language Institute (1980–2004) *The Vulcan Language* (unpublished). <http://surak.nu/vulcanlanguage.pdf>

Haspelmath, M. (2006) 'Against markedness (and what to replace it with)', *Journal of Linguistics* 42 (1): 25–70.

Kogan, V. V. and Reiterer, S. M. (2021) 'Eros, beauty, and phonaesthetic judgements of language sound. We like it flat and fast, but not melodious. Comparing phonetic and acoustic features of 16 European languages', *Frontiers in Human Neuroscience* 15: 1–22.

Kohler, K. (1990) 'German', *Journal of the International Phonetic Association* 20 (1): 48–50.

Köhler, F. (1947) *Gestalt Psychology: An Introduction to New Concepts in Modern Psychology*. Oxford: Liveright.

Le Guin, U. K. (2016) *Always Coming Home*. London: Gollancz.

Leibniz, G. W. (1981) *New Essays on Human Understanding* (eds P. Remnant and J. Bennett). Cambridge: Cambridge University Press.

Locke, J. (2004) *An Essay Concerning Human Understanding* (ed. R. Woolhouse). London: Penguin.

Lockwood, G. and Dingemanse, M. (2015) 'Iconicity in the lab: a review of behavioral, developmental, and neuroimaging research into sound-symbolism', *Frontiers in Psychology* 6: 1–14.

Maddieson, I. (2013a) 'Presence of uncommon consonants', in M. S. Dryer and M. Haspelmath (eds) *The World Atlas of Language Structures Online*. Leipzig: Max Planck Institute for Evolutionary Anthropology. <https://wals.info/chapter/19>

Maddieson, I. (2013b) 'Uvular consonants', in M. S. Dryer and M. Haspelmath (eds) *The World Atlas of Language Structures Online*. Leipzig: Max Planck Institute for Evolutionary Anthropology. <https://wals.info/chapter/6>

Mooshammer, C., Bobeck, D., Hornecker, H. and Meinhardt, K. (2021) 'Does Orkish sound evil? Perception and phonology of constructed fantasy languages' [Poster presentation at the conference *Phonetik and Phonologie* 17. Goethe-Universität, Frankfurt am Main, 29 October).

Okrand, M. (1992) *The Klingon Dictionary* (2nd edn). New York: Pocket Books.

Okrand, M. (1996) *The Klingon Way: A Warrior's Guide*. New York: Pocket Books.

Peterson, D. J. (2015) *The Art of Language Invention: From Horse-Lords to Dark Elves to Sand Worms, the Words Behind World-Building*. London: Penguin.

Plato (1997) 'Cratylus', in J. M. Cooper and D. Hutchinson (eds) *Plato: Complete Works*. Cambridge: Hackett Publishing Company, pp. 101–56.

Podhorodecka, J. (2007) 'Is lamatyave a linguistic heresy? Iconicity in J. R. R. Tolkien's invented languages', in O. Fischer, C. Ljungberg and E. Tabakowska (eds) *Insistent Images*. Amsterdam: John Benjamins, pp. 103–30.

Ramachandran, V. S. and Hubbard, E. M. (2001) 'Synaesthesia: a window into perception, thought and language', *Journal of Consciousness Studies* 8: 3–34.

Reiterer, S. M., Kogan, V., Seither-Preisler, A. and Pesek, G. (2020) 'Foreign language learning motivation: phonetic chill or Latin lover effect? Does sound structure or social stereotyping drive FLL?', in K. D. Federmeier and H.-W. Huang (eds) *Adult and Second Language Learning, Psychology of Learning and Motivation*. Amsterdam: Elsevier, pp. 165–205.

de Saussure, F. (1916) *Cours de Linguistique Générale*. Cambridge: Payot.

Tolkien, J. R. R. (1981) *The Letters of J. R. R. Tolkien* (eds H. Carpenter and C. Tolkien). London: HarperCollins.

Tolkien, J. R. R. (2005) 'Guide to the names in *The Lord of the Rings*: nomenclature of *The Lord of the Rings*', in W. Hammond and C. Scull (eds) *The Lord of The Rings: A Reader's Companion*. London: HarperCollins, pp. 750–83.

Tolkien, J. R. R. (2016) *A Secret Vice* (eds D. Fimi and A. Higgins). London: HarperCollins.

Tolkien, J. R. R. (2021) *The Lord of the Rings: One Volume*. London: HarperCollins.

Vennemann, T. (1988) *Preference Laws for Syllable Structure and the Explanation of Sound Structure*. Berlin: De Gruyter Mouton.

Part II
Interpretation

CHAPTER 8

Tolkien's use of invented languages in *The Lord of the Rings*

James K. Tauber

In this chapter, James Tauber, Director of the Digital Tolkien Project, considers the ways in which J. R. R. Tolkien uses a variety of presentational techniques to negotiate the many different fictional languages in *The Lord of the Rings* and other writings. The chapter sets out Tolkien's skill in providing a reader with an immersive experience of these invented languages, while rarely being direct or explicit about the grammar and morphology of, for example, the Elvish languages. Even in the paratextual material that Tolkien appended to his novels, and in his letters, Tolkien refrains from the highly technical descriptive register that he was certainly expert in. Tauber argues that Tolkien's negotiation of the fictional languages in his novels is for readerly linguistic engagement rather than world-building alone.

Representing invented languages

In number 483 'Fiction rule of thumb' of his humorous webcomic *XKCD*, Randall Munroe (2008) suggests that the probability that a book is good is inversely proportional to the number of words made up by the author. The mock example given is:

> The Elders, Or *Fra'as*, guarded the *farmlings* (children) with the *krytoses*, which are like swords but *awesomer*. . . .

Notably, he adds 'Except for anything by Lewis Carroll or Tolkien, you get five made-up-words per story. I'm looking at you, *Anathem*' (a reference to Neal Stephenson's 2008 novel, notorious for its excessive use of invented words).

Quite apart from any exceptions that need to be made for him, though, Tolkien is actually surprisingly restrained in his use of his invented languages in *The Lord of the Rings* and does not use them in the way being mocked by Munroe. This restraint is even more remarkable when we consider that, for Tolkien, language invention was not so much in the service of world-building as world-building in the service of language invention. Tolkien, a philologist by day, was driven by language invention itself to construct his elaborate mythology or 'legendarium' that would come to underpin his novels and which, in one form edited by his son (Tolkien 1977), would be posthumously published as *The Silmarillion*. Tolkien wrote in the foreword to the second edition of the first book of *The Lord of the Rings* that his mythology

> was primarily linguistic in inspiration and was begun in order to provide the necessary background of 'history' for Elvish tongues.
> (Tolkien 1966: 7)

The depth and detail of Tolkien's language invention over his lifetime was unprecedented but this chapter is not primarily an account of the linguistic details of his invented languages *per se*, nor their biographical origins (for that see Tolkien 2016) but rather the way in which they are presented in *The Lord of the Rings*. How are Tolkien's invented languages used within the main narrative text? And does Tolkien really need the free pass afforded him by Munroe in *XKCD*?

Before coming to *The Lord of the Rings*, though, it is worth a small note about the book which preceded it, *The Hobbit* (Tolkien 1937). *The Hobbit* was not initially part of Tolkien's world-building, although he occasionally borrowed names of places in the legendarium like 'Gondolin' and made references to different groups of Elves consistent with those described in his mythology. Many of the Hobbit-related names were intended to sound English but the names of most of the dwarves as well as the name 'Gandalf' came from the 10th century Old Norse poem *Vǫluspá* (compiled in 1220).*The Lord of the Rings* (Tolkien 1954a, 1954b, 1955), starting out as a mere sequel to *The Hobbit*, was also not initially intended to take place in Tolkien's grand legendarium but, as writing commenced, that legendarium was woven in as the distant back-story of the novel. This involved incorporation of his invented Elvish languages but gave rise to a problem: if the Elves had *their* languages, why did the Hobbits and the Men and the Dwarves speak English and why did the Dwarves have Old Norse names?

The initial part of Tolkien's solution was to become a common one in the genre: Tolkien presented himself as merely acting as a *translator* of a work written in another (fictional) language. The characters didn't speak English but rather the 'Common Speech' or 'Westron' which Tolkien (so he claimed) had translated into English. As Tolkien wrote in Appendix F at the end of the trilogy (Tolkien 1955: 375–87) (and notice his use of the word 'history' to describe the novels):

> The language represented in this history by English was the Westron or Common Speech of the West-lands of Middle-earth in the Third Age.
> (*LR* F.1.001)

(References of this form (book.chapter/appendix.paragraph) make use of the Digital Tolkien Project's citation system, for which see <https://digitaltolkien.com/citation-systems/>)

For example, 'Frodo Baggins' wasn't the main character's real name, and he didn't call his home 'Bag End'. Rather, these were suitable *representations* of the real names.

People are often surprised that, with the exception of the Elvish names, most of the names in *The Lord of the Rings* are translations. Some were transliterations, like 'Brandywine' (from Baranduin) and 'Took'. But the Hobbits actually called themselves 'kudukin' and the Shire 'Sûza'. Bilbo and Frodo's surname was actually 'Labingi', and they lived at 'Laban-nec'. Tolkien just translated these into a sort of representative English equivalent: 'Baggins' and 'Bag End'. Similarly, names such as 'Buckland', 'Bucklebury', 'Bracegirdle', 'Budgeford', and 'Bridgefields' were intended to be English-sounding equivalents of the underlying Hobbit names. Sam's real name (or nickname anyway) was 'Banazîr', Hobbitish for 'half-wit' and the Old English for 'half-wit' is 'samwís'. Rivendell is one of the few truly translated Elvish names. In Westron it was 'Karningul' or in Elvish, 'Imladris'.

What then of the use of Old Norse names for Gandalf and the Dwarves in *The Hobbit*? Tolkien's solution here was particularly clever. He claimed firstly that these weren't the Dwarves' own names for themselves (which they kept secret) but rather the names given to them by Men in the region in which they lived. The Men in turn spoke a language that had a *relationship* to the Common Speech that was *equivalent* to the relationship Old Norse has to Modern English. Thus, the apparent Old Norse names were a type of representative translation into an analogical equivalent based on the historical relationship of the in-world languages.

Where this technique was used to great effect was in the portrayal of Rohirric, the language of Rohan. In *The Lord of the Rings*, the names of people and places in the region of Rohan, as well as some of their expressions, are drawn directly from Old English. Hence, we find examples like the names 'Dwimordene', 'Elfhelm', 'Éomer', 'Eorlingas', 'Éowyn', 'Erkenbrand', 'Gúthwinë', 'Mundburg', and 'Théoden'. We find expressions such as 'Westu Théoden hál!' (*Be thou well, Théoden!*) and extensive use of alliteration, as in Old English verse. The local name of a flower is given as 'simbelmynë', a fictitious but plausible Old English word. It is important to emphasise, Rohirric is not Old English. Théoden's real name was actually 'Tûrac'. 'Théoden' is just an attempt at an Old English equivalent to give English readers a flavour of what Rohirric might have sounded like to Westron speakers.

Where this sort of analogical representation was not used is with the Elvish languages, which constituted the bulk of Tolkien's language invention. These languages, as well as a couple of others, were, for the most part, just transliterated in the text. When an Elvish name, such as 'Elrond', is given, it is the actual form in the original invented language.

And so we see three types of language use in *The Lord of the Rings*:

1. **Common Speech Representation** – the *lingua franca* of the world being 'translated' into English or English-like words.
2. **Analogical Representation** – languages being translated into equivalents based on the same historical relationship to Modern English as the constructed language had to the Common Speech.
3. **Invented Languages** – constructed languages that are just transliterated.

It is the third category, mostly Elvish with some Dwarvish, that I will explore most in more detail in the rest of this chapter.

Patterns of usage in *The Lord of the Rings*

Much of the research for this chapter came out of an adult continuing education course taught at Signum University with Elise Trudel Cedeño. Our goal was to introduce students to the constructed languages of Tolkien as they appear in *The Lord of the Rings* and to give a flavour for the sort of detective work that a philologist might do when faced with a new language. In order to prepare for the course, and more broadly as part of the Digital Tolkien Project (https://digitaltolkien.com/), I undertook a search for all constructed words in the text by:

1. Tokenising the main text of *The Lord of the Rings*.
2. Automatically removing words that also appeared in numerous English spell check dictionaries.
3. Manually reviewing the remaining words and excluding obviously English words and novel-but-clearly-English-inspired names.
4. Classifying the remaining 683 words by language and whether a name (proper nouns) or not (common nouns, but also in larger utterances: verbs, adjectives, function words, etc).

The overall counts by language were as follows:

Quenya	159
Sindarin	345
Black Speech/Orkish	42
Khuzdûl (Dwarvish)	10
Old English (representing Rohirric)	84
Entish	18

These are plotted by individual chapter in Graphics 8.1 and 8.2

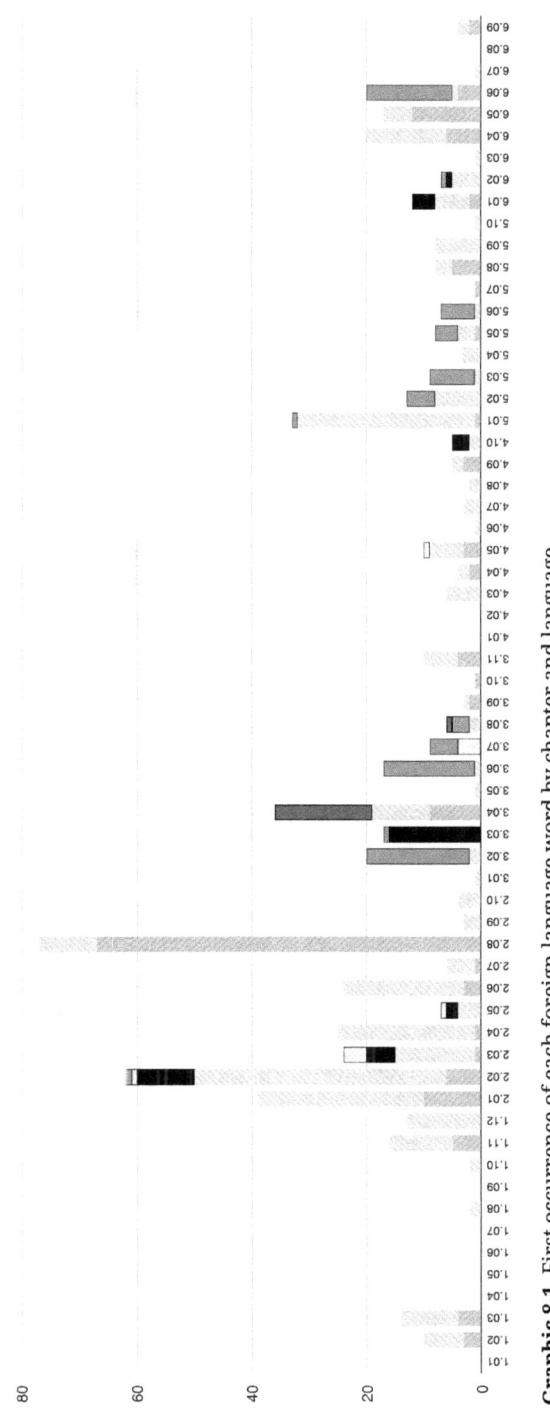

Graphic 8.1 First occurrence of each foreign-language word by chapter and language

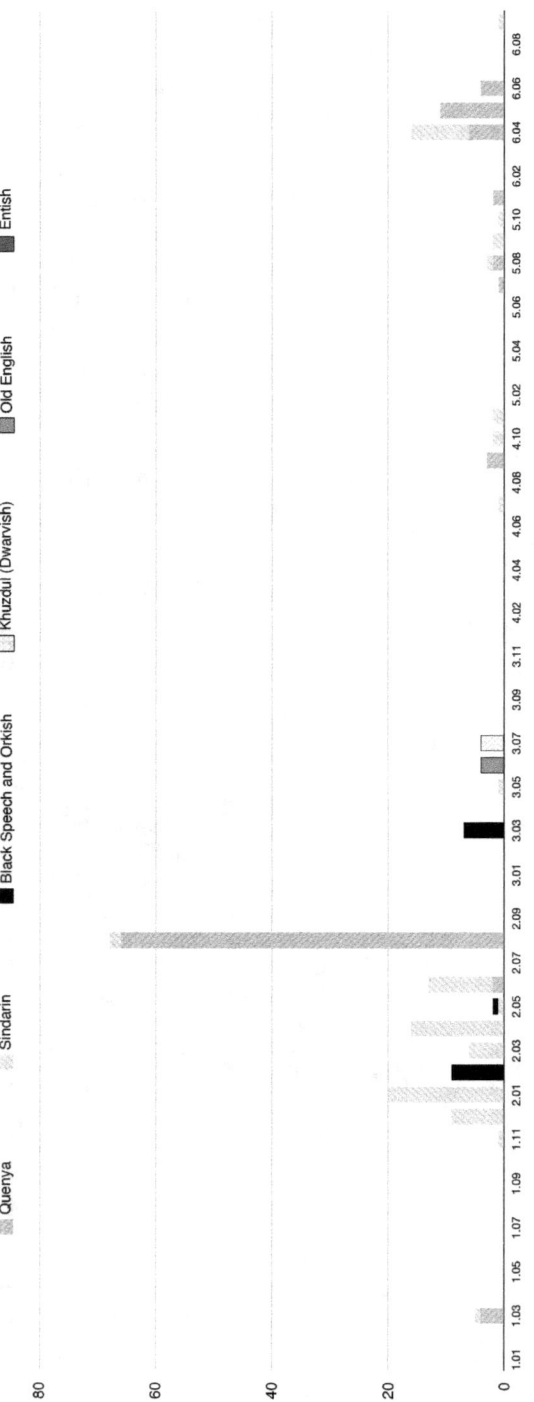

Graphic 8.2 First occurrence of each foreign-language word other than names of people and places by chapter and language

Quenya is the 'ancient tongue' 'used for ceremony, and high matters of lore and song, by the High Elves'. Sindarin is the everyday language of the Elves still in Middle-earth and is also used by certain groups of Men of more 'noble' ancestry (*LR* F.1.05).

The picture becomes particularly interesting if we exclude names of people and places as in Graphic 8.2. Most of the peaks are utterances or songs with very few isolated invented words within English sentences (of the type mocked in the *XKCD* comic).

Overall, there are several means by which invented languages are inserted into the main narrative:

1. Names of people and places.
2. Parallel translation.
3. Individual common nouns.
4. Greetings.
5. Verse and song.
6. Direct linguistic description.

In addition to the main text, two of the appendices to *The Lord of the Rings* (in Tolkien 1955) deal with linguistic matters. Appendix E primarily focuses on pronunciation and writing systems. Although there is no additional grammatical information nor explicit vocabulary, various example words are given to illustrate points of pronunciation and glosses are generally given for these, providing additional insight into words whose meaning might not otherwise be explicable from the main narrative. Appendix F briefly describes the different languages, their history and relationship, and talks about the particular approach taken in 'translating' into English, as we touched on above.

Names of people and places

Within the main narrative text, the names of people and places in the invented languages are fairly common. The meaning is sometimes indicated through what I have called a 'parallel translation' (see below) but even if not, there is a well-thought-out etymology to them, and roots are often identifiable.

For example, we come across 'Angband', 'Angmar', 'Angrenost' with the common element ANG meaning 'iron'. 'Angrenost' is the Sindarin name for 'Isengard' which is itself just Tolkien translating the archaic Westron name into an Old English equivalent ('isen' being one form of the Old English for 'iron').

In 'Doriath', 'Gondor', and 'Mordor', the common element is DOR and they are all lands. 'Doriath' means 'land that is fenced', 'Gondor' means 'stone land', and 'Mordor' means 'black land'. In 'Angrenost', 'Belegost', and 'Fornost', 'OST' means a 'fortress'. 'Angrenost' is an 'iron fortress',

'Belegost' is a 'great fortress', and 'Fornost' is a 'northern fortress' (we also find 'Forochel' and 'Forodwaith'). And we find 'Ered Mithrin', 'Mithril', 'Mithlond', and 'Mithrandir'. 'Mithlond' is the Sindarin name of the 'Grey Havens'. The 'Ered Mithrin' are the 'Grey Mountains'. 'Mithrandir', or 'Grey Pilgrim' was Gandalf's Sindarin name. The element 'MITH' means 'grey'.

There is very little in the way of grammatical explanation in the main text (we shall discuss Appendix E in a moment). There is one example of word formation explained, in *LR* 2.01.135. Here we are not only taught explicitly in direct speech that 'Dúnadan' means 'Man of the West' (and are told an alternative name, 'Númenórean') but we are also given the components DUN and ADAN. We are not yet explicitly told which morpheme means 'West' and which means 'Man', although we are given enough clues elsewhere to work it out.

Parallel translation

A common technique used for introducing names, especially place-names, in *The Lord of the Rings* is to give the name in multiple languages, as used by different peoples. For example,

> 'I am afraid we must go back to the Road here for a while,' said Strider. 'We have now come to the River **Hoarwell**, that the Elves call **Mitheithel**.'
>
> (*LR* 1.12.020)

Here we have an English name 'Hoarwell' (supposedly translated from whatever the Common Speech would be) and the corresponding Elvish (in this case, Sindarin) name 'Mitheithel'. As we have already seen, MITH means 'grey', corresponding to the 'hoar-' in the English equivalent.

This giving of a name of a place in multiple languages is certainly not unique to Tolkien. We find it, for example, in the New Testament where we are told:

> When Pilate heard these words, he brought Jesus outside and sat on the judge's bench at a place called **The Stone Pavement,** or in Hebrew **Gabbatha**.
>
> (John 19.13)

> ... and carrying the cross by himself, he went out to what is called **The Place of the Skull**, which in Hebrew is called **Golgotha**.
>
> (John 19.17)

In the underlying Greek text, 'The Stone Pavement' is *lithostrōton* but Gabbatha is given just as *gabbatha* even in the Greek. 'The Place of the Skull' is *kraniou topon* but again 'Golgotha' is *golgotha* in the Greek text.

Notice that the Greek name is *translated* into English, but the Hebrew name is *transliterated*. This is what Tolkien is essentially doing with the river 'Hoarwell' or 'Mitheithel': the former is a translation into English from the Common Speech and the latter is a transliteration of the Elvish. The fact that Tolkien chose to use 'hoar-' in his 'translation' of the river name suggests the underlying Common Speech name was probably archaic sounding at the time. As a Germanic philologist, Tolkien was acutely aware of the dates of usage of English words.

This technique of parallel translation is found for the names of people as well, for example when Faramir is recounting the words of Gandalf in this passage:

> 'The **Grey Pilgrim**?' said Frodo. 'Had he a name?'
> '**Mithrandir** we called him in elf-fashion,' said Faramir, 'and he was content. *Many are my names in many countries, he said.* **Mithrandir** *among the Elves,* **Tharkûn** *to the Dwarves;* **Olórin** *I was in my youth in the West that is forgotten, in the South* **Incánus**, *in the North* **Gandalf**; *to the East I go not.*'
>
> (*LR* 4.05.064–065)

It is important to note that parallel names do not always mean the words themselves are calques (translated loanwords from another language), merely that they have the same referent. The name 'Gandalf' is, recall, an Old Norse name (note he is called that 'in the North' and this is of course not what those men actually called him, which is not given here, but rather is Tolkien's *representation* of that name). But 'Mithrandir' does mean 'Grey Pilgrim'. Notice also that the parallel names here are given sociolinguistic context, both racially and geographically: 'my names in many countries', 'among the Elves', 'to the Dwarves', 'in the West', 'in the South', 'in the North'.

We see another example of parallel translation with a common noun, a herb that is of some significance to the plot at multiple points:

> Thereupon the herb-master entered. 'Your lordship asked for **kingsfoil**, as the rustics name it,' he said; 'or **athelas** in the noble tongue, or to those who know somewhat of the Valinorean . . .'
> 'I do so,' said Aragorn, 'and I care not whether you say now **asëa aranion** or **kings-foil**, so long as you have some.'
>
> (*LR* 5.08.065–066)

Notice the herb-master gives the name both in representative English ('kingsfoil') as well as Sindarin (called here 'the noble tongue', itself an interesting sociolinguistic hint) 'athelas' – and is about to give the Quenya (or, here, 'Valinorean', a reference to the place Quenya was most associated with) when Aragorn interrupts making it clear he knows all three languages but that is far from what matters right now.

We occasionally get small bits of implicit parallel translation. On two occasions (*LR* 2.06.113–14 and *LR* 2.09.048–049) an Elf exclaims 'Yrch!' and non-elf responds 'Orcs!', revealing the Sindarin word for 'orcs'. But there is perhaps no more interesting example of parallel translation than the dwarf Gimli's description of the key mountains that characterise his ancestral homeland. Gimli explains that he doesn't need a map because the dwarves

> 'have wrought the image of those mountains into many works of metal and of stone, and into many songs and tales. They stand tall in our dreams: **Baraz, Zirak, Shathûr**.'
>
> (*LR* 2.03.103)

Those three words are given untranslated but, as we shall soon see, it is possible to work out their meaning. They are not the names of the mountains themselves but something more poetic and mnemonically useful.

Gimli continues, giving the name of the underground kingdom and the three mountains each in three different languages:

> 'Only once before have I seen them from afar in waking life, but I know them and their names, for under them lies **Khazad-dûm**, the **Dwarrowdelf**, that is now called the **Black Pit**', **Moria** in the Elvish tongue. Yonder stands **Barazinbar**, the **Redhorn**, cruel **Caradhras**; and beyond him are **Silvertine** and **Cloudyhead**: **Celebdil the White**, and **Fanuidhol the Grey**, that we call **Zirakzigil** and **Bundushathûr**.'
>
> (*LR* 2.03.104)

'Khazad-dûm' (in Khuzdûl) is also given as 'the Dwarrowdelf' (in the Common Speech), which was also later called 'the Black Pit (Common) and is 'Moria' (in the Elvish Sindarin). We are told in Appendix F (*LR* F.2.19) that the actual Westron name is 'Phurunargian' but, in keeping with the translation into English representatives, 'Dwarrowdelf' is used here. As Tolkien explained in a note at the start of *The Hobbit*, 'Dwarrow' is what the plural of 'Dwarf' would have been if certain analogical levelling had not taken place. And so 'Dwarrowdelf' is English (representing the Westron) but deliberately archaic sounding. The alternative English name given, 'the Black Pit', is a translation of the Sindarin 'Moria'. We find the root 'MOR' in Mordor (Black Land), Morgul (Black Sorcery), and other words in the legendarium.

And then we have the names of the mountains themselves, each given in the Common Speech, Sindarin, and Khuzdûl:

Redhorn [Common]	= Caradhras [Sindarin]	= Barazinbar [Khuzdûl]
Silvertine [Common]	= Celebdil [Sindarin] the White	= Zirakzigil [Khuzdûl]
Cloudyhead [Common]	= Fanuidhol [Sindarin] the Grey	= Bundushathûr [Khuzdûl]

A few things may be observed. Firstly, each of the Common Speech names is a compound: red+horn, silver+tine, cloudy+head. Secondly, Celebdil contains the root CELEB which is found in numerous other names and in Appendix E is glossed 'silver' (in passing, in the context of the word as an example of how to pronounce C in Elvish languages). Note that the Sindarin name is further qualified with 'the White' even though the Sindarin name, like the Common Speech name, contains 'silver'. Similarly, Fanuidhol means 'cloudy head' and is also further qualified with a colour: 'the Grey'. The Sindarin 'Caradhras' is not further qualified by a colour but does contain the root meaning 'red'.

The reason two of the Sindarin names are qualified with a colour is that the Sindarin names, like the English translations of the Westron (potentially themselves translations from the Elvish) use the qualifiers 'red', 'silver', 'cloudy' whereas the colour words in the Khuzdûl translate to 'red', 'white', and 'grey'. The additional modifiers in two of the Sindarin names are to line them up with the Khuzdûl names. And this leads us back to Gimli's initial names of the mountains 'wrought ... into ... songs and tales': 'Baraz', 'Zirak', 'Shathûr'. Far from merely a shortening of the full mountain names, this is the Dwarven tricolour: red, white, and grey.

Gimli does continue with another three-way parallel translation:

'There the Misty Mountains divide, and between their arms lies the deep-shadowed valley which we cannot forget: **Azanulbizar**, the **Dimrill Dale**, which the Elves call **Nanduhirion**.'

(LR 2.03.105)

Gandalf then explains it is this dale they are heading to and names a few more locations. But observe the style of Gandalf's speech in contrast to how Gimli responds with the corresponding Khuzdûl names.

'It is for the Dimrill Dale that we are making,' said Gandalf. 'If we climb the pass that is called the Redhorn Gate, under the far side of Caradhras, we shall come down by the Dimrill Stair into the deep vale of the Dwarves. There lies the **Mirrormere**, and there the **River Silverlode** rises in its icy springs.'

'Dark is the water of **Kheled-zâram**,' said Gimli, 'and cold are the springs of **Kibil-nâla**. My heart trembles at the thought that I may see them soon.'

(LR 2.03.106–7)

Gandalf's description is matter-of-fact, the words of someone who is familiar with the landscape and knows where they are going. Gimli's response is formulaic as if recalling one of the 'songs and tales'. He seems not to have ever been there himself.

That 'Dark is the water of Kheled-zâram and cold are the springs of Kibil-nâla' is part of a shared tradition among the Dwarves is later confirmed when Gimli meets the Elf Galadriel and she speaks:

> '**Dark is the water of Kheled-zâram, and cold are the springs of Kibil-nâla, and fair were the many-pillared halls of Khazad-dûm in Elder Days before the fall of mighty kings beneath the stone.**'
> She looked upon Gimli, who sat glowering and sad, and she smiled. And the Dwarf, hearing the names given **in his own ancient tongue**, looked up and met her eyes; and it seemed to him that he looked suddenly into the heart of an enemy and saw there love and understanding. Wonder came into his face, and then he smiled in answer.
> (*LR* 2.07.028)

Galadriel's recitation of Gimli's exact words and her continuation of it in iambs suggests this is one of the traditional Dwarven songs. But, significantly, it is her knowledge of it, and Gimli's hearing the names given 'in his own ancient tongue' that first draws him to her in wonder and causes him to recognise that love and understanding were possible, even with a traditional enemy.

Individual common nouns

As has already been remarked, there are very few invented language common nouns used within English sentences in the main text of *The Lord of the Rings*. They are shown in Graphic 8.3 with their overall counts, a gloss or object type, and the location of the first token.

Each of these is a Sindarin word. Many of them have identifiable etymology (for example, the MITH in mithril, the LAS in athelas, the EL and the ANOR in elanor). We see the plural 'mellyrn' alongside the singular 'mallorn' (exhibiting vowel harmony, for which see below).

Notice that the majority of words refer to flora or fauna and food or drink. In each case, the word usage emphasises the otherness of the object or the environment to the Hobbits. Half of the words are introduced in the other-worldly realm of Lothlórien in chapters 6 and 8 of Book 2. Unlike in Munroe's *XKCD* webcomic example, Tolkien never renames things already familiar to the reader. As is often the case with Tolkien, the thing being introduced is no less foreign to the focalised character than it is to the reader and so the explanation of the term never feels forced. A good example of this is the introduction of 'lembas', a type of Elvish waybread. Over five paragraphs (*LR* 2.08.022–25), we are told that the food given to the Fellowship by the Elves was mostly of a form of 'very thin cakes, made of a meal that was baked a light brown on the outside, and inside was the colour of cream'; that Gimli was doubtful about it but after trying a bite 'ate of the rest of the cake with relish'; that it is 'more strengthening than any food made by Men'; and finally that it is a type of waybread called 'lembas'.

word	count	object type or gloss	first occurrence
ann-thennath	1	mode of Elvish verse	1.11
athelas	9	herb	1.12
mithril	15	metal	2.01
crebain	2	bird	2.03
miruvor	3	drink	2.03
talan	3	platform	2.06
mallorn/mellyrn	6/1	tree	2.06
elanor	5	flower	2.06
niphredil	2	flower	2.06
lembas	20	waybread	2.08
hithlain	1	fibre used to make rope	2.08
lebethron	2	tree	4.07

Graphic 8.3 Invented common nouns in LOTR

The term 'lembas' is used a total of twenty times in the main text of the book across thirteen chapters. In the paragraphs above, the appearance and characteristics of the food are described, and a gloss, 'waybread', is given. Tolkien did not arbitrarily choose to give an alternative name to a well-known foodstuff. Instead, this was something new and foreign that turns out to be of some relevance later. It is well-described and then given a 'local' name so it can be referred to clearly later on.

Greetings in Elvish

The first example of a more extended invented language utterance is appropriately when the Hobbits first encounter a group of Elves. It is, perhaps surprisingly, spoken by the Hobbit Frodo.

> 'O Fair Folk! This is good fortune beyond my hope,' said Pippin. Sam was speechless. 'I thank you indeed, Gildor Inglorion,' said Frodo bowing. **'Elen síla lúmenn' omentielvo, a star shines on the hour of our meeting,'** he added in **the High-elven speech.**
> 'Be careful, friends!' cried Gildor laughing. 'Speak no secrets! Here is a scholar in **the Ancient Tongue.**'
>
> *LR* 1.03.140–1

Notice that a parallel translation is given inline. This is likely a narratorial addition, although it is not so indicated, and it is possible that Frodo actually translated it for the rest of his companions (contrast the other greeting described below). The language is described as 'the High-elven speech' by the narrator and 'the Ancient Tongue' by Gildor. In Appendix F, we are given the name of the language: Quenya.

In a letter to his son, Christopher, Tolkien (perhaps only half-) jokingly suggests that *The Lord of the Rings* was created merely as place to use that particular Elvish greeting:

> Nobody believes me when I say that my long book is an attempt to create a world in which a form of language agreeable to my personal aesthetic might seem real. But it is true. An enquirer (among many) asked what the L.R. was all about, and whether it was an 'allegory'. And I said it was an effort to create a situation in which a common greeting would be elen síla lúmenn' omentielmo, and that the phase long antedated the book.
>
> (Tolkien 1981: Letter 205)

The use of 'omentielmo' in this letter versus 'omentielvo' in the quoted book text is actually due to Tolkien reworking the verb inflections of Quenya subsequent to the first edition of *The Lord of the Rings* – a detail that would otherwise have no relevance to the book but which was important to him to get right.

We encounter a second Elvish greeting a few chapters further in *The Lord of the Rings*, this time spoken by an Elf to the Dúnadan, Aragorn (called Strider in the narration): 'Ai na vedui Dúnadan! Mae govannen!' (*LR* 1.12.088) This greeting is in Sindarin rather than Quenya and is not translated. One potential in-world reason for this is that Sindarin was well understood and in regular use among Elves and certain Men whereas Quenya, Tolkien tells us in Appendix F, was more akin to (neo-)Latin in its usage.

Verse and song

There are a number of examples of extended verse in constructed languages in *The Lord of the Rings*. For example, while Gandalf only gives a translation of the verse on the One Ring in *LR* 1.02, at the Council of Elrond in *LR* 2.02 we get the transliterated Black Speech (although a figure in *LR* 1.02 does show the Black Speech written in Tengwar so, with the aid of Appendix E, the sounds can be worked out in that earlier chapter).

In *LR* 2.01.168 we get the Sindarin song to Varda, 'A Elbereth Gilthoniel'. It is this song that leads to that chapter having the second highest occurrence of newly introduced non-name foreign words in our earlier charts. A translation is not given although many of the words can be worked out from their elements.

In *LR* 2.08.078–81 we have the Quenya song 'Namárië'. We are told Galadriel 'sang in the ancient tongue of the Elves beyond the Sea, and [Frodo] did not understand the words'. We are given a translation this time, seemingly from the narrator, along with a parallel translation remark that the 'Varda' mentioned in the song is 'the name of that Lady whom the Elves in these lands of exile name Elbereth' (*LR* 2.08.082). This explanation of Elbereth being the name used by 'the Elves in these lands of exile' (contrasted with being told the song is in 'the ancient tongue of the Elves beyond the Sea') reinforces the physical sundering of the Elves that is the historical reason for the split between the Sindarin and Quenya languages. Notice too that, as with the greeting, the Quenya song is given a translation whereas the Sindarin song is not. Again, it seems that Tolkien imagined the in-world narrator would feel the need to provide a translation for the Quenya but would assume the reader would understand the Sindarin.

Direct linguistic description

In the main text we encounter various examples of languages being directly described from the perspective of non-speakers or speakers of different dialects. For example, on hearing some Khuzdûl place-names, Sam declares 'A fair jaw-cracker dwarf-language must be!' (*LR* 2.03.128). And the first time an Elf is heard by the Hobbits, we are told his 'speech and clear ringing voice left no doubt in their hearts: the rider was of the Elven-folk. No others that dwelt in the wide world had voices so fair to hear' (*LR* 1.12.088).

Sometimes as readers we are given dialectal or sociolinguistic cues such as where a Rider is described as 'using the Common Speech of the West, in manner and tone like to the speech of Boromir, Man of Gondor' (*LR* 3.02.112). Or where the 'language of the Rohirrim', 'a slow tongue unknown to the Elf and Dwarf' is described as having 'a strong music in it'. Legolas the Elf says 'for it is like to this land itself; rich and rolling in part, and else hard and stern as the mountains' (*LR* 3.06.013–014). When Frodo first encounters the Dúnedain of the South, they are said to speak 'using the Common Speech, but after the manner of older days' (*LR* 4.04.091). When they switch to their own dialect of Sindarin, 'Frodo became aware that it was the elven-tongue that they spoke, or one but little different'.

Some of these dialect differences (at least as pronunciation goes) are described in Appendix E.

When Merry first meets a Wild Man, the Wild Man's 'voice was deep and guttural, yet to Merry's surprise he spoke the Common Speech, though in a halting fashion, and uncouth words were mingled with it' (*LR* 5.05.012). And we find out in the main text that apparently different Orc groups spoke distinct, non-mutually intelligible languages: 'Presently two orcs came into view [. . .] As usual they were quarrelling, and being of different breeds they used the Common Speech after their fashion' (*LR* 6.02.061).

The only substantial metalinguistic descriptions in the book come in two of the Appendices. We have already seen that Appendix F discusses the relationship and history between the various languages. Appendix E is concerned with the pronunciation of the invented languages and with their writing systems. In many ways this reflects the way in which a typical grammar for a historical language like Gothic or Greek would begin: here are the sounds of the language and here is how they are written.

Unlike a historical language, however, Tolkien does give hints of variation in pronunciation.

> For vowels the letters *i, e, a, o, u* are used, and (in Sindarin only) *y*. **As far as can be determined** the sounds represented by these letters (other than *y*) were of normal kind, though **doubtless many local varieties escape detection**.
>
> (*LR* E.1.006)

He then makes a remarkable mention of diphthongisation of Quenya long vowels by non-native speakers. In a footnote to *LR* E.1.007 he writes as if making a sociolinguistic commentary on a real language. The particular pronunciation discussed is 'fairly widespread', 'usual in the Shire', but 'regarded as incorrect or rustic'. Notice also it gives him an opportunity to gloss *yéni únótime* as 'long-years innumerable'. This is a phrase that appears in *LR* 2.08.078.

There are also hints given here of historical development:

> Sindarin alone **among contemporary languages** possessed the 'modified' or fronted *u*, more or less as *u* in French *lune*. It was partly a modification of *o* and *u*, **partly derived from older diphthongs** *eu, iu*. For this sound *y* has been used (as in ancient English): as in *lŷg* 'snake', Q. *leuca*, or **emyn pl. of amon 'hill'**. In Gondor this *y* was usually pronounced like *i*.
>
> (*LR* E.1.008)

This continues to be an in-world description of the languages, rather than a simple example of world-building. The sound changes had been mapped out in detail by Tolkien privately (as evident in the posthumous publication of many of his language notes in the journal *Parma Eldalamberon* and elsewhere). It is the underlying detail that allows Tolkien to give hints in passing. Far from merely giving the *illusion* of depth, Tolkien is showing us the iceberg above the water. The rest of the iceberg is very much there underneath, fully worked out.

We also get an important example of a Sindarin plural noun alongside its singular: 'emyn pl. of amon "hill"' (incidentally following exactly the format we would expect in a grammar like Joseph Wright's [1910] on the Gothic language). This pluralisation exhibits vowel harmony that is similar to the i-mutation or umlaut that underlies English alternations such as *foot~feet*.

Amon > Emyn	(Amon Sûl – a hill; Emyn Muil – a range of hills)
barad > beraid	(tower; towers)
Orod > Eryd/Ered	(Orodruin – Mount Doom; Ered Mithrin – Grey Mountains)
craban > crebain	(crow-like birds) *LR* 02.03.123,125
mallorn > mellyrn	(a species of immense tree) *LR* 02.06.082
Dúnadan > Dúnedain	(Man of the West; Men of the West)

The <i> is still seen in Quenya, e.g. 'palantíri' (the Seeing Stones), 'atani' (men).

Concluding remarks

Tolkien generally uses three methods to present his languages: the *lingua franca* of the imagined world being 'translated' into English or English-like words; languages being translated into equivalents based on the same historical relationship to Modern English as the constructed language had to the Common Speech; and, finally, the invented languages themselves that are just transliterated. Perhaps unsurprisingly for a fantasy novel requiring world-building, there is a heavy focus on the names of people and places. There is extensive word formation going on which is almost never made explicit but which can be used to work out the meaning of many of the words. Common nouns are used sparingly and, with only a few exceptions, are glossed and explained, sometimes in great detail. The common nouns refer to things unfamiliar to both the reader and at least one of the characters first encountering them. There is occasional use of extended expressions and poems or songs that are translatable but not necessarily translated, although the word formation makes it possible to work out the gist of many of the untranslated words. There is a frequent use of parallel translation where the names of people or places are given in more than one language (sometimes in English, representing the Common Speech).

Any linguistic explanation outside the Appendices is almost entirely characters speaking to other less-informed characters (focalising the most ignorant character in the scene, usually a Hobbit).

In short, *The Lord of the Rings* not only reveals some of Tolkien's incredibly rich language invention but illustrates the various ways in which such an invention can be revealed within a narrative. It is not just the invented languages themselves but Tolkien's use of invented language in his fictional writing that make his example so worth following.

References

Munroe, R. (2008) '483 Fiction rule of thumb', *XKCD: A Webcomic of Romance, Sarcasm, Math, and Language* 483. <xkcd.com/483/>

Stephenson, N. (2008) *Anathem*. London: Atlantic Books.

Tolkien, J. R. R. (1937) *The Hobbit*. London: George Allen and Unwin.

Tolkien, J. R. R. (1954a) *The Lord of the Rings: 1 The Fellowship of the Ring*. London: George Allen and Unwin.

Tolkien, J. R. R. (1954b) *The Lord of the Rings: 2 The Two Towers*. London: George Allen and Unwin.

Tolkien, J. R. R. (1955) *The Lord of the Rings: 3 The Return of the King*. London: George Allen and Unwin.

Tolkien, J. R. R. (1966) *The Lord of the Rings: 1 The Fellowship of the Ring* (2nd edn). London: George Allen and Unwin.

Tolkien, J. R. R. (1977) *The Silmarillion* (ed. C. Tolkien). London: George Allen and Unwin.

Tolkien, J. R. R. (1981) *The Letters of J. R. R. Tolkien* (ed. C. Tolkien and H. Carpenter). London: George Allen and Unwin.

Tolkien, J. R. R. (2016) *A Secret Vice: Tolkien on Invented Languages* (eds D. Fimi and A. Higgins). London: HarperCollins.

Wright, J. (1910) *Grammar of the Gothic Language*. London: Clarendon Press.

CHAPTER 9

Changing tastes: reading the cannibalese of Charles Dickens' *Holiday Romance* and nineteenth-century popular culture

Katie Wales

> Several chapters in this collection consider the emotional response to particular conlangs as experienced outside of their literary contexts. The chapters by Beinhoff and by Mooshammer et al. (Chapters 6 and 7) focus primarily on responses to the design of phonology and phonoaesthetics. In this chapter, however, Wales argues for the importance of context in the study and appreciation of artlangs. Focusing on the representation of *cannibalese*, a coinage of her own for the language of fictional cannibals, Wales examines the language and style of Dickens' *Holiday Romance* (1838) in the context of nineteenth-century politics and reception. She analyses cannibalese within its co-text and in line with its intertextual relations, considering such phenomena as 'Robinsonade fiction', children's literature, pantomime, and music hall performance.

'He'll speak like an Anthropophaginian unto thee'
(Host to Simple about Falstaff) *The Merry Wives of Windsor* IV.v.9–10.

In this chapter I focus on the importance of context in the consideration of a constructed fictional language or what Tolkien termed an 'art-language' (Fimi and Higgins 2016: 33), indeed several contexts: of the language within its co-text; its intertextual relations with other kinds of texts and cultural and literary schemata; and the context of its readerly reception. Since my chosen art-language is based on representations in nineteenth-century texts the issue of reception is potentially political, because of changing tastes across time. And since my particular 'case study' is taken from a story primarily written for children, the issue of reception is made more complex because of likely differences in reading expectations between children and adults in any period. The art-language itself I am calling *cannibalese*: my own coinage for the language of cannibals, by which I mean those non-Western peoples particularly associated in the nineteenth-century ethnographic imagination with Caribbean or Pacific cultures (Obeyesekere 1998: 79). I am not using the term, therefore, to refer to survival cannibalism, or the language of serial killers. The *-ese* suffix emphasises its fictionality, which is important to remember in the discussion which follows, since the representation of cannibalism generally has been a much-debated topic in the field of post-colonial studies: for example, Barker, Hume and Iverson (1998) and Brown (2013). I shall return to this issue below and in my conclusion.

My case study is taken from a work for children by Charles Dickens, not a writer normally associated with children's literature, except perhaps for his *Child's History of England* (1851–3). These writings have generally been ignored by critics, undeservedly. In 1868, two years before his death, he published four comic tales or 'parts' under the heading of *Holiday Romance*. They first appeared in an influential American children's magazine, *Our Young Folks*, during his tour of America (November 1867–April 1868), and also in Dickens' own periodical for families *All the Year Round* in the first four issues of 1868. They have been published separately or altogether since 1874, four years after his death, and were re-edited in 1995 by Gillian Avery (the edition I will be using here). In 1981 they were dramatised for children's television by Adrian Mitchell: I shall return to this later. What makes the tales particularly unusual in the field of children's fiction even today is that they purport to be composed by two boys and two girls and hence are 'narrated' by them: aged 'eight', 'six', 'nine', and 'half-past six'. Following Wydryzynska (2021: 232), citing Currie (2010), the children are the 'internal authors', and hence their voices and focalisations are those of children – a significant point to which I shall return.

I am focusing on the third part of the text, 'Romance. From the pen of Lieut.-Col. Robin Redforth [aged nine]', about a swash-buckling pirate-hero 'Captain Boldheart' at war with his Latin-grammar master on the high seas (Dickens 1995: 418–28). It is very clearly a parody of the sea-adventure stories for children, especially boys, and yarns, travellers' tales, and penny dreadfuls, featuring pirates and cannibals. R. M. Ballantyne's *The Coral Island* (1858) is probably the best-known example, set in an imaginary locale, and itself based on Defoe's *Robinson Crusoe* (1719): the archetype, as it were, for what has been termed 'Robinsonade' fiction (see Hanlon 2001: 612–13). It is also a novel which has been much critiqued for its cultural hegemony. There is a sense that Dickens, in his later middle age and a grandfather, is remembering his own childhood reading, and the impressions it made. John Forster, in his *Life of Dickens*, recounts how, as a boy, inspired by his father's collection of books, including *Robinson Crusoe*, he had a 'greedy relish' for voyages and travels; and went about the house 'armed with the centre-piece out of an old set of boot-trees, the perfect realisation of Captain Somebody, of the Royal British Navy, in danger of being beset by savages' (Forster 1936: 319).

In this story of Captain Boldheart, the hero is faced one day by 'fifteen hundred canoes, each paddled by twenty savages [...] advancing in excellent order. They were of a light green colour (the savages were), and sang, with great energy, the following strain:

Choo a choo a choo tooth.
Muntch, muntch. Nycey!
Choo a choo a choo tooth.
Muntch, muntch. Nycey!'

(Dickens 1995: 423)

My own first reaction, a gut reaction perhaps, to this apparent piece of 'nonsense' was to laugh out loud, as I did when I read the rest of this story and the three others. Despite the re-spellings of *chew* and *munch* which suggest 'exoticness', the song works best when read aloud. It follows closely two desirable characteristics Tolkien advocates in his paper written in 1931 on invented languages: the use of word forms that sound aesthetically pleasing, such as reduplication; and a sense of fitness between symbol and sense (Fimi and Higgins 2016: xv, xxii). We can note the repetition or reduplication of 'choo' and 'muntch' in the couplets themselves repeated; the assonance of the high long vowel in 'choo' and 'tooth', the enunciation of which demands extended exhalation; and the onomatopoeia of 'muntch'. From the 'spitting out' of the affricates in 'muntch' and 'choo', sounds which physically involve the teeth (and 'tooth' is repeated here), we are acutely reminded of the fact that the same parts of the mouth are used for speaking and eating. Deleuze (2003: 189), commenting on this fact, adds 'orality is naturally prolonged in cannibalism'. There's a synaesthetic physicality to the song, taste mingling with sound: Dickens' 'greedy relish' quoted above reinforced by the repetition of 'Nycey!'

My second reaction, however, is to wonder whether I should be laughing: is it a perverse kind of pleasure, double-edged, a kind of 'gallows humour' (Warner 1994: 68). To what extent am I, a modern reader, conspiring with the long-held view that the British and Europeans are guilty of a linguistic hegemony or colonialism that views the language of 'Others', especially exotic others, as 'Non-sense', because it is unknown and hence unintelligible. *Nonsense* in this context is synonymous with the de-humanising *babble*, *barbarism*, *gibberish*, *jabbering*, or *mumbo-jumbo* (a word not found until the end of the nineteenth century). Linguistic xenophobia certainly lies behind *barbarism*, from Greek via Latin, meaning 'a foreign mode of speech' ('Other'; one essentially not Greek), and may contain onomatopoeic reduplication. For Shakespeare's Host cited at the head of this chapter, Falstaff is likely to be quite incoherent or inarticulate when he wakes up, and hence 'speak[ing] like an Anthropophaginian', a people-eater – Shakespeare's own coinage. For cannibals, what is 'unspeakable' is doubly so: both alien (in speech) and also taboo (in actions). In Dickens' defence, however, I would argue that the song is not mere 'babble': despite having no recognisable syntactic frame, its lexis and phonology are all recognisably to do with eating.

I would argue, moreover, that Dickens' cannibalese needs to be put into context, or rather several contexts: the co-text, the immediate context of the whole text itself, and its cultural and literary contexts, including the larger tradition of nonsense and fantasy writing for children in the nineteenth century. First it is to be recalled that the focalisation of the tale is that of the 'internal author', the boy-narrator. While it might be argued that this enables the 'real' author to abnegate responsibility, as it were, for what is written, it is doubtful whether he or his readers at this moment in time would have had any of the qualms I have mentioned above. Much more significant is the fact that the sheer inventiveness of the word-play can be viewed through the lens of a childish innocence and exuberance. As Tolkien notes (Fimi and Higgins 2016: li), children take delight in nonsense and imaginary or private languages. Indeed, Dickens himself as a schoolboy at Wellington House Academy between the ages of twelve and fourteen invented what he termed a 'lingo', adding 'a few letters of the same sound to every word', so that he and his school-friends might be considered 'foreigners' when walking down the street (Forster 1936: 343). It seems highly plausible, then, that both the 'internal author' and a child reader would equally have a 'taste' for cannibalese.

Moreover, the two couplets are not merely a simple 'song', but a chant of exertion, as the cannibals row towards the Captain. It has the rhythm of pulling: the trochaic /x on 'choo a choo a' and 'Nycey'; the double stresses of 'choo tooth' and 'muntch'; and the extended exhalation already referred to of the long vowel in 'choo' and 'tooth'. Indeed, the spelling 'choo' and its sixfold repetition might also conjure the image of a steam train, and hence the 'puffing' of breath. Similar nonsensical rowing chants like 'yo ho heave ho' also have patterns of noises of bodily and oral exertion formalised or verbalised. William Endicott, writing about his Fiji explorations (1829–32) describes carriers of dead savages 'singing a war song to the rhythm of the gait' (cited in Obeyesekere 1998: 66). Choruses of sea shanties have similar formalisations. Indeed, Captain Boldheart himself sings a song on his schooner which has a chorus of 'Heave yo':

O landsmen are folly!
O pirates are jolly!
O diddleum Dolly,
    Di

(Dickens 1995: 418)

The chant is also made the subject of dark humour. The Captain and his crew believe it embodies 'this simple people's views of the evening hymn'. But it soon appeared that the song was a translation of 'For what we are going to receive' (Dickens 1995: 424): so, a kind of grace before a meal, like a music-hall joke. Later the cannibals sing it again while dancing round the captured Latin-grammar master, the real enemy in the story. He is discovered 'in a hamper with his head shaved, while two savages floured him, before putting him to the fire to be cooked' (the cannibals later resolve 'that he should not be cooked, but should be allowed to remain raw . . .', p. 424). This is just the sort of detail that can be found in pantomime, to which I return below. Importantly, however, the story is very much the internal author's wish-fulfilment fantasy: getting revenge on schoolmasters (the Latin-grammar master is eventually 'hanged at the yard-arm', Dickens 1995: 426); and part of a larger mental schema in which little boys dream of becoming heroes, readers as well as internal authors. Bratton (1990: ix) notes of Ballantyne's *The Coral Island* that it contains no adult guides or mentors: so too the world of this romance and the three others in Dickens' collection. This she believes contributes to the 'sense of freedom' in Ballantyne's novel, a sense which could also have inspired Dickens' own title of *Holiday Romance.* (See further Wales, in preparation).

In its cultural context I would argue here for the significance of pantomime and music-hall for Dickens' cannibalese, and for the representation of the discourses and images of cannibalism in the nineteenth century generally. Again, the influence of *Robinson Crusoe* is unmistakable: there were at least 200 pantomime versions of the novel in the nineteenth century (Richards 2015: 20); and the playwright Richard Sheridan wrote a pantomime on it as early as 1781 (Eigner 1989: 22). These versions were very much intertwined with pantomimes on people-eating giants (*Jack and the Giant-Killer*; *Jack and the Beanstalk*), to which I shall return below; and on exotic adventurers like *Sinbad the Sailor* and even *Dick Whittington.* Dickens was a life-long devotee of the pantomime, from the same age as his 'writer' Robin Redforth; he also directed and acted in family shows and wrote about pantomime in his periodical *Household Words* (see further Eigner 1989). Amidst lots of comic stage business involving manic gestures, cooking, sneezing from pepper, and making pies, pantomimic cannibals characteristically have onomatopoeic or rhyme-reduplicative names like *Hoity Toity, Hokee Pokee,* and *Wanky Fum.* These names would have been familiar to audiences from broadside ballads circulating in the early nineteenth century and surviving in folk songs well into the twentieth century about 'The King of the Cannibal Islands'. One version has a chorus beginning 'Hokey Pokey winky wong'; another, 'Hokey Pokey Wongkee fum' (see, for example, the English Folk Song Project on YouTube.) That Dickens himself knew the tune of 'The King of the Cannibal Islands' is revealed in a vignette of his family holiday in Broadstairs (1844). Buying a collection of ballads for a penny from a street-hawker, including one about Queen Victoria, he 'launched immediately into the chorus', to the tune of the Cannibal ballad (Harman 2018: 65). In one pantomime, *Hoopdedoodendoo* is a King of the 'Caribee' Islands, with *Piccalilee,* his favourite squaw

(Booth 1976: 247–8). In another, Friday tells Crusoe that his name is 'Kill-ee-gowollop-um-skully-go cracky' (cited in Davis 2010: 114). At a Lyceum production of *Robinson Crusoe* in 1895–6, *The Times* praised Charles Lauri as Man Friday for his 'wonderful barbarian language' (cited in Booth 1976: 394): unfortunately no examples are given.

This same editor, in a discussion generally of nonsense refrains in music-hall, pertinently points out (Booth 1976: 457 fn1) that the name 'Hoopdedoodendoo' mentioned above was actually a nonsense chorus line in more than one music-hall song; and there was a song of that title by Earl Pierce of the American black-faced Christy Minstrels, who appeared in England from 1857–60. The blending of the cultural stereotypes of cannibal and black-faced minstrel leads to a kind of cannibalese in both pantomime and fiction which echoes the representation of the American South in works like Harriet Beecher Stowe's (1852) *Uncle Tom's Cabin*: so, in words like *mudder, nebber, lub, berry* (very) (see, for example, Thorne and Grove Palmer's *Robinson Crusoe* pantomime, 1882–3). Generally, the syntax in pantomime cannibalese is what Crusoe calls 'broken English' – a pidgin-type English, particularly striking in its non-standard concord: 'Me got no heir'; 'Him not de King of Naples'. In Henry James Byrom's version of the Crusoe story, or *Harlequin Friday and the King of the Caribee Islands* (1860), Friday hides from Hokey Pokey who cries: 'De pris'ner am escaped! Oh Wankey Fum! De Indian drum! Tum, tum! Come fum!' (cited in Booth 1976: 264). Similar non-standard forms are found also in Robinsonade fiction through the ages. Man Friday's pidgin English is acquired from Crusoe's efforts to teach him English: for example 'Yes, my nation eat mans too, eat all up' (Defoe 1719: 254); 'you teachee me good, you teachee them good' (p. 268). This hint of pidgin Chinese might be evoked in Dickens' 'Nycey'; but it also hints at the historical development of pidgins from the interchanges of sailors, traders, and missionaries with local communities. In Ballantyne's *The Coral Island* (1858) it is interesting that more than one of the pirate crew could 'imperfectly speak dialects of the language peculiar to the South Sea Islanders' (Bratton 1990: 215). It is just possible that such 'exotic' languages have partly inspired the characteristic feature of reduplication in cannibalese. LeCercle (1994: 21) makes a distinction between the imitation of the sounds of one's own language (*charabia*) and the imitation of the sounds of another language (*baragouin*): cannibalese would thus illustrate a combination of the two techniques.

For Dickens, cannibalese is confined to the song: it is not a feature of spoken discourse in the story. The cannibal chief in the tale, as it turns out, actually 'understood English perfectly' (Dickens 1995: 424). Convenient as this is for many representations of cannibal speech, in both fiction and pantomime (but inconvenient for those like myself searching for examples), it testifies to the significant historical role of missionaries in their endeavours to convert the peoples of the South Seas to Christianity in the early nineteenth century: a particular kind of cultural hegemony that predates the domination of the Empire. Bratton (1990: xviii) recognises the significance of this; but Brown (2013: 26), in mis-dating *The Coral Island* to 1893 rather than 1858, undervalues missionary imperialism in her emphasis on the expansion of the British Empire. The work of the missionaries actually provided a schema for the representation of cannibals well into the twentieth century: inextricably associated together in people's minds and so the stuff of music-hall, comic postcards, and jokes. For example:

'What did the cannibal say when he saw the sleeping missionary?'
'Oh look! Breakfast in bed!'
(See further Wales 1990)

In a version of *Robinson Crusoe* performed at Drury Lane in 1893–4, Man Friday learns English from a missionary before eating him (cited in Booth 1976: 377–8); and in one version of the broadside ballad *The King of the Cannibal Islands* the king dies from eating his clergyman cold.

The quotation closest to Dickens' cannibalese I have found so far actually comes from a pantomime about people-eating giants, cited by Warner (1998: 317–18): *The Ogre and Little Thumb; Or The Seven League Boots*, performed at Covent Garden in 1807. The ogre's name is 'Anthropophagos', and one of his victims fears his 'Crunch, crunch, munch, munch, crunch, crunch, crunch, crunch, munch, munch, crunch, crunch'. It is this context of fantasy and fairy tale which must also be considered here, overlaid with the silly and the whimsical. The story of Captain Boldheart is but one of Dickens' four 'romances', all playing unashamedly with the conventions of fairy tale (see further Wales, in preparation), and, like fairy tales, primarily oriented to a child readership accustomed to hearing stories and rhymes from the nursery to schoolroom. From a Victorian child's perspective, Dickens' people-eating cannibals with their light-green faces and strange language were not 'real' people, they were as exotic or alien as blood-sucking vampires or little men from Mars in present-day children's schemata, and comparable to the fantastic beings of child-eating giants and even witches in the popular tales of the period. The giant's catchphrase in the fairy tale, 'Fee, fi, fo fum', with its ablaut-reduplication, echoes through the ages. There was a pantomime *Faw, Fee, Fo Fum* in 1867–8, according to Richards (2015: 48), where the rest of the rhyme originates:

...I smell the blood of an Englishman.
Be he alive or be he dead,
I'll grind his bones to make my bread.

An early example can be found in *King Lear*. Edgar, disguised as mad Tom the beggar, recites:

> Childe Roland to the dark tower came.
> His word was still 'Fie, foh and fum.
> I smell the blood of a British man.'
>
> (*King Lear* III.iv.185–6)

The images or schemata of giants, like cannibals, are simultaneously stereotypical and yet continually 'refreshed' in Cook's (1994) terms. Present-day children are as enthralled by Roald Dahl's *The BFG* as those young readers of forty years ago with the nine 'human beans'. People-eating ogres have more than a passing resemblance to popular representations of cannibals: 'fearsome, ugly, half-naked, fifty-feet-long brutes' (Dahl 1982: 128), with a 'sort of short skirt around their waists, and their skins ... burnt by the sun' (p. 22). The spoken syntax of the Friendly Giant, though he himself is not a people-eater, echoes the cannibalese tradition, with its non-standard forms 'I is hungry', etc.; and his vocabulary has a Dickensian phonaesthetic word-play in 'whiffswiddle', 'fizzwiggler', 'snozzcumbers', and so on.

About the same time as *The BFG*, Adrian Mitchell wrote a play with music for the children's television series *Theatre Box*, directly based on *Holiday Romance*. Its very title, *You Must Believe All This*, is taken from the opening to the first story. The four children (now all part of the same family) act out the stories in their attic. In their version of the pirate story the cannibals' chant is repeated verbatim, but Mitchell also expands on Dickens' cannibalese. So, the 'Chief' of the cannibals standing in the canoe says 'Oola. Gumber umber. Eee?' which is translated as the Chief wanting to step aboard. Reduplication abounds: 'umber gumber', 'oomer goomer', 'wummer dummer', 'oomper groomper', and ('grumpily') 'oovo, oovo' (Mitchell 1981: 37–8).

Finally, there is another context for Dickens that needs to be considered, if briefly. At the time of the publication of *Holiday Romance* there had appeared a remarkable wave of writing for children, striking for its general whimsicality, absurdity and word-play. *Alice in Wonderland* by Lewis Carroll was published just three years previously in 1865; and Edward Lear's *Book of Nonsense* in 1846, enlarged in 1861. In Lear, themes of sea-voyages and nonsense words and rhyme-reduplications abound: 'Quangle Wangle', 'Soffsky-Poffsky' trees, the 'Yonghy-Bonghy-Bo'. The Old Man of Spithead says nothing but 'Fil-jamble, fil-jumble, / Fil-rumble-come tumble', echoing the nursery rhyme jingles of 'Hey, diddle, diddle', etc. The Old Man of Peru is baked in a stew, and the Old Man of Berlin is mixed up in a cake, admittedly both by mistake. The Jumblies, like Dickens' cannibals, had green heads, but not until 1877.

Carroll, Lear, and Dickens have not forgotten what it is like to be a child: in Beer's words (2016: 116) 'they are in dialogue with their past'. Peter Hollindale (1997) calls this quality 'childness'. Dickens' *Holiday Romance*, with its childlike internal authors, narrators, focalisation, and style, takes this to an extreme. However, while it cannot be denied that the mid-nineteenth century saw a definite category of children's literature emerging, with a specific readership or audience of children in mind, at the same time their authors knew their readers were adults as well as children, nannies, parents, tutors, and governesses, who could equally appreciate the whimsicality, just as they enjoyed pantomime. Dickens himself envisaged a dual readership, a dual response. In a letter to Percy Fitzgerald (21 July 1867) he describes his 'romances' as 'a queer combination of a child's mind with a grown up joke' (in Storey 1999: 399); using the same expression in a letter to Charles Kent (3 September 1867) (Storey 1999: 420). We know that *Holiday Romance* did appeal to adults. In a letter to J. T. Fields, his American publisher, before his visit (25 July 1867) Dickens writes: 'It made me laugh to that extent that my people here [in Gad's Hill, his home] thought I was out of my wits, until I gave it to them to read– when they did likewise' (Storey 1999: 402–3). In a letter to John Forster (2 July 1867) he urges him to read the 'pirate story' in particular, 'for I am very fond of it' (Storey 1999: 387). Percy Fitzgerald, again, apparently liked this same story very much (28 July 1867, Storey 1999: 707).

In the twenty-first century the dual readership of children and adults is potentially a more complex consideration, because of changes of taste, ideology, and even language (see further Burke and Coats 2022). The representation of South Seas cannibals is now seen by many cultural critics through the prism of racism and imperialism. The noun *savage*, for example, so prevalent in Ballantyne's *The Coral Island* as in *Robinson Crusoe*, and appearing in Dickens' story of Captain Boldheart, is now labelled as 'inappropriate and offensive' in dictionaries (though *cannibal* is not). Non-expert child readers of Dickens are likely to enjoy the cannibalese and the whole story and remain as 'innocent' as their nineteenth-century counterparts; but they can also be educated by teachers and parents or caregivers about changes of language use. There is the danger of their being over-protected, in trends to censor, rewrite, or 'cancel' well-known stories. Even Adrian Mitchell's play from the 1980s, if revived today, would doubtless be prefixed by a warning. However, it is important for all readers not to judge earlier literature too harshly by modern standards: we need to reach back, try and see it in its contemporary contexts, and so engage in a 'dialogue' between the present and the past, as Gadamer has argued (1976). Most significantly, in the words of Nodelman with children's literature specifically in mind, we have to be 'willing and able to imagine ourselves as being the specific [implied] reader' of the original historical context, in order to 'laugh at the jokes as children [did and] do' (Nodelman 1996: 19–20, 23). I have tried here to make a case for seeing Dickens' cannibalese in the many creative and cultural contexts I believe to be relevant, so that we can continue to enjoy his *Holiday Romance*.

References

Ballantyne, R. M. (1858) *The Coral Island*. Edinburgh: Thomas Nelson and Sons.
Barker, F., Hulme, P. and Iversen, M. (eds) (1998) *Cannibalism and the Colonial World*. Cambridge: Cambridge University Press.
Beer, G. (2016) *Alice in Space: The Sideways Victorian World of Lewis Carroll*. Chicago: University of Chicago Press.
Booth, M. R. (ed.) (1976) *English Plays of the Nineteenth Century, Vol.5 (Pantomimes, Extravaganzas and Burlesques)*. Oxford: Clarendon.
Bratton, J. S. (1990) 'Introduction' to R. M. Ballantyne's *The Coral Island*. Oxford: Oxford University Press, pp. vii–xxi.
Brown, J. (2013) *Cannibalism in Literature and Film*. London: Palgrave Macmillan.
Burke, M. and Coats, K. (2022) 'Stylistics and children's literature', *Language and Literature* 3 (1): 3–10.
Cook, G. (1994) *Discourse and Literature: The Interplay of Form and Mind*. Oxford: Oxford University Press.
Currie, G. (2010) *Narratives and Narrators: A Philosophy of Stories*. Oxford: Oxford University Press.
Dahl, R. (1982) *The BFG*. London: Jonathan Cape.
Davis, J. (2010) 'Only an undisciplined [nation] would have done it': Drury Lane pantomime in the late nineteenth century', in J. Davis (ed.) *Victorian Pantomime: A Collection of Critical Essays*. Basingstoke: Palgrave Macmillan, pp. 100–17.
Defoe, D. (1719) *Robinson Crusoe*. London: William Taylor.
Deleuze, G. (2003) *The Logic of Sense*. London: Continuum.
Dickens, C. (1995) *'Holiday Romance' and Other Writings for Children* (ed. G. Avery) [original story 1868]. London: Dent.
Eigner, E. (1989) *The Dickens Pantomime*. Berkeley: University of California Press.
Fimi, D. and Higgins, A. (eds) (2016) *A Secret Vice: Tolkien on Invented Languages*. London: HarperCollins.
Forster, J. (1936) *Life of Dickens* [original 1872]. London: Hazell, Watson & Viney.
Gadamer, H.-G. (1976) *Philosophical Hermeneutics*. Berkeley: University of California Press.
Hanlon, B. (2001) 'Robinsonade', in V. Watson (ed.) *The Cambridge Guide to Children's Books in English*. Cambridge: Cambridge University Press, pp. 612–13.
Harman, C. (2018) *Murder by the Book*. London: Penguin.
Hollindale, P. (1997) *Signs of Childness in Children's Books*. Stroud: Thimble Press.
LeCercle, J.-J. (1994) *Philosophy of Nonsense: The Intuitions of Victorian Nonsense Literature*. London: Routledge.
Mitchell, A. (1981) *You Must Believe All This*. London: Thames Methuen.
Nodelman, P. (1996) *The Pleasures of Children's Literature*. New York: Longman.
Obeyesekere, G. (1998) 'Cannibal features in nineteenth-century Fiji: seamen's yarns and the ethnographic imagination', in F. Barker, P. Hulme and M. Iversen (eds) *Cannibalism and the Colonial World*. Cambridge: Cambridge University Press, pp. 63–86.
Richards, J. (2015) *The Golden Age of Pantomime*. London: Taurus.
Storey, G. (ed.) (1999) *The Pilgrim Edition of the Letters of Charles Dickens: Vol.11 (1865–7)*. Oxford: Clarendon Press.

Thorne, G and Grove Palmer, F. (1882–3) *Mr Emery's Seventh Pantomime Robinson Crusoe and Billy Taylor, or Harlequin, Man Friday and the King of the Cannibal Islands*. Liverpool: Prince of Wales Theatre, no publisher.
Wales, K. (1990) *Shark-Infested Custard: The Joke-book to Get Your Teeth Into*. London: Piccolo.
Wales, K. (in preparation) 'The *mooreeffoc* effect: Charles Dickens' *Holiday Romance*'.
Warner, M. (1994) *Managing Monsters: Six Myths of Our Time*. London: Vintage.
Warner, M. (1998) *No Go the Bogeyman: Scaring, Lulling and Making Mock*. London: Chatto & Windus.
Wydryzynska, E. (2021) '"I shouldn't even be telling you but I shouldn't be telling you the story": Pseudonymous Bosch and the postmodern narrator in children's literature', *Language and Literature* 30 (3): 229–48.

CHAPTER 10

Dialectal extrapolation as a literary experiment in Aldiss' 'A spot of Konfrontation'

Israel A. C. Noletto

> In this chapter, Israel Noletto devotes particular attention to the language of SpEEC (Speech of the European Economic Community), a dialectal extrapolation of English invented by Brian W. Aldiss for his 1973 short story 'A spot of Konfrontation'. Focusing on the language's descriptive and rhetorical functions, he considers the ways in which SpEEC impacts upon the readability and interpretation of Aldiss' short story. Throughout his analysis Noletto builds a case for glossopoesis as experimentation, analysing Aldiss' neologistic innovation, creative representation of speech, and textual aesthetics, alongside the language's sociolinguistic implications.

Introduction

The study of experimental fiction, narratives that manipulate language in intriguing ways, exploiting its potential through form and meaning, has frequently drawn on such fields as stylistics and narrative theory. This seems appropriate since both style and theme hinge on language discussions in this type of literature. Examples of other works that have, broadly speaking, followed this route include Bernaerts (2017), Scott (2018), and Tykhomyrova (2018). In this chapter, I set out to analyse the short story 'A spot of Konfrontation' (1973) (henceforth 'Konfrontation') deploying a stylistic frame of reference. Via close reading, I place particular emphasis on SpEEC (Speech of the European Economic Community), a dialectal extrapolation of English invented by Brian W. Aldiss (all references are from the 1979 *New Arrivals, Old Encounters* collection) from the perspective of the most salient narrative functions the fictional language seems to have: namely, the descriptive and rhetorical functions (see Noletto 2022 and the introduction to this volume). This will involve analysing the text from a critical viewpoint, highlighting how SpEEC may impact both readability and interpretation.

'Konfrontation' is set in Papeete in 2073 and describes a highly bureaucratic world whose international government, headquartered in Brussels, uses travel allowances to balance the trade between the rich and the developing nations, tackling postcolonial issues with a distinct dystopian overtone. This means that the citizens from the 'Market States', as the wealthy countries are called, must spend their mandatory holidays in the third world as a way to fund deprived states, which apparently have no other source of revenue (Aldiss 1979: 80).

Early on in the story, the reader is greeted by the invented words of SpEEC – *apologio, Politzei, mambo-jet,* and *temperturo* – which adumbrates the stylised language in which part of the tale is rendered. Told in third-person narration, the narrative focalises Gunpat Smith, a British national who travels with his family to Tahiti. Upon learning that he had been involved in a romantic affair with a sex worker named Flavia, Gunpat's wife flies back home, spends all that is left of their travel allowance, and leaves Gunpat behind as a 'displaced tourist' (Aldiss 1979: 91). Being a displaced tourist means that Gunpat is stranded in Tahiti, virtually penniless, and cannot expect any practical help from the British Vice-Consul, Mr Skinner, a caricature of a government official. As Gunpat tries to get by, he can only rely on the Polynesian bartender Rosie, the only local who does not shun him for being a displaced tourist, and Abe Hakabendassi, a troublesome Germano-Tahitian smuggler. Gunpat now fears he might spend the rest of his life there, talking to the natives in SpEEC, a language that he, like most other characters, has not mastered yet.

As a satire, besides the humorous content, the over-encoding of SpEEC invites a symbolist reading that I mean to explore under the assumption that Aldiss deployed *glossopoesis* (language invention) as a tool for interfacing style and theme. In doing so, I argue that the presence of an unfamiliar fictional language interlaced with English as the narrative medium does not necessarily constitute a barrier to understanding as might otherwise be expected.

Generally, dialectal extrapolations retain the original language's syntax to some extent and take a large number of loanwords, neologisms, and neosemes. Creating a specific register or dialect that pertains to the story world but remains somewhat intelligible can operate at differing levels of communication 'while not making undue demands on the reader to engage in detailed decoding' (Stockwell 2006: 5).

As Beauchamp (1974: 474) pointed out, however history unfolds, language will adjust to echo the changing reality. Representing futuristic changes in society or embedding a symbolist critique of the present in language invention is an artifice recurrently utilised in science fiction and dystopia. The two genres constantly overlap, which offers abundant plot possibilities for discussing linguistic issues and implementing innovative narrative devices. Similarly, Meyers stated that:

> Only one job requires its practitioners to put down on paper their estimates of the language of the next decade, the next century, or the next millennium – the job of writing science fiction. Science fiction has, therefore, a special relationship within the field of language to historical linguistics.
>
> (Meyers 1976: 131)

An instance of text with this formula is the well-known *A Clockwork Orange* (1962) by Anthony Burgess. It was written amidst the Cold War and features Nadsat, a blend of British English and Russian. Likewise, *Riddley Walker* (1980) by Russell Hoban imagines a deteriorated form of English that reflects both the brutality of the time and the lack of education of the characters who live in a post-apocalyptic England in tune with the nuclear holocaust threat at the time of writing. *Ambient* (1987) by Jack Womack presents an English patois heavily influenced by Rasta and Spanish in a twenty-first-century alternate New York as a social critique.

Before writing 'A spot of Konfrontation', Brian Aldiss experimented with non-traditional narratives and glossopoesis, inventing a portmanteau of various European languages to represent the psychedelic effects of a chemical bombing in *Barefoot in the Head* (1969). The language of that novel was so intricate that some have considered it an extravagant stylistic experiment with too much emphasis on form and little concern with meaning (Ketterer 1974: 260).

Fictional languages frequently function as elaborative or characterising tools for the settings in which they appear and the characters who speak them, in addition to informing the plot at a secondary discourse level (Stockwell 2006, Cheyne 2008, Noletto and Lopes 2019). Paying attention to the historical moment when these fictional languages were invented can be enlightening. However, reading them against the fictional context is also critical to interpreting their meaning and function. These two points of departure, both contingent on the reader's schematic knowledge, are indispensable for a fuller appreciation of literary glossopoesis.

Because most stories that feature dialectal extrapolations are either written in the fictional language itself or at least intertwined with English, they establish a point of intersection with literary experimentalism, which is characterised by an iconoclastic impetus that can defy traditional aesthetic and narratorial norms. Generally, such experiments focus considerably on form, explore textual sites, and are programmatic and metadiscursive. They can incorporate exceptional narrative modes and inventive language or build up as recondite puzzles that require reading between the lines (Glicksberg 1974). Although the diction used in the narration can still be viewed as pedestrian, as happens in most science fiction stories, in terms of narrative style, 'Konfrontation' is highly creative.

Making a stylistic choice to employ an invented language requires some measure of language learning and code-switching from the reader. This means that readers may initially have to grapple with 'an alienating form of their own language', which 'must eventually become knowable if the interface between style and theme is to be effective' (Mandala 2010: 39; see Stockwell 2000: 155, and Myers 1983: 306). Stockwell (2000: 62) explains that the thorough use of literary dialects, fictional or natural, constitutes a narrative experiment that aims to 'foreground the language to the extent that the reader is likely to thematise the stylistic form itself, in a way that would not happen in traditional' writing. In other words, in addition to being the narrative wherewithal, a fictional dialect is also a means to inform the story's theme.

'Konfrontation' has been described as a 'broad farce, skilfully constructed and richly ornamented', combining 'the mellow bawdry of [Aldiss'] mainstream novels [...] with the verbal ingenuities of *Barefoot in the Head*' (Disch 2005: 106). Unlike *Barefoot*, however, the way Aldiss experimented with language in 'Konfrontation' evinces a more perceptible preoccupation with readability and intelligibility. The glossopoeic technique in both cases displays the same fundamental strategy – language hybridism – which spotlights the narrative's future setting and the story's thematic issues. Nevertheless, to create SpEEC, Aldiss did not deploy metaplasmic figures, such as *oronyms*, strings of words or phrases that sound the same but are spelt differently and have different meanings (I scream vs. ice cream), and *zeugma*, the use of one word to join together phrases or strings of words (Farmers *grew* potatoes, barley, and *bored*). Rather, he borrowed words from several European languages, keeping them reasonably unchanged, using mostly English lexes and creating similar syntax.

Style and readability

A concern arising from any analysis of experimental texts with some sort of multilingualism, even if only in part, as in 'Konfrontation', is to what extent such text will be readable. Some could argue that these texts are discouraging rather than immersive or engaging, leading most readers to give up reading almost immediately. Interestingly, however, a reading-ease test based on Flesch-Kincaid metrics, for which I used an application called Datayze Readability Analyzer, gave the text a score of 3.91. This means the narrative is likely to be understood by a reader with at least a seventh-grade education (age twelve) and should be easy for most adults to read (see Kincaid et al. 1983). This ease seems mainly to be because SpEEC comprises roughly only 6 per cent of the text, including repetitions and instances of neosemy (words from SpEEC that appear in the English portion of the text), most of which are German and Romance roots, and excluding the names of characters and places. This is consistent with other cases of dialectal extrapolation, such as *A Clockwork Orange*, whose percentage of Nadsat words is approximately 5 per cent (Jackson 2011: 67).

'Konfrontation' oscillates between orthodox prose and the fictional language. The shifts between the narratorial voice and the characters are mediated mainly by SpEEC-English switches. Dialogues are often marked by SpEEC and inverted commas rather than by reporting verbs, as in Gunpat's exclamation, 'Phew, dies temperturo!' (Aldiss 1979: 73). This makes the short story much easier to read and engage with than novels with a denser texture, such as *Riddley Walker*. Characters' lines are presented in the fictional language to indicate their speech patterns. In contrast, free indirect discourse is represented in relatively formal language with grammatically accurate sentences, exhibiting a high concentration of Latinate vocabulary, thus suggesting precision: voluntary, secure, inevitable, conviction, etc. (Mandala 2010: 60).

The story starts *in media res* in fluid prose with only occasional SpEEC words and expressions in direct speech (*Politzei, temperturo*, etc.) as the reader learns about Gunpat's romantic affair. One morning, he wakes up to see Flavia has already left. He sees 'a note lying folded on the room's only chair' (Aldiss 1979: 74). The note written in SpEEC, the very first nomination of the language, reads, 'Helo, Gunny! Jeg exita. Apologio fur absenso. Too much temperturo in dies rummet fur somno, als eterno. Jeg reviendra par middago. Somna vohl! Amor, Flavia' (Aldiss 1979: 75), which can be translated as: 'Hello, Gunny! I went out. Sorry for my absence. Too hot in this room to sleep as always. I will be back by midday. Sleep well! Love, Flavia.'

This second occurrence of SpEEC seems to 'serve to train the reader to cope with the estranged text' (Mandala 2010: 64), promoting solidarity with the reader and helping him or her pick up the language's features and subtleties. For example, besides the quasi-perfect cognates, *helo, exita, in, too much, apologia,* and *absenso*, which are easy to decode in isolation, words like *jeg* and *fur* occur twice in similar positions, allowing contextual decoding: 'I' and 'for', respectively. The initial sentences also operate to hint at some morphosyntactic features of the language that are subsequently confirmed and reinforced as the words are repeated in similar circumstances.

Aldiss adopts interesting conlanging strategies that contribute to an overall organic and natural feel to the language regardless of sophistication. This includes a few morphological markers that facilitate learning. Most nouns end in '-o' (*temperturo, apologio, absenso, middago*), whereas most verbs end in '-a' (*exita, reviendra, somna*). This marks, for instance, cases of anthimeria, or using one part of speech as another, in this case, a noun as a verb, and vice versa, just by changing the final vowel of the word. Accordingly, *somna* (possibly from French *sommeil* via Latin *somnus*, both meaning 'sleep'; coincidently cognate with Swedish for 'to fall asleep', *somna*), then, becomes the noun *somno*, 'sleep', a feature that seems to have been borrowed from Esperanto. Of course, there are exceptions. *Rummet*, for instance, means 'room' and comes from Swedish *rum* (*rummet* = the room) and does not end in 'o'. Also, *eterno*, an adverb, ends in 'o', whereas *amor* does not.

Dialectal extrapolation in Aldiss' 'A spot of Konfrontation' 149

There are other inconsistencies as well. For instance, the copular 'to be' is simply omitted on several occasions, as in 'Ven jeg fortunato' (Aldiss 1979: 76), 'If I am lucky' and 'U.K. lange wego from Tahiti' (Aldiss 1979: 76), 'The U.K. is a long way from Tahiti.' In other sentences, the verb 'to be' is used in 'Is es totaal doomwatch?', 'Is it completely blown?' This is found again in Rosie's utterances for which she is characterised as speaking 'broken SpEEC'. These rules help give consistency and learnability to SpEEC. In contrast, sporadic irregularities and inconsistencies can enhance the language's verisimilitude, although they might be simply authorial error or carelessness.

Overall, SpEEC bears a consistent use of the definite article *die*, the demonstrative pronoun *dies*, the adverb *rialto*, 'really', as well as the personal pronouns *jeg*, 'I', *vous*, 'you', *elle*, 'she', *wir*, 'we', and *uns*, 'us'. Prepositions are also relatively consistent: *als*, meaning 'as', and *par*, 'for' or 'by', although 'by' appears instead on occasion. Parenthetically, it is curious that Aldiss decided to incorporate the French formal personal pronoun *vous* and make it standard. The T-V distinction (*tu-vous*) is used in Romance languages to mark familiarity and formality. So, this could be a way to lend politeness to the language. Lastly, the conjunction 'and' is rendered *unt* (phonetic *und*) by all characters, except for Gunpat, who insists on using 'and'.

Deducing from the excerpts, SpEEC can be described as a pastiche of English, Danish, German, Dutch, Swedish, French, Spanish, and Italian (see Graphic 10.1). In addition to some words kept in English, the word order and other syntactic features remain relatively unchanged. This allows reasonable ease of decoding, especially for the informed reader interested in conlanging who probably has a working knowledge of European languages. Since English and the other languages Aldiss used as a basis for SpEEC share a great deal of their lexes, reading for cognates, or at least guessing from the context, makes the text somewhat transparent.

As Graphic 10.1 shows, concerning most pronouns, prepositions, and nouns, Aldiss' glossopoeic strategy basically consisted of borrowing words and keeping them completely unaltered (*jeg* – 'I' in Danish; *amor* – 'love' in

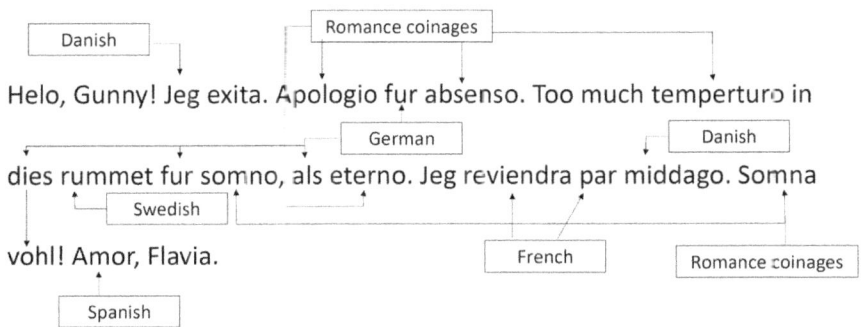

Graphic 10.1 Etymological breakdown of SpEEC lexes (Aldiss 1979: 75)

Spanish; *als* – 'as' in German; *dies* – 'this' in German; *par* – 'by' in French), slightly modified loanwords (*fur* from *für*, 'for' in German; *vohl* from *wohl*, 'well' in German), and creative coinages from Romance roots that remain cognate with their English equivalents (*apologio*, 'apologies', from French *apologie* via Latin; *absenso*, 'absence', from Latin *absentia*; *temperturo*, 'temperature', from French *température*).

Although Aldiss seems to have paid some attention to the contextual position of terms with potential for misinterpretation, a few SpEEC words may be read as false cognates if pronounced according to English phonology, which could theoretically interfere with readability. This is the case of *jeg*, *als*, and *dies*. *Jeg* /jaj/, Danish for 'I' would likely be pronounced /dʒeg/. *Als* /als/ or /alts/, 'as' in German might be pronounced /ɔːlz/, thus resulting in a possible confusion with 'all's'. And *dies* /diːs/, 'this' in German is a false cognate with English 'dies' /daɪz/. Other words, however, can phonetically aid in their decoding. *Eterno*, for instance, would possibly be pronounced /iˈtɜːnəʊ/, which is close enough to 'eternal', and *fur*, /ˈfyə/ from German 'for', would probably be read /fɜː/, which is reasonably close to the unstressed pronunciation of 'for'.

From these examples, in addition to cases of Anglicised spellings such as *ven*, 'if', from German *wenn* /ven/ and *mine*, 'my', from German *mein* /main/, it is possible that SpEEC is meant to sound somewhat like English, in terms of prosody. However, each separate word should retain its original pronunciation in order to generate the intended estranging effect properly.

Other curious morphosyntactic choices Aldiss made have to do with word order, verbs, and spelling. Some of these choices have apparently been imported directly from the languages that form the basis of SpEEC; others, however, are entirely new. Graphic 10.2 shows that the word order of SpEEC is considerably similar to Standard English (SVO) in the present tense and conditional mode in affirmative sentences. Interrogative sentences look

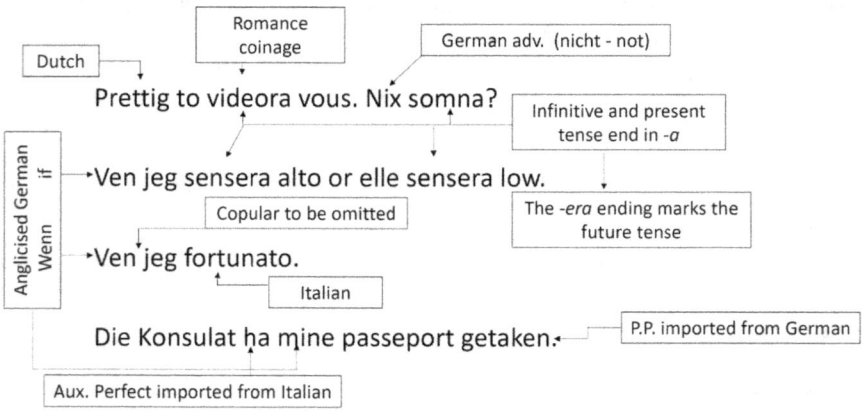

Graphic 10.2 SpEEC etymological and syntactic rundown (Aldiss 1979: 76, 83)

more related to colloquial English because of the ellipsis of the auxiliary 'did' and the subject in sentences such as 'Nix somna?', or 'Didn't you sleep?', thus dispensing with any past tense marker. Also, verbs end in -*a* in the infinitive or get the French endings -*era* or -*iendra* in the future (e.g. *amora* [pres.] vs. *amorera* [fut.], 'to love'; *fluging* [cont.] vs. *fugera* [fut.], 'to fly'). Again, there are many transparent loanwords from Dutch, Danish, German, French, and Italian (*prettig* – pretty; *jeg* – I; *nix* – not; *elle* – she; *fortunato* – fortunate, lucky) as well as creative coinages (*videora* – see, meet; *sensera* – feel).

A last noteworthy syntactic feature concerning word order is how Aldiss organised the present perfect. Rather than using the English structure (subject+to have+past participle+object), Aldiss borrowed *Das Perfekt* from German, both in terms of word order (subject+haben[ha in SpEEC]+object+past participle) and strong verb inflexion (ge+verb[in its past form]), as in 'Die Konsulat ha mine passeport getaken', 'The consulate has taken my passport.' This general rule even follows the exceptions found in German (for instance, verbs ending in -*ieren* do not take the *ge-* prefix, as in '*Mine passeport is komandeert*', 'My passport has been commandeered').

There are also some cases of semantic metanalysis by blending, reduplication, and metaphor (see Campbell 1999: 118, 256). Blending is seen in *waz-wot* when Gunpat tells Flavia about his passport trouble; she encourages him to talk to Abe because 'Abe kenna waz-wot in Papeete' (Aldiss 1979: 83) or 'Abe knows what's-what in Papeete'. Reduplication, when Gunpat tells Abe not to shoot his partner, Cancer Thouars, 'Nix bang-bang ' (Aldiss 1979: 89) as well as in *zo-zo* (from Dutch *zo*, 'so', or phonetic German, '*so*'), 'so-so', a reply for *Common' geht?*, in itself a pun for being an oronym for 'come on!' And metaphor is seen in *high-rise* and *dock-strike*. For instance, when Gunpat is asked how he liked Tahiti, he answers, 'Jeg high-rise to be here' (Aldiss 1979: 77), or 'I am thrilled to be here'. In this context, 'high-rise', a noun meaning a multistorey building or the corresponding adjective, is metaphorically used to refer to an emotion of joyous thrill, possibly by analogy with the feeling of being on top of a high-rise building, perhaps on a balcony or close to the edge. Additionally, Rosie uses the adjective *dock-strike* along with *wunderbar* and other positive adjectives to portray her daughter as attractive (Aldiss 1979: 79). *Wunderbar* is simply 'wonderful' in German. *Dock-strike*, despite the apparently negative denotation, is also used by Mr Skinner to tell Gunpat his documents are in order (Aldiss 1979: 80), thus expressing a positive connotation, perhaps in a similar inversion of meaning as in 'sick' or 'nasty' which shifted meaning to 'awesome' in British slang.

A few SpEEC words have been incorporated into the vocabulary of some characters even when they speak English, such as *rialto*, meaning 'really', or *mambo-jet* (mammoth jumbo jet), a gigantic airliner in use in the future, from 'Jumbo Jet', a nickname given to the Boeing 747 due to its sizable dimensions. Most of these are formed by semantic metanalysis or neosemy and carry political commentary. *Nixon*, for instance, can be glossed as 'nothing' if deduced from the context in the following excerpt (taking from Mr Skinner's 'thank you' and Gunpat's subsequent response to it, 'that's really nothing'), a possible critique of Nixon's performance as the 37th President of the USA, which is quite telling of the writer's political stance:

> 'I have to dine with the Governor at the Jockey Club tonight,' he says. 'Thank you.' 'Uh – oh, well, that's a rialto nixon. Never mind – uh, some other time...' [...]
> 'Why do you need my passport? [...] to which Mr Skinner replies, 'Mere thatcher. Just in case anything sputniks.'
>
> (Aldiss 1979: 81)

The context in which *thatcher* and *sputnik* appear seems to suggest that they mean 'formality' or 'bureaucracy' and 'to go wrong'. These could be read respectively as critiques of Margaret Thatcher's close economic regulation (she was Secretary of State for Education 1970–4) in and how the Soviet satellite may have triggered the Space Race that financially destroyed the USSR.

Other examples of this use of proper nouns to coin new vocabulary include *to taiwan* and *koestler*. As suggested by the context, *to taiwan* could be glossed as 'to rot', meaning 'to remain unwillingly in one place for a long period', perhaps as a reference to the fact that Taiwan does not want to remain a part of China. Similarly, *koestler* could possibly mean 'OK' or 'fine' since Mr Skinner tells Gunpat not to worry, for 'everything will turn out koestler' (Aldiss 1979: 81). This is indeed a curious pun. Arthur Koestler, an author who criticised science fiction novels for lacking linguistic inventiveness (Beauchamp 1974), ironically becomes a neoseme, meaning 'OK' in a story marked by outstanding linguistic inventiveness.

These more complicated features may interfere with reading comprehension due to the distancing from English and the consequent disorientating effect. Nonetheless, a few decoding aids seem to have been used in some parts of the text. For instance, Aldiss couples a few sentences in English with the equivalent in SpEEC. Although this could be viewed simply as a way to render the texture less dense and keep the engagement of those who are not so interested in decoding a fictional language, it again serves to train the reader as it prompts a contrastive analysis of the sentences.

This decoding cue is disguised by Gunpat's lack of fluency, who still translates from English whenever he has to speak SpEEC. Similar reading aids are found at the beginning and again halfway through the short story: 'If I'm lucky, Rosie. Ven jeg fortunato!' (Aldiss 1979: 76); 'Hello, Abe, nice to see you again so soon. Prettig to videora vous' (Aldiss 1979: 82). Additionally, Aldiss signals contextual cues by adding introductory or explicatory statements such as 'Perhaps she was surprised' followed by an expression of surprise in SpEEC, 'Unt dies vesto vento?', which Gunpat translates before answering, and 'He bared his teeth to her' to explain 'Jeg high-rise to be here'.

Rosie glanced round at the other men in the bar and then asked, 'Common' vous amora Tahiti, Mister Smeet?'
'Oh, jeg mucho amora. Rialto wunderbar.'
Perhaps she was surprised. *'Unt dies vesto vento?'*
'Ooh, lovely warm wind, rialto! Jeg high-rise to be here.'
He bared his teeth to her.

(Aldiss 1979: 77; my emphasis)

As the story advances, the dialogues build up in complexity, incorporating idiolectal variation, characters' errors, and more abrupt code-switching. So, while SpEEC operates to estrange the language of the text, later, provided that the reader reads on, it is likely to result in immersion, taking the reader into the short story's constructed world and increasing the reader's involvement with the focaliser and other coadjutant characters (Stockwell 2006).

This enhanced complexity is mainly found in Flavia's utterances, the most skilled SpEEC speaker, and in Abe Hakabendassi's utterances, which are overloaded with German. In a conversation in which Gunpat, apparently tired of struggling with SpEEC, resorts to English, Hakabendassi replies,

'Englisch nix speec! Speec SpEEC!' [. . .]
'Wir nix kaput yet, Schmit! Kom! Wir transportera unser kommodities nach ein neu hide-out. Politzei nix find. Okay?'

(Aldiss 1979: 84)

Here the only help the reader can use is contextual cues and cognates. There are no translations or any other sort of textual aid other than those previously provided. At this point, the immersed reader must use their schematic knowledge and the authorial cues scattered throughout the narrative to decode this denser text. The paradigm repeats itself subsequently in Flavia's utterance:

'Jeg kenna die rialto perfecto hide-out!' Flavia said. 'Zu votre fratello villa nach Vaitoto.' To Smith she explained, 'Abe ha ein brudder, Hans, in Vaitoto. Die kommodities restera fail-safe in Hans' villa. Gang mit Abe unt assistera cargo die schip. Jeg restera hier unt dekoyera die Politzei. Common' overkill!' She laughed.

(Aldiss 1979: 84)

The experimental style Aldiss employed to represent direct speech in 'Konfrontation' may have resulted in a text that is relatively more difficult to read than most sf stories, especially due to the dense examples cited above. However, this style is precisely the text's instrument to convey its theme and subtextual information. As Meyers (1980: 69) would put it, the medium (the fictional language) has become the message itself. Therefore, considering the information conveyed or implied by SpEEC is key to interpreting 'Konfrontation', which is analysed in the next section.

Theme and subtext

As the neosemes *thatcher, nixon,* and *to sputnik* reveal, the theme in 'Konfrontation' has a strong political component. By and large, dystopian writers must reconcile the opposing concerns of aestheticism and didacticism (Sisk 1997: 80). The premise and the theme of dystopian texts invariably include both 'wit or humor founded on fantasy [or scientific discourse] or a sense of the grotesque or absurd' with a scathing attack on something, usually some idea or organisation (Frye 1990: 224). Another characteristic common to many dystopian texts, whether they overlap with science fiction or not, is the description of an implausible solution for a social problem or condition as the means to criticise, teach a lesson, or cast a warning about something in the actual world. Therefore, the activity of reading dystopias involves grappling with textual aesthetics in order to access the didacticism, usually in the shape of a pseudo prophecy and frequently a self-negating idea (see Noletto and Lopes 2019: 7). By the same token, SpEEC is both a stylistic device and a thematic vehicle. Hence, understanding SpEEC and its sociolinguistic implications are integral to any analysis of 'Konfrontation'.

For Mandala (2010: 71), SpEEC should be construed as a pidgin, which, as I elaborate on later, directly impacts the interpretation of the narrative. As Wardhaugh (2006: 61) explains, real-world pidgins are no one's first language because they are contact languages. This means actual pidgins are normally born out of the contact of three or more speech communities which do not have a common language but need to communicate. Pidgins are formed by an amalgamation of languages that find themselves in close contact. They usually have a limited vocabulary and a reduced grammatical structure compared to the languages that originated them. Since they do not have native speakers, pidgins can often vary significantly in their use from individual to individual.

Viewing SpEEC as a pidgin makes sense, at least at a superficial level, given some pertinent elements that could define SpEEC as such. First, there is the multicultural setting, Papeete, filled with different language groups in contact. Some characters serve to epitomise the language groups that make up the fictional language: Smith, English; Flavia, Italian; Abe, German; each one either stranded as a displaced tourist forever or a native, mixing up their languages as they try to communicate. Also in the setting, an alternative reality, English is no longer the global language. According to Mandala (2010: 60), a few characteristics of the language, such as some word formation via metaphorical extension, reduplication and the broad adoption of colloquial terms for formal registers, seem to replicate the process of pidginisation.

Furthermore, as Mandala (2010: 58) points out, the European travellers who take their mandatory holidays 'have no incentive to learn each other's languages', and this is the typical scenario in which natural pidgins emerge. In such a scenario, the premise in 'Konfrontation' would suggest a shift in the 'global balance of power' (Mandala 2010: 67), as the pidgin establishes itself as the new norm, abandoning the stigma of a devalued language and resulting in the empowerment of the ones that had been oppressed. However, I wish to offer an alternative reading that may be more in tune with the dystopian overtone of the text and Aldiss' pessimistic frame of understanding existence as inherently entropic, which is observed in most of his stories.

As previously mentioned, SpEEC is an acronym for the 'Speech of the European Economic Community (EEC)', an organisation established in 1957 by Germany, the Netherlands, Luxembourg, Belgium, France, and Italy, including all of their colonies in the third world. It aimed to integrate the economies of its six members. The United Kingdom, Denmark, and Ireland joined it later in 1973. At the time of writing, Portugal and Spain were expected to join as well, which they eventually did in 1986, following their turn away from dictatorships. So, Aldiss probably decided to anticipate this since the story is set in 2073. This justifies the languages represented in SpEEC, except for Swedish, which, given its similarity with Danish, must have been included due to authorial error. Alternatively, not knowing that the organisation would be replaced with the European Union, Aldiss might have imagined that Sweden would have joined the EEC by 2073.

All the languages of the organisation's members are represented in the story by the fictional language even if through a single word, as though SpEEC were metafictional, admittedly constructed to represent all the participating linguistic groups. Hence, rather than a pidgin, as Mandala (2010) stated, I argue that SpEEC is more likely an IAL (International Auxiliary Language) created by the EEC's central administration to replace English as the international language in the narrative. The status of English as a global language is a frequent theme in Aldiss' stories. Besides 'Konfrontation', *Barefoot* also addresses it. Interestingly, Mandala (2010: 13) initially contemplates the IAL argument, although she maintains that there is more evidence in favour of the pidginisation hypothesis. Two factors, nevertheless, support my claim.

First, there are apparent references in 'Konfrontation' to two IALs: a salient grammar regularity and simplicity, in which nouns end in '-o' and verbs end in '-a' (Esperanto nouns end in '-o' and verbs end in '-as' in the present tense); the representation of various European languages; and of course, the *lingua franca* status seem to be referencing Esperanto. Zamenhof – the creator of Esperanto – argued that his IAL was indeed an international language since he had incorporated features of several different languages. In reality, however, Esperanto was not more than a Romance language heavily influenced by Slavic and Germanic languages with only scarce roots from Asian languages and none from less prestigious groups such as African, Aboriginal, or Indigenous languages. This denounced a narrow view of the world and its linguistic diversity, just like the diversity represented by SpEEC.

Overall, Esperanto was a failed attempt to create a language that could equally represent all linguistic groups. Partly due to this failure, a large number of other languages followed it as contenders for the IAL position: Ido, Novial, Occidental, Esperantido, and so forth. All of them deployed the same recipe, language hybridism and simplified grammar. They also failed to captivate supporters and represent linguistic diversity. The movement essentially died out in the late twentieth century; however, it grew exponentially between the two World Wars, and the Esperantist movement was still largely active in the 1970s (see Large 1985: 93).

The language name, SpEEC, containing an acronym for EEC, could likewise be read as a reference to Basic English, an IAL created by C. K. Ogden in 1930, whose name is also an acronym for *B*ritish *A*merican *S*cientific *I*nternational *C*ommercial English. As can be noted from the excerpts in the previous section, SpEEC speakers use a very basic vocabulary, and their utterances display simplified syntax: often no grammatical subject and no copulas. Incidentally, Ogden described Basic English as 'a careful and systematic selection of 850 English words which will cover the needs of everyday life for which a vocabulary of 20,000 words is frequently employed' (Large 1985: 163). Additionally, the characteristics Mandala has pointed to that may theoretically resemble pidginisation are typical conlanging strategies adopted by science fiction writers and dystopia writers. Aldiss implemented it in *Barefoot*, and it is also observed in *Riddley Walker*, to name just a few examples.

Second, Mr Skinner tells Gunpat, SpEEC could become considerably more complex since the USSR and Greece were applying to join the Market States (Aldiss 1979: 80). Consequently, the lexicon and possibly grammatical features of Russian and Greek would have to be incorporated into the language as well, artificially rather than naturally. That SpEEC occupies a higher social position than that of a pidgin developed by a community of displaced tourists is also emphasised by the fact that SpEEC words have even influenced the language spoken by British authorities. For instance, Mr Skinner's speech pattern is filled with curious loanwords: the previously mentioned *thatcher*, *nixon*, *to sputnik*, *to taiwan*, and *koestler*.

These SpEEC words entering the vocabulary of prominent people such as Mr Skinner when they are speaking English further reinforces the view that SpEEC appears to be a top-down phenomenon, not the other way around. Typically, languages borrow words for two reasons, need or prestige, or both; to incorporate a new concept or because the foreign term is more highly esteemed than the vernacular due to strong cultural influence (Campbell 1999: 64). Rather than developing a pidgin to converse with the locals, it makes more sense to expect that these first-world travellers would bring their own international language with them, one already in use in their own regions. It is worth noting that some Market States' institutions also have names in SpEEC, such as the *Out-Tourist Departement*, located in Brussels. Moreover, songs in SpEEC, e.g. *Elle Donata Me Blow fur Blow*, were 'an overkill hit throughout the Pacific Urbanizacion' (Aldiss 1979: 82), demonstrating that the language was not a local occurrence.

Fictional languages should also be read within the context in which they are featured rather than just through their implications in the actual world. In this case, the setting is a future world ruled by a global government. SpEEC can be understood as a sort of parody of Esperanto and the IAL movement or the idea of inventing a language to solve all communication problems. This is consistent with the satirical aesthetics of other narrative entities in the short story.

It seems that Aldiss applied the *reductio ad absurdum* dystopian principle (see Beauchamp 1974: 470). Everything in 'Konfrontation' is presented as absurd and precarious: the EEC as a sort of global government, the bloated bureaucracy, mandatory holidays as a strategy to balance international trade, the persistent colonialist policy of the wealthy nations, Gunpat's and Flavia's awful circumstances as displaced tourists, and even the weather that is repetitively portrayed as too warm and uninviting. No wonder the *lingua franca* of the time is also an absurd language which, combined with the fact that 'Konfrontation' is a satire, undoubtedly excuses the apparent lack of conlanging sophistication. As Ruppert (1986: 150) elucidated, dystopias have consistently relied on absurd contrast as a rhetorical device. Accordingly, SpEEC is a rich source of contradictions. The presence of V-pronouns in a language of reduplications, metaphorical extensions, and other informalities is an example of that.

If my understanding is accurate, it has a direct impact on the interpretation of the text. While a pidgin carries a stigma of marginalisation and disfavour, an IAL that the wealthy nations have adopted must be regarded as a language of prestige. Accordingly, rather than a local language that emerged spontaneously from the contact among different speech communities with almost no consequence stemming from power relationships, SpEEC appears to be a language that has spread through conquest and continued control (see Wardhaugh 2006: 379). In this light, 'Konfrontation' becomes a synecdoche for cultural suppression, a satire of the 'first-world' current imperialist policy, its exclusionist character, and the problem with decisions taken by a minority for the majority, and, at a secondary level, a sort of metonymic mockery on the IAL movement.

Curiously, the fact that another language has displaced English as the international language tells the reader not to take for granted the significant changes in the geopolitics of the short story. Ultimately, it appears Aldiss has deployed SpEEC as the means to practise the show-do-not-tell rhetorical principle anchored in immersive strategies and a highly descriptive fictional language (see Beauchamp 1976: 475).

Conclusion

This chapter has argued that SpEEC likely functions as an IAL that consists of a dialectal extrapolation of English with heavy influence from other European languages rather than a pidgin that emerged spontaneously. This view directly impacts the interpretation of 'Konfrontation'. For this reason, any critical appraisal of the text must pay close attention to the fictional language's roles in the plot. The thematised language both estranges the reader and serves to characterise narrative entities. Its presence in the text may be a bit challenging to the reader. Nonetheless, thanks to the larger proportion of English in comparison with SpEEC in the text and the decoding aids provided, the estranged language is learnable, which validates the interface between style and theme.

'Konfrontation' probably takes longer to read than one would expect from a 5,446-word short story. However, the oscillation between English and SpEEC does not necessarily impede comprehension. Decoding the fictional language requires schematic knowledge and contextual inference, but these are staples of the science fiction genre. In effect, this deciphering exercise could even help with the reader's engagement as the sense of discovery could work as a significant part of the reading pay-off.

As a thematised language, SpEEC performs stylistic and thematic functions. It describes the constructed world of 'Konfrontation', elaborating details that activate the readers' knowledge of their actual world, fleshing out the characters and other narrative entities, and giving access to ideologies. So, SpEEC operates on a diegetic level to support the main narrative about Smith's misfortune. As a signpost, it supplements contextual information that may prompt the reader to consider possibilities not fully realised in the text and to consider how the world became so nonsensical.

In a way, I could argue that the influence every linguistic group has on SpEEC directly corresponds to the power that linguistic group has in the EEC within the story world. Accordingly, the British would be the most powerful nation since English is clearly the framework within which the fictional language was constructed. Then, the second most influential language would be German, followed by French and Spanish. It seems that Dutch, Italian, and Danish are all at the same level.

Aldiss' fictional language is quite eloquent. It not only tells a cohesive back-story but also informs the subtext as a diegetic tool. However, SpEEC is even more eloquent in what is excluded. There is no representation of Polynesian languages whatsoever. French Polynesia is home to several languages, of which the most widely spoken are Tahitian, Marquesan, and Tuamotuan, and yet not a single word of those languages is included. Thus, the Tahitians are not really part of the Market States; they are but a marginalised extension. As happens with IALs, there is simply not enough room for all languages to be represented. Finally, through this interpretative lens, 'Konfrontation' must be regarded as symbolist fiction in that it treats the future as a metaphorical world for critical reflection on the present.

References

Aldiss, B. W. (1969) *Barefoot in the Head*. London: Faber.
Aldiss, B. W. (1979) 'A spot of Konfrontation', in *New Arrivals, Old Encounters* [original 1973]. London: Jonathan Cape, pp. 73–90.
Beauchamp, G. L. (1974) 'Future words: language and the dystopian novel', *Style* 8 (3): 462–76.
Bernaerts, L. (2017) 'The blind tour: spatial abstraction in experimental fiction', in J. Douthwaite, D. F. Virdis and E. Zurru (eds) *The Stylistics of Landscapes, the Landscapes of Stylistics*. New York: John Benjamins, pp. 61–79.
Burgess, A. (1962) *A Clockwork Orange*. London: Penguin Books.
Campbell, L. (1999) *Historical Linguistics: An Introduction*. Cambridge: The MIT Press.
Cheyne, R. (2008) 'Created languages in science fiction', *Science Fiction Studies* 35 (5): 386–403.
Data.Yze Readability Analyzer [Computer software] (1998): <https://datayze.com/readability-analyzer>
Disch, T. M. (2005) *On SF*. Ann Arbor: University of Michigan Press.
Frye, N. (1990) *Anatomy of Criticism*. Princeton: Princeton University Press.
Glicksberg, C. I. (1974) 'Experimental fiction: innovation versus form', *The Centennial Review* 18 (2): 127–50.
Hoban, R. (1980) *Riddley Walker*. New York: Summit Books.
Jackson, H. (2011) 'Invented vocabularies: the cases of Newspeak and Nadsat', in M. Adams (ed.) *From Elvish to Klingon: Exploring Invented Languages*. Oxford: Oxford University Press, pp. 49–73.
Ketterer, D. (1974) *New Worlds for Old: The Apocalyptic Imagination, Science and American Literature*. Bloomington: Indiana University Press.
Kincaid, J. P., Braby, R. and Wulfeck, W. H. (1983) 'Computer aids for editing tests', *Educational Technology* 23: 29–33.
Large, A. (1985) *The Artificial Language Movement*. New York: Blackwell.
Mandala, S. (2010) *Language in Science Fiction and Fantasy: The Question of Style*. London: Continuum.
Meyers, W. E. (1976) 'The future history and development of the English language', *Science Fiction Studies* 3 (2): 130–42.
Meyers, W. E. (1980) *Aliens and Linguists: Language Study and Science Fiction*. Athens: University of Georgia Press.
Myers, V. (1983) 'Conversational technique in Ursula LeGuin: a speech-act analysis', *Science Fiction Studies* 10: 306–16.
Noletto, I. A. C. (2022) *Language Extrapolation. Glossopoesis in Science Fiction* (unpublished doctoral thesis). Federal University of Piauí, Teresina.
Noletto, I. A. C. and Lopes, S. A. T. (2019) 'Language and ideology: glossopoesis as a secondary narrative framework in Le Guin's *The Dispossessed*', *Acta Scientiarum. Language and Culture* 41 (2): 1–7.
Ruppert, A. (1986) *Reader in a Strange Land: The Activity of Reading Literary Utopias*. Athens: University of Georgia Press.

Scott, J. (2018) 'The experimental short story', in P. Delaney and A. Hunter (eds) *The Edinburgh Companion to the Short Story in English*. Edinburgh: Edinburgh University Press, pp. 193–210.

Sisk, D. W. (1997) *Transformations of Language in Modern Dystopias*. Westport: Greenwood Press.

Stockwell, P. (2000) *The Poetics of Science Fiction*. London: Routledge.

Stockwell, P. (2006) 'Invented language in literature', in K. Brown (ed.) *Encyclopedia of Language and Linguistics* (2nd edn). Oxford: Elsevier, pp. 3–10.

Tykhomyrova, O. (2018) 'Metafiction in contemporary English-language prose: narrative and stylistic aspects', *Lege Artis: The Journal of University of SS Cyril and Methodius in Trnava* III (1): 363–416.

Wardhaugh, R. (2006) *An Introduction to Sociolinguistics*. Malden: Blackwell.

Womack, J. (987) *Ambient*. London: Grafton.

CHAPTER 11

Women, fire, and dystopian things

Jessica Norledge

This chapter explores the language of Láadan, a functional artlang created by Suzette Haden Elgin for her *Native Tongue* trilogy. Designed as a perception-based women's language, Láadan embodies early feminist thinking, reflecting the ideology and principles of the second feminist wave. Taking a mixed-methods approach, Norledge examines the peculiarities of Láadan considering its role and function as a dystopian conlang, before moving on to examine the impact of Láadan on our existing 'idealised cognitive model' of LANGUAGE. Norledge follows the work of George Lakoff, as set out in his seminal text, *Women, Fire, and Dangerous Things* (1987) on which she has based the title of this work. As part of her analysis, she considers the challenges and difficulties of presenting a women's language, addressing the stylistic successes and failures of Láadan both within and beyond the boundaries of Elgin's fiction.

Reading dystopian languages

Language in dystopia is a dangerous thing. It is the key to rebellion and the tool of the dystopian maverick. It is unsurprising, therefore, that there is a salient pattern across the genre whereby a character's use of language is manipulated, restricted, or in some way suppressed, held up by a totalitarian regime or inexplicable authority as a marker of absolute societal or individual control. Linguistic creativity is often proscribed, communication is characteristically monitored, and branches of linguistic expression such as reading or writing may be prohibited or even criminalised (Norledge 2023). So commonplace are these particular tropes that critics have gone as far as to argue that language, as a concept, is 'so crucial to the dystopia that we are justified in labelling it a generic structural element', without which a fiction cannot be considered dystopian at all (Sisk 1997: 174). Though this may seem a grand claim – especially given the wealth of dystopian texts in which language plays only a minor role – language, either in its use or its loss, is frequently identifiable as the primary dystopian *novum*. The novum, a term taken from the work of Suvin (1979), identifies the specific defamiliarising feature of a given fiction that prompts cognitive estrangement and the recognition of an imagined world as a refraction of our own (Norledge 2022).

Consider, for example, the regulation of women's language in Christina Dalcher's (2018) *Vox*, which sees female characters penalised physically for speaking above their allocated one hundred words a day. 'Precise' language is enforced in Lois Lowry's (1993) *The Giver*, which presents a world in which characters cannot exaggerate or lie. The use of particular letters is restricted in Mark Dunn's (2001) progressively lipogrammatic dystopian fable *Ella Minnow Pea*, with the graphology of the epistolary reflecting the omission of letters and the depletion of language within the fiction. The creation and enforcement of Newspeak lies at the heart of George Orwell's (1949) *Nineteen Eighty-Four*, with the language itself being a cornerstone of Big Brother's totalitarian regime. Alex's use of Nadsat, a russified generational argot, distracts from his character's violence in *A Clockwork Orange* (Burgess 1962), whilst euphemism and nonsensical dogma conceal the indoctrination of the World State in *Brave New World* (Huxley 1932).

In each of these texts, language *is* power, being in some way foundational to the dystopian impulse, and the projection of ostensibly *utopian* aspirations. It is the desire to uphold the utopian dream – to solidify or impose the illusion of a peaceful and mechanically perfect society – that drives the creation of the genre's most complete *artlangs*, the aforementioned Newspeak and the perception-based language of Suzette Haden Elgin's *Native Tongue* trilogy, Láadan. Both languages are central to the depiction of dystopian society, with the design of each helping to signal or satirise the principal logic on which their respective narratives stand. Though Láadan will take the analytical focus of this chapter, it is useful first to contextualise the language in relation to Newspeak, given the resounding influence upon each of the 'Sapir-Whorf hypothesis' (Sapir 1949, Whorf 1957).

Originally proposed across the works of Edward Sapir and Benjamin Lee Whorf, the Sapir-Whorf hypothesis – or the hypothesis of linguistic relativity – presents the observation that language and experience are indissolubly linked, with an individual's perceptions or worldview being influenced by the language they have available to them. Over time, the hypothesis has been divided into two distinct versions, having both a 'strong' version, typically aligned with 'linguistic determinism', and a 'weak' version. Linguistic determinism posits a binding and causative relationship between language and experience in which language effectively determines and consequently limits one's understanding of, and engagement with, reality. The weaker version of linguistic relativism, though holding to a shared premise that language shapes and guides experience, reflects more specifically the ways in which different languages, in offering discrete vocabularies, aspects, and grammars, impact upon the categorisation, organisation, and verbalisation of lived experience.

It is the extreme view of linguistic relativism – that which hinges on the determinist perspective that language motivates or restricts cognition – that fuels *dystopian* relativism, with the connection between language and thought being exaggerated and then realised through the suppression or control of language use, and the creation of dystopian languages. As argued by Barnes (1975: 150–1), 'all dystopian languages technically belong to Whorf', given their characteristic association with the manipulation of consciousness and social observation. After all, '[t]he Whorf hypothesis has a corollary: if it is true that our language determines our perception of reality, then whoever controls language controls the perception of reality as well' (Meyers 1980: 163), a consequence that dystopian power structures often seek to exploit and eventually instil.

Designed to diminish the range of thought experienced by citizens of Oceania – one of the three world states in Orwell's *Nineteen Eighty-Four* – the language of Newspeak, for example, aims to project the 'world-view and mental habits proper to the devotees of Ingsoc', and Big Brother's infamous Party, 'Ingsoc' being a shortening in Newspeak of English Socialism (Orwell 1949: 343–4). Through Newspeak, the connection between language and reality is magnified and corrupted, enabling members of the Party to internalise the often-paradoxical doctrine of the One State. Take, for instance, the Newspeak word 'doublethink', which defines 'the power of holding two contradictory beliefs in one's mind simultaneously, and accepting both of them' (Orwell 1949: 244). Here, we see directly the impact of Newspeak on the citizens of Oceania, with the language offering a purpose-built term through which experience can be rationalised, and the 'Oldspeak' meaning of 'reality control' can be ameliorated. Newspeak effectively softens the process it embodies, redefining conscious experience and limiting patterns of free thought through the manipulation of linguistic expression.

In order to influence the thoughts of Oceanian citizens, Newspeak seeks to impose a minimal tripartite vocabulary which, divided into distinct classes, is representative of the business of everyday life (the A vocabulary), political discourse (the B vocabulary), and scientific or technical terminology (the C vocabulary). The lexicon in this way is designed 'to give exact and often very subtle expression to every meaning that a Party member could properly wish to express, while excluding all other meanings' (Orwell 1949: 344). The combination of neologistic innovation with the removal of 'undesirable words' and 'unorthodox meaning' from the lexicon, presents a language that by its very design 'make[s] all other modes of thought impossible' (Orwell 1949: 343). (For a more complete discussion of the design of Newspeak see Chilton 2006, López-Rúa 2019, Stockwell 2000, and Norledge 2022).

Despite the detail of Newspeak's linguistic blueprint and the nuance of its projected ideology, the language is, however, primarily paratextual, being mapped out in the novel's extensive appendices in the guise of the eleventh edition of the Newspeak dictionary. At the time of Winston's narrative, the tenth edition is being revised, with the aim of removing Oldspeak completely by the year 2050. Newspeak is said to appear in the language of the *Times* newspaper and the work of specialists, whilst being used by Party members only sparingly. The narrative of the novel proper is presented in Standard English with Newspeak words appearing only occasionally within the body of the text. The language acts primarily, therefore, on a compositional level, serving as a strategic world-building device, used to colour readerly conceptualisations of the fictional world and enrich the plot, if not always the represented dialogue of Orwell's characters.

In a similar way to Newspeak, the language of Láadan appears only occasionally across the three novels which make up Elgin's trilogy: *Native Tongue*, *The Judas Rose*, and *Earthsong*, published between 1984 and 1994. Described as 'a language constructed by a woman, for women, for the specific purpose of expressing the perceptions of women' (Elgin 2019d: n.p.), Láadan is conceived by the linguists of Chornyak Barren House, an underground retirement home for the women of the Lines. 'The Lines' is the name given to the collective households of the thirteen Linguist families, a network who within the fictional world hold political monopoly over intergalactic relations and interplanetary trade. The Linguists' power is determined by this monopoly, which in itself results from their unparalleled ability to learn and communicate in alien languages.

The novels' focus on interplanetary affairs, references to space travel, and the colonisation of worlds beyond the Earth, alongside their futuristic world-building elements, place the *Native Tongue* trilogy at the boundary line of dystopia and classic science fiction. It is in the oppression of the novels' female characters that the dystopic presents itself, with the novels taking on issues surrounding gender politics and relating the struggle for women's rights following the repeal of the nineteenth Amendment to the American constitution. In order for the nineteenth Amendment to be reinstated and the role of women to revert back to that of the fictional past – a time seemingly aligned with that of the modern reader's real-world present – the women of the Lines believe that a specialised language must be created that better reflects the experiences of women. The creation of such a language, which in the course of the series is realised as Láadan, underpins *Native Tongue*'s narrative arc, with the eventual teaching and dissemination of Láadan taking the focus of the second book in the series, *The Judas Rose*.

For the men of the Lines, Láadan (or its believed alias, Langlish), is 'as dangerous as any plague [...] it represents danger, and represents corruption' (Elgin 2019a: 309). For this reason, Láadan is kept secret throughout the course of the first book and for much of the second. It is because of this secrecy, and the thematic focus of *Native Tongue* on the process of language creation, that Láadan, like Newspeak, develops paratextually. In fact, the first edition of *Native Tongue* contains only two examples of Láadan, with the original copy even foregoing the eventual Láadan glossary that would appear in later editions of the text. Over time, the language was developed both by Elgin and by followers of the conlang, being presented in full –

alongside teaching materials, paradigms, and set texts – in the separately published Láadan dictionary (Elgin 2019d), now in its third iteration. Given the limited use of Elgin's artlang across the *Native Tongue* trilogy, the Láadan dictionary will be also drawn upon throughout the remainder of this chapter, as I move on to look specifically at the construction of Láadan in the next two sections. I then return to the representation of a women's language, exploring the modelling of a seemingly gendered and perceptual language variety in line with Lakoff's (1987) work on 'idealised cognitive models', proposed most fully in his seminal text, *Women, Fire, and Dangerous Things*.

The conceptualisation of Láadan

During the 1970s, feminist linguistics began exploring the view that language plays a significant part in upholding patriarchal social structures, in that language use which 'excludes and marginalizes women translates into patriarchal societies that do the same. Consequently, feminist linguists argued the need either to transform the English language so that it was no longer androcentric, or to invent new languages that would allow women to be free and equal' (Bruce 2008: 44–5). To this end, several feminist dictionaries were published throughout the late 1970s and early 1980s in which the experiences of women were emphasised or highlighted through particular lexical entries. Take, for instance, *A Feminist Dictionary*, a purpose-built 'word-book', which, presenting an alternative to the practice of 'male dictionary-making', aimed to

> document words, definitions, and conceptualizations that illustrate women's linguistic contributions; to illuminate forms of expression through which women have sought to describe, reflect upon, and theorize about women, language, and the world; to identify issues of language theory, research usage, and institutionalized practice that bear on the relationship between women and language; to broaden knowledge of the feminist lexicon; and to stimulate research on women and language.
>
> (Kramarae and Treichler 1985: 1)

Kramarae and Treichler drew influence for their work from such texts as the *Woman's New World Dictionary*, presented originally as part of a feminist journal edited by Midge Lennert and Norma Wilson (1973), and Monique Wittig's and Sande Zeig's (1979) *Lesbian Peoples: Material for a Dictionary* which sought to correct the 'lacunary', the empty spaces of history in which the contributions and experiences of women are obscured or overlooked.

Within the bounds of science fiction, works such as Mary Daly's (1987) *Webster's First Intergalactic Wickedary of the English Language* added further nuance to such explorations, with Daly's text seeking to 'expose what she [considered] the masculinist dystopia we live in and to create a vision of a feminist utopia' in its place (Anderson 1992: 2). The history of the Wickedary claims to free 'words from the cages and prisons of patriarchal patterns', declaring through its creation that 'words and women have served the fathers' sentences long enough' (Daly 1987: 3). Elgin's creation of Láadan rests on a similar albeit realist perspective, with *Native Tongue* drawing 'fundamentalist views on women to their "logical" conclusion', highlighting through the principles and ideology of the language 'that until women find the words and syntax for what they need to say, they will never say it, nor will the world hear it' (Heilbrun 1987: n.p.).

In discussing the motivations for creating Láadan, the women of the Lines present a similar view, stating that 'no more powerful instrument for change exists than language' (Elgin 2019b: 393). The argument presented here directly reflects the external motivations of Elgin herself, who is known to have written the *Native Tongue* trilogy as a kind of thought experiment, as a means to test her theories surrounding women's language and the Whorfian relationship between language and perception. As a guide for her experiment, Elgin hypothesised the following:

1. that the weak form of the linguistic relativity hypothesis is true [that human languages structure human perceptions in significant ways];
2. that Gödel's Theorem applies to language, so that there are changes you could not introduce into a language without destroying it and languages you could not introduce into a culture without destroying it;
3. that change in language brings about social change, rather than the contrary; and
4. that if women were offered a woman's language one of two things would happen – they would welcome and nurture it, or it would at minimum motivate them to replace it with a better women's language of their own construction.

(Elgin 2000: n.p.)

The first proposition is directly realised throughout the course of *Native Tongue* and *The Judas Rose*, with the prologue of *Native Tongue* projecting a future world in which women are once again free. Presented metafictionally, as a joint publication by the 'The Historical Society of Earth', 'WOMANTALK, Earth Section', 'The Metaguild of Lay Linguists, Earth Section', and 'The Láadan Group', *Native Tongue* is described as 'the only work of fiction ever written by a member of the Lines' (Elgin 2019a: 4). The novel within the fictional world is signed by the women of Chornyak Barren House and, as seen throughout the narrative proper, details the origins of Láadan (see Cheyne 2008, Sisk 1997 for analysis). Given the reference to 'The Láadan

Group' it can be assumed that in the present of the preface, Láadan has already been properly established and is recognised as a successful language variety. As women are also able to publish and be published, there is an implication here that since the writing of the fictional novel, society *has* changed. The 'constitution of reality through language' is consequently more than 'a psychological effect in *Native Tongue*' (Squier and Vedder 2000: 344), with language having altered the socio-political order of the fictional world, as hypothesised in proposition 3 in the quotation above.

Through the design of Láadan, Elgin also fulfils the second proposition, extrapolating on the self-destruction of American culture in a world in which women's perceptions are embraced by the dominant language variety. The fourth and final proposition highlights the potential consequences of the second, reflecting upon the after-effects of substantial language and social change. These remaining hypotheses will be returned to at the close of this chapter as I draw together my discussion of Láadan in both the fictional world of Elgin's trilogy and in the actual world beyond its textual borders. For now, I would like to turn to the peculiarities of Láadan and the ways in which the construction of the language reflects the ideology underpinning its design, as set out in Elgin's propositions 1 through 3.

Defining a women's language

Translated into English, Láadan means 'perception language'. The name reflects the mirrored motivations of the variety's fictional and actual-world creators in that it offers the words to describe experiences that have never been verbalised before, experiences that are particular to women, and intrinsic to a distinct female reality. The foundational premise of Láadan lies in the understanding that 'women's perceptions find inadequate expression in male languages, if they can be communicated at all' (Sisk 1997: 119) and that it is only through the creation of a purpose-built women's language that female experience can be validated in any social world, fictional or otherwise. The classification of what actually constitutes a 'female reality', or indeed 'female experience' is, however, problematic, and before moving on to unpick the language of Láadan it is important to pause here and acknowledge the difficulties of identifying women (in the real world and in the boundaries of fiction) as comprising a homogenous group.

During its second wave, feminist thought was characterised by the belief that men and women viewed the world differently, and that language, by this logic, could not express both the perceptions of men and women (Bruce 2008). It is the apparent essentialism of the second wave – the belief in opposing and irrefutable biological difference – that informed the creation of Láadan, with Elgin's work and her own political stance being reflective of the particular feminism of the 1960s and 1970s. The notion of what constitutes 'womanhood' and 'female experience' within the fictional world of the

Native Tongue trilogy is consequently entwined with the novels' socio-historical context, being tied to the gender binary, and the stereotypical experiences of cis-hetero individuals at the time of publication. That being said, the novel (and the language of Láadan more broadly) is not exclusionary in its definition of women nor does it refute the diversity of female experience. Instead, it is primarily reflective of a particular kind of female experience – that which is embodied by the Chornynak women and inscribed by the ideology and experience of Elgin and her contemporaries. For the purposes of my analysis, I consequently situate and define Láadan as a gendered language, which aims to lexicalise and highlight some of the felt differences in perception and experience that are believed to be unique to the majority of women, as set against the backdrop of early feminist thought.

Looking to the linguistic formation of Láadan, then, what we see first is a language in which the feminine is normative and consequently unmarked. Unlike in English where we find '-ess' used to mark the feminine form of particular lexical items (e.g. 'waitress', 'actress'), it is the masculine in Láadan that is marked in the morphology, indicated through the addition of '-id'. For example, the Láadan word for woman is *with*, and the word for man is *withid*. Items ending in '-ess' are becoming increasingly outdated in contemporary English, with the masculine form broadening in meaning to encompass all genders, as with the use of 'actor', for example. That being said, the inverted Láadan morphology remains notable for its distinct privileging of the feminine form. For Bruce (2008: 53), it is through this inversion of markedness that 'Elgin makes it clear that, if a language defines women as deviations from a masculine norm, the speakers of that language will not perceive women and men as equals'. It is for this reason that I imagine the feminine was selected over a neutral morphological form, as although the gendered nature of Láadan upholds the gender binary, it does so to destabilise and challenge directly the masculine norm in language construction.

The selection of a feminine system is one of several ways in which Láadan draws attention to the notion of a women's language, with additional aspects of its grammar and vocabulary serving to highlight early linguistic hypotheses regarding women's speech. Take, for instance, Láadan's unique set of function words that explicitly mark the language for particular speech acts. A sentence formed in Láadan begins with a 'speech act morpheme', the most common of which is *bíi*, used to mark a sentence as a declarative: 'I say to you as a statement'. There are five further speech act morphemes in addition to *bíi*, each of which take a sentence initial position as set out in Graphic 11.1. English also contains these lexical items (e.g. 'I promise you', 'I warn you'), but such elements are optional in English where in Láadan they are not.

By opening all propositions with a speech act morpheme, the reliability of Láadan speech is emphasised, with intention, purpose, and commitment being made explicit in the language. In a sentence such as *Bíi ada with wa* ('The woman laughs'), for example, the perlocutionary morpheme, *bíi*,

	Láadan Speech Act Morphemes
bíi	I say to you as a statement
bó	I say to you as a command
báa'	I say to you as a question
bé'	I say to you as a promise
bée	I say to you as a warning
bóo	I say to you as a request

Graphic 11.1 Láadan speech act morphemes

marks the utterance as a statement, rendering the full translation as 'I say to you as a statement – the woman laughs – as perceived by me, the speaker.' All utterances in Láadan appear to have illocution and perlocution, meaning there can be no 'failed' perlocutions (i.e. misunderstandings) as we often encounter in English and other real-world languages.

The concepts of intentionality and truth are, in fact, prioritised in Láadan, with the language also containing a series of 'evidentials', which are not found in English. The evidential is placed at the end of the sentence to indicate the speaker's positioning in relation to a particular statement or claim, indicating whether a statement is made in truth. The closing use of *wa* in the previous example, *Bíi ada with wa* ('The woman laughs'), holds such a function. Láadan comprises eight evidence morphemes as set out in Graphic 11.2.

As a final step in its pursuit of linguistic transparency, Láadan sentences can then also be marked for feeling, detailing the emotions of the speaker and the attitude with which they present certain information. Returning to the speech act marker *bíi*, for example, the morpheme can take a variety of modified forms: a Láadan speaker stating information in anger would begin their sentence with *bíid*, as compared to when speaking in pain (*bíith*), with love (*bíili*), in celebration (*bíilan*), in jest (*bíida*), as a teacher (*bíidi*), or in fear (*bíiya*). In specifying the speaker's attitude, conversational approach, intention, and commitment, opportunities for pragmatic miscommunication or deceit are significantly decreased. Emphasis is placed instead on authenticity, honesty, and emotional openness. Such qualities serve to counter characteristic impressions of female speakers as non-assertive or tentative, as suggested in early accounts of women's language (such as Lakoff 1973) whilst highlighting those attributes (honesty, emotional intelligence, integrity) that were typically assigned to women during the second wave.

Láadan Evidentials

waálh	indicating a proposition is assumed false by the speaker because the source is not trusted, assumed false and considered evil
waá	indicating a proposition is assumed false because the speaker distrusts the source
wi	used when a proposition is considered self-evident
wóo	where the speaker has no knowledge as to a proposition's validity
wa	where a proposition has been perceived directly by the speaker
wo	used to indicate information has been imagined or invented by the speaker
wáa	to signal a proposition is assumed true because the speaker trusts the source
we	where the content of the discourse has been perceived by the speaker in a dream

Graphic 11.2 Láadan evidentials

In addition to determining tone, stance, and locutionary force, Láadan also seeks to more clearly categorise and lexicalise female experience, as seen through its extended, purpose-built vocabulary. Consider, for instance, the precision with which the language distinguishes particular action processes, as exemplified by the variant forms of the verb *osháana*, 'to menstruate'. In English there is but one verb form to describe menstruation, with additional detail being added through forms of pre- or post-modification, if at all. Láadan by comparison has six additional verb forms, each of which recognises a particular aspect of menstrual experience. An individual's first cycle, for example, would be described using the verb *elasháana* ('to menstruate for the first time'). One might menstruate early (*desháana*) or late (*wesháana*), or experience pain (*husháana*) or in some instances joy (*ásháana*). As Láadan is a language of connection that glorifies shared experience, it even presents a term to describe menstruation that falls in sync with another (*zhesháana*). Similar distinctions are also offered for additional biological processes associated with the female reproductive system such as pregnancy and menopause, adding linguistic nuance to experiences that are typically under-lexicalised or even taboo (Bray 1986).

In this way Láadan accepts the challenge set by Elgin to recognise and naturalise the lived experiences of women, both in the fictional world of her novels and in the actual world of her readers. The language is consequently empathetic (as evidenced by the examples set out above), and occasionally politically pointed. After all, it is Láadan's rich neologistic innovation that gives the language its biting, almost satirical, texture. Consider, for example, words such as *radíídin*, defined in the Láadan dictionary as a 'non-holiday', a holiday (in the American sense) that is 'more work than it's worth, a time allegedly a holiday but actually so much a burden because of work and preparations that it is a dreaded occasion; especially when there are too many guests and none of them help' (Elgin 2019d: 183). The underlying meaning here concerns the expectations of stereotypical female domesticity and the characteristic pressures placed on a presumably female host. Though the experience described is one which we can certainly imagine, it is an experience that has no single name in English. Such words are foundational to Láadan, with each new term offering 'a word for a perception that had never had a word of its own before' (Elgin 2019a: 175). These words are described in the fiction as 'Encodings', and they reflect those perceptions or experiences that 'yearn for being lexicalized and thus brought into being' (Koparan 2020: 5). The practice of Encoding is specific to the construction of the Láadan language and illustrates an atypical form of language creation. The practice itself destabilises the real-world practice of lexical encoding, suggesting instead a more direct and empathetic connection between language and experience.

Doing strange things with language

Encoding, here presented with a capital 'E', is an unusual process, one which is unique to Láadan and uncharacteristic of language creation in the actual world. As set out in the Chornyak Barren House, *Manual for Beginners*:

> The linguistic term lexical encoding *refers to the way that human beings choose a particular chunk of their world, external or internal, and assign that chunk a surface shape that will be its name; it refers to the process of world-making. When we women say 'Encoding,' with a capital 'E,' we mean something a little bit different. We mean the making of a name for a chunk of the world that so far as we know has never been chosen for naming before in any human language, and that has not just suddenly been made or found or dumped upon your culture. We mean naming a chunk that has been around a long time but has never before impressed anyone as sufficiently important to deserve its own name.*
>
> *You can do ordinary lexical encoding systematically – for example, you could look at the words of an existing language and decide that you wanted counterparts for them in one of your native languages. Then it's*

> *just a matter of arranging sounds that are permitted and meaningful in that language to make the counterparts. But there is no way at all to search systematically for capital-E Encodings. They come to you out of nowhere and you realize that you have always needed them; but you can't go looking for them, and they don't turn up as concrete entities neatly marked off for you and flashing NAME ME. They are therefore very precious.*
>
> (Chornyak Barren House, *Manual for Beginners*, page 71)
> (Elgin 2019a: 22; italic in the original)

Capital 'E' Encodings are categorised as words which seemingly 'emerge from an intuitive "nowhere"' (Mahoney 1995: 125); they are active and decidedly rare. It is noted that there is no systematic way to uncover these terms; they cannot be found or created with any form of purposeful intent. Capital 'E' Encodings are only ever perceived, as indicated by the mental process 'they come to you' but cannot be sought by the senser, evidenced by the deictic relationship carried by 'come'. The relationship between the Encodings and the speaker is one of necessity, evidenced by the embedded use of 'need' in 'always needed them' and framed by the cognitive realisation of the universal female enactor, embodied by the generic 'you'. Representing terms that are in some way desired, capital 'E' Encodings have a high inherent value, recognised by Elgin's formulation 'very precious'.

The heightened emotional process of Encoding recognises the extent of the women's belief that language can and will change reality with the women who create the Encodings being described as figures of renown: '"a woman who gives an Encoding to other women is a woman of valour, and all women are in her debt forevermore"' (Elgin 2019a: 175). As argued by Cavalcanti (2000: 163) the Encodings are consequently 'metonymic for the Láadan Project' and as such 'render a fictionalized version of this phenomenon and foreground the human factor behind linguistic change'. In placing attention on the 'human factor' of language creation, Elgin effectively repositions our understanding of language as a force, consequently reimagining pre-established idealised cognitive models (ICM) of language itself.

The term 'idealised cognitive model' is here taken from the work of Lakoff (1987), used to define those complex conceptual structures with which we organise our knowledge of the world. For example, if we consider the overall ICM to which the concept LANGUAGE relates, it likely contains information pertaining to the human, both the human body (that is, the physical capability to generate language, either verbally or gesturally), and the specifically human need to communicate with others; the presence of a society in which communication is frequent and/or required; the understanding of language as a purpose-built conceptual system through which communication can be achieved; and crucially an understanding of a language system, in terms of grammar, vocabulary, and semantics.

Branching out from this definition, we can also perceive of LANGUAGE as part of a 'cluster model' in which we find various converging ICMs. Consider for example the connections between 'spoken' and 'written' models of language, or the specification of more nuanced subcategories of LANGUAGE such as a 'digital model' (in which we have an understanding of language as 'code') or a 'non-human model' (in which the principle of 'humanness' is expanded to recognise such phenomena as animal communication). As explored throughout this edited collection, we can also recognise a 'fictional model' in which the base principles of the LANGUAGE ICM may or may not apply, given the potential differences amongst imagined species and fictional cultures.

Though Láadan meets the conditions of the foundational LANGUAGE ICM, it does present an unusual realisation of the above principles, challenging our understanding of language as a system and as a tool. Aligned with the expectations of the 'fictional model', Láadan invites a reimagining of the typical conceptual structure of LANGUAGE in order to present a communication system that is at times spontaneous, automatic, and, in some way, unconscious. On discussing the use of Láadan by the children of the Lines, Susannah Chornyak (one of the retired women of Barren House) recounts, for instance, the following interaction in which the non-standard acquisition of Láadan is exemplified:

'I thought I'd introduce a new word yesterday, for that new way of dancing that we saw on the threedies. You remember, Grace? The one that looks as if the youngsters are all trying to dislocate their shoulders?'

[...] 'Well I thought I had a decent proposal for a word, and I suggested it. And one of the littlebits *corrected* me, I'll have you know!'

'Corrected you? How could that be – did you make an error in the morphology? At your age?'

'Of course not, it was a perfectly good Láadan word, formed in accordance with every rule. But she did. She said, "Aunt Susannah, it could not be that way. I'm very sorry, but it would have to be this way."'

'And she was right?'

'Goodness, how would I know that? I don't have native intuitions about Láadan, you know!'

'Nor do the children.'

'Ah, but they seem to think they do. Already.'

'It's not possible.'

'No ... but she said, "This way, my mouth knows that its right."'

(Elgin 2019a: 294)

Here we see 'a prioritising of the instinctive and intuitive – the "native" – over the "perfectly good" and linguistically "correct"' (Mahoney 1995: 125).

The workings of the child Láadan speaker are prioritised over that of an original Láadan creator, the former presenting an inexplicable command of the Encoding process. The exclamations of the child projects clear epistemic commitment, exemplified by the metonymic construction, 'my mouth knows that its right'. It is suggested that such commitment is indicative of 'native intuition', as supported by the modelling of the child character, who, like her peers, 'seems to think' she possesses innate knowledge of yet to be lexicalised Láadan. In comparison, Susannah's working, which is based in systematic linguistic fact and representative of 'perfectly good Láadan', is negated and corrected. In this way the knowledge of the trained Linguist (who possesses a detailed understanding of Láadan as a language system) is brought into question, whilst the language of the child (as with the capital-E Encodings more broadly) is positioned in line with an undefinable and emotional form of felt perception.

The underpinning conceptual structure of the Láadan language is also foregrounded in the metaphoric mappings drawn across the *Native Tongue* trilogy. 'Metaphoric ICMs' (Lakoff 1987, Lakoff and Johnson 1980) reflect the structuring of an ICM through processes of 'source' to 'target' conceptual mappings, where a target domain (here the concept recognised by the ICM, i.e. 'language') is metaphorically structured in terms of another typically rich source. When considering the existing conceptual mappings which ground our understanding of language as an abstract concept we have, for instance, Metaphoric ICMs in which language is structured in terms of force, as in such uses of 'strong language' (here the force of an animate entity) or 'loaded language' (here the force of a weapon). We find this mapping in visible metaphor (where the domains are represented directly by lexical items), as in the adage 'language is power', and also through invisible metaphor. Consider, for example, such phrasing as 'they made me do it' or 'they convinced me' in which we have the conceptual metaphor LANGUAGE IS FORCE. The domains are not indicated by linguistic tokens and the metaphoric domains must be inferred by the reader. To unwrap this example, language as used here is metonymic – it is the speaker's words (as a part of themselves) which does the 'making' and the 'convincing'. Language, once realised, then becomes the target of the mapping, LANGUAGE IS FORCE. (See Stockwell 1992 and 2000 for explication of visible and invisible metaphor.) We also see an extension of this conceptualisation in constructions such as 'a war of words' or 'verbal sparring' in which the conceptualisation of language as powerful or forceful is realised through the metaphoric mapping ARGUMENT IS WAR.

Within the fictional world of *Native Tongue* and *The Judas Rose*, established patterns are backgrounded against an expressive series of Metaphoric ICMs that highlight a nuanced emotional connection between language and the speaker/hearer. Consider, for example, the positioning of Láadan as akin to a friend or a lover, as epitomised in such examples as: 'you couldn't have gotten them to betray Láadan'; 'it is a language worth caring about, and the readings are carefully chosen to seduce the ear'; or, it 'would cause the nurses to begin loving it and wondering what it was they loved'. Such mappings personify the language, positioning Láadan as the recipient of various mental reaction processes ('betray', 'care', 'love') and the actor of typically human behavioural processes ('seduce'). In these particular examples, the power of language as persuasive rhetoric is heightened, being realised through the metaphoric ICM, LANGUAGE IS HUMAN.

Language is also structured in relation to magic (as in, it 'would lull them the way an incantation lulls'), and as medicine ('she knew how much better she felt, listening to the language, how soothed she was afterward, how it made the tension inside her melt away'; 'it would continue to keep the women of the Lines, and all the women who knew it beyond, immune to the state of violence that the men struggled with so incessantly'). Láadan is here described as evocative (evidenced by the mental perception process, 'lull'), healing (as indicated through mappings of health and immunisation), and bonding, evidenced by the consistent reference to 'all women' as a unified collective. Such mappings recognise how '[a]long with its constitutive and manipulative powers, language also has the power to produce emotional comfort through consensual validation' (Squier and Vedder 2000: 345). It brings its speakers together as much as it frees them from the restrictions of patriarchal society.

Returning to the original discussion of 'language' with which I opened this section, the conceptualisation of Láadan, as developed across *Native Tongue* and *The Judas Rose* in particular, presents readers with a revised cognitive profile of 'language' itself, in which language is considered agentive and self-materialising. Though highly structured and designed in line with established and systematic linguistic patterns, Láadan is also intuitive and emotionally connected to its native speakers, marked as a complementary (albeit hidden) aspect of their biological, spiritual, and cognitive make-up. Such a proposition challenges or at least repairs the established ICM of LANGUAGE proper, adding an additional proposition in which language is understood to be animate and existentially affective. These new additions to the ICM would in effect confirm Elgin's earlier hypotheses that language has the power to affect social change, and that the Sapir-Whorf hypothesis holds true – at least within the boundaries of her fiction.

What language reveals about dystopia

Throughout *Native Tongue* and *The Judas Rose* the representation of Láadan consequently challenges our overarching ICM for language itself, at the foundational level. Within the fiction, it is suggested that there are specific qualities that would define a 'women's language', qualities that go beyond the formal structures and expectations of language acquisition and use, such as the ability to 'soothe' or 'calm' the speaker, 'seduce' the listener, and formulate intuitively, perceptions for which no words have previously existed. Such qualities are presented as peculiar to women, proposing another strand to the LANGUAGE cluster model – a women's model. These findings align with the ideologies of second wave feminism, realising the belief that women and men think differently and establishing a world in which the language of women leads to a more peaceful and accepting society.

These facets are, however, unique to Láadan and, more specifically, to the fictional variant of Láadan. The use of Láadan in the actual world had no such effects, being relatively ignored by Elgin's contemporaries. Unlike other fictional languages such as Klingon, the language was not widely picked up and though Láadan is now fully developed, it has received only limited critical and public attention. Despite Elgin's hypotheses for her women's language, it was consequently unsuccessful in her lifetime, with her fourth hypothesis – that women would take up the language or conversely create their own – being notably unfulfilled. The 'failure' of Láadan is reflected in the breakdown of the language in her final novel, *Earthsong*, in which it is revealed that outside of the Lines, women "'didn't give a *fig* for it'" (Elgin 2019c: 62). Beyond the fiction, our standard ICM of LANGUAGE remains, then, unchanged. What we have instead, is a variant of language under the 'fictional model', with Láadan presenting a thoughtful and experimental language variety that pushes the boundaries of the conlang experience, and the characteristic presentation of language in dystopia.

Taken together, Láadan and the language of Newspeak (with which I introduced this chapter) are compositionally iconic of the dystopian dialectic. Newspeak, with its colourless and restrictive design, reflects the distinguishing oppression of dystopian society. Láadan, by contrast, realises the resistance of the dystopian maverick, standing as 'an instrument of change, not of preservation' (Anderson 1991: 98). Though the notion of a women's language is inherently flawed, Láadan's unique encodings 'reveal significant lacunae in our own languages, which should encourage us to find ways of voicing the perceptions of marginalised and silenced groups' (Bruce 2008: 67), recognising the potential for language to influence social perception and ideology as a positive rather than oppressive force. Láadan, unlike Newspeak, is a language of hope and though as a force for change it proved unsuccessful (both within the final throes of the fiction and within the actual world), it reflects a pivotal ideal in the development of feminist thought and a defining narrative moment in the evolution of the feminist dystopia.

References

Anderson, K. J. (1991) 'To utopia via the Sapir-Whorf hypothesis: Elgin's Láadan', *Utopian Studies* 3: 92–8.

Anderson, K. J. (1992) 'Places where a woman could talk: Ursula K. Le Guin and the feminist utopia', *Women and Language* 15: 1–7.

Barnes, M. E. (1975) *Linguistics and Language in Science-Fiction Fantasy*. New York: Arno Press.
Bray, M. K. (1986) 'The naming of things: men and women, language and reality in Suzette Haden Elgin's *Native Tongue*', *Extrapolation* 27 (2): 49–61.
Bruce, K. (2008) 'A woman-made language: Suzette Elgin's Láadan and the *Native Tongue* trilogy as thought experiment in feminist linguistics', *Extrapolation* 49 (1): 44–69.
Burgess, A. (1962) *A Clockwork Orange*. London: Heinemann.
Cavalcanti, I. (2000) 'Utopias of/f language in contemporary feminist literary dystopias', *Utopian Studies* 11 (2): 152–80.
Cheyne, R. (2008) 'Created languages in science fiction', *Science Fiction Studies* 35 (3): 386–403.
Chilton, P. (2006) 'Newspeak', in K. Brown (ed.) *Encyclopaedia of Language & Linguistics* (2nd edn). Amsterdam: Elsevier, pp. 618–19.
Dalcher, C. (2018) *Vox*. London: HarperCollins.
Daly, M. (1987) *Webster's First Intergalactic Wickedary of the English Language*. Boston: Beacon Press.
Dunn, M. (2001) *Ella Minnow Pea*. London: Methuen.
Elgin, S. H. (2000) 'Láadan, the constructed language in *Native Tongue*', Suzette Haden Elgin's website: <www.sfwa.org/members//elgin/Laadan.html>
Elgin, S. H. (2019a) *Native Tongue* (2nd edn) [original 1984]. New York: Feminist Press.
Elgin, S. H. (2019b) *The Judas Rose* (2nd edn) [original 1987]. New York: Feminist Press.
Elgin, S. H. (2019c) *Earthsong* (2nd edn) [original 1994]. New York: Feminist Press.
Elgin, S. H. (2019d) *A Third Dictionary and Grammar of Láadan* (eds J. Gomoll and D. Martin). Morrisville: Lulu Press.
Heilbrun, C. (1987) 'Cover endorsement'. Credited to *Women's Review of Books*. *Native Tongue* (1st edn). New York: Feminist Press.
Huxley, A. (1932) *Brave New World*. London: Chatto and Windus.
Koparan, C. (2020) 'Subversion and the Sapir-Whorf hypothesis in contemporary science fiction', *Journal of Science Fiction and Philosophy* 3: 1–19.
Kramarae, C. and Treichler, P. A. (1985) *A Feminist Dictionary*. Boston: Pandora.
Lakoff, G. (1987) *Women, Fire, and Dangerous Things. What Categories Reveal About the Mind*. Chicago: University of Chicago Press.
Lakoff, G. and Johnson, M. (1980) *Metaphors We Live By*. Chicago: University of Chicago Press.
Lakoff, R. (1973) 'Language and woman's place', *Language in Society* 21: 45–80.
Lennert, M. and Wilson, N. (eds) (1973) *A Woman's New World Dictionary*. Lomita: 51% Publications.
López-Rúa, P. (2019) 'VPS, goodthink, unwomen and demoxie: morphological neologisms in four dystopian novels', *Miscelánea: A Journal of English and American Studies* 59: 117–36.
Lowry, L. (1993). *The Giver*. New York: Houghton Mifflin.
Mahoney, E. (1995) 'Claiming the speakwrite: linguistic subversion in the feminist dystopia', in S. Mills (ed.) *Language and Gender*. London: Routledge, pp. 121–31.
Meyers, W. E. (1980) *Aliens and Linguists: Language Study and Science Fiction*. Athens: University of Georgia Press.
Norledge, J. (2022) *The Language of Dystopia*. London: Palgrave.
Norledge, J. (2023) '"It is a sin to write this": the prohibition of language in dystopia', *emagazine* 100: 28–31.

Orwell, G. (1949) *Nineteen Eighty-Four*. London: Penguin.
Sapir, E. (1949) *The Selected Writings of Edward Sapir* (ed. D. G. Mandelbaum). Berkeley: University of California Press.
Sisk, D. W. (1997) *Transformations of Language in Dystopia*. Westport: Greenwood Press.
Squier, S. M. and Vedder, J. (2000) 'Afterword: encoding a woman's language', in S. H. Elgin (ed.) *Native Tongue* (2nd edn, 2019). New York: Feminist Press, pp. 337–62.
Stockwell, P. (1992) 'The metaphorics of literary reading', *Liverpool Papers in Language and Discourse* 4: 52–80.
Stockwell, P. (2000) *The Poetics of Science Fiction*. Harlow: Pearson Education.
Suvin, D. (1979) *Metamorphoses of Science Fiction: On the Poetics of a Literary Genre*. New Haven: Yale University Press.
Whorf, B. L. (1957) *Language, Thought, and Reality: Selected Writings of Benjamin Lee Whorf* (ed. J. B. Carroll). Cambridge: MIT Technology Press.
Wittig, M. and Zeig, S. (1979) *Lesbian Peoples: Material for a Dictionary*. New York: Avon.

CHAPTER 12

Building the conomasticon: names and naming in fictional worlds

Rebecca Gregory

In this chapter Gregory introduces the idea of a conomasticon, a repository of created names belonging to a constructed naming system. In presenting her argument, she considers the presentation of fictional names and fictional naming within a variety of texts and fictional settings, ranging from the post-apocalyptic future of Sandra Newman's (2014) *The Country of Ice Cream Star* through to the medieval past of James Meek's (2019) *To Calais, in Ordinary Time*. Along the way, she examines how names can act as world-building elements and contribute to authenticity in the representation of fictional worlds and their languages, whether they be speculative, alien, or pseudo-historical.

The 'human' universal

Names are often referred to as a human universal, in that 'labelling people and their surrounding landscape seems to be something which is ingrained into human cultural practice' (Bramwell 2016: 264) and is not limited to any one cultural or linguistic context. Any fully realised fictional world in which a new language or dialect is created, therefore, must also contain names for people, places, and things: in other words, to accompany its lexicon – its store of vocabulary words – every conlang also needs a *conomasticon*, a constructed store of names. This chapter aims to demonstrate some of the ways in which literary fictional worlds have incorporated names and naming into their linguistic landscapes, considering not only the analysis of names in and of themselves, but also the craft of name creation – what Robinson (2011: 130) has termed 'a shift from literary onomastics [...] to literary onomaturgy'. I examine both *toponyms* (place-names) and *anthroponyms* (personal names) in their fictional settings, extending the idea of a 'human universal' to cover both human and non-human languages.

A genre-based approach is often considered a productive one in approaching fictional naming (see Cavill 2016: 356, Falck-Kjällquist 2016: 330), although the genres in which conlangs are often found, such as fantasy, dystopia, and science fiction, have notoriously fuzzy boundaries. In this chapter, therefore, I examine three settings – as opposed to genres – for fictional languages and fictional names. The chapter begins with names in post-apocalyptic, futuristic, dystopian worlds, looking at *Riddley Walker* and *The Country of Ice Cream Star*. I then turn backwards in time and examine two novels with medieval settings, *The Wake* and *To Calais, in Ordinary Time*. Finally, we take one small interstellar step to examine two settings on alien planets, in *The Book of Strange New Things* and *The Dispossessed*. This selection of novels contains a mixture of *a posteriori* and *a priori* languages, from dialects of English to entirely alien tongues. I hope that the analysis which follows will provide some useful perspectives on the role of names in creating a linguistically and culturally coherent (or intentionally incoherent) fictional society.

Post-apocalyptic future namescapes

The two books in this section, *Riddley Walker* and *Ice Cream Star*, are set in fictional worlds following disaster and upheaval. In both novels, the authors have their characters speaking languages which reflect the world around them, with their vocabulary and syntax primarily rooted in present-day English but having undergone changes reflective of societal and cultural transformation. In this way, the authors create fictional dialects rather than whole new languages, using first-person narration as a crucial worldbuilding element. In Norledge's (2022: 43) words, 'dialectal extrapolation is an effective form of dystopian language projection, signalling significant socio-cultural change without the complexities of building a wholly new language'. Given that the language of the novels is intended to reflect their respective worlds and fictional communities, we would expect that the names of people and places in the texts similarly signal societal and cultural change over the short (*Ice Cream Star*) and long (*Riddley Walker*) period since their respective apocalypses.

'These stolen children lose their name'

Ice Cream Star (Newman 2014) is set in a post-apocalyptic east-coast USA, where a pandemic has swept through the population and left behind it mainly Black and Hispanic children who themselves live short lives, succumbing to illness by the age of twenty. 'The survivors cling together in racially and linguistically distinct bands' (Bollinger 2016: 255) which have formed over a span of around eighty years. We experience most of the novel in the dialect of Ice Cream, the internal first-person narrator, but witness other dialects through the voices of characters we meet. Newman's fictional dialects are based in US English, and are 'highly stylized' (Bollinger 2016:

255), including phonetic French and Spanish alongside their English base. The protagonist and her immediate community are known as 'Sengles'.

Names are of paramount importance to identity in *Ice Cream Star*, with the names and naming systems belonging to each community we meet through Ice Cream's eyes being distinctive in their practices. When characters move between communities, they are renamed according to the expectations of new social groups. The protagonist's story begins: 'My name be Ice Cream Fifteen Star. My brother be Driver Eighteen Star, and my ghost brother Mo-Jacques Five Star, dead when I myself was only six years old. Still my heart is rain for him, my brother dead of posies little' (Newman 2014: 1). From these two sentences, we learn that Ice Cream has one living brother, and one dead. She and her brothers share a last name, so we can deduce that the community she lives in names its children with a family name, although at this stage we do not know whether the family name is hereditary, and, if so, whether it is inherited from mother or father. The names also contain a number: *Fifteen*, *Eighteen*, and *Five*. Only a small logical leap is required to deduce that these indicate the children's ages. So, our protagonist and her immediate family each have a given name (*Ice Cream*, *Driver*, *Mo-Jacques*); a second, optional name indicating their age (which changes through their life); and a family name shared between siblings. From this, Newman conveys the importance her characters place on family, and on age. In a world where people rarely live past twenty, and where children are orphaned young, raised by a combination of siblings and other members of the community, this naming pattern fits perfectly.

It is initially unclear how Sengle given names are chosen, or by whom, but later in the novel we are given some insight: 'Then I remember ice cream been a food I never taste. I wonder what my mama dream to name me for this food, as if she name me Something Lost' (Newman 2014: 13). We learn, here, that Ice Cream's mother chose her name. Newman allows the reader to piece together further information about Sengle naming, as Ice Cream recounts all the members of her community one by one, beginning: 'These be the Sengles in the time I speak of, when my trouble grown' (Newman 2014: 53). Working on the information Ice Cream provides, we can construct the names and relationships of forty-eight members of the Sengle group and observe patterns of naming.

What becomes immediately apparent is that family names are indeed hereditary and pass from mother to child. We learn, for example, that *Lolina-tina One Diouf* is the daughter of *Mari's Ghost Fourteen Diouf* and *Crow Sixteen Doe*. Where there are siblings, there are sometimes patterns of given names: *Mohammed Three* and *Mustapha Five Insulting* both bear names of Muslim origin; *Marlboro Ten*, *Kool Ten*, and *Bowl Thirteen Tete-Brisee* may derive from brand names or packaging; *Bother Zero* and *Problem Four Tool* also share a theme. Within the group, there is a mixture of more traditional given names –*Mohammed, Jermaine, Naomi*, and *Jennifer* – and more creative ones, made either from proper or common nouns (*Marlboro*,

Mouse, Maple, Jeep Cherokee) or from lexically transparent phrases (*Hate You, My Sorrow, Best Creature*). The family names are also sometimes easily recognisable as twenty-first-century family names (*Wilson, Wang, Duval, Ndiaye*), while others seem to have been invented more recently, such as *Insulting*, which is given to a girl who joins the Sengles from another community, and who then passes it to her children. Evidently there is a mixture of invention and tradition taking place in the naming of children in this community.

The creativity and sense of community and family within the Sengles' names comes in direct contrast to two of the other social groups presented in *Ice Cream Star*. The Lowells inhabit Lowell's Mill, and are friendly with the Sengles, although they operate a more structured way of life. Ice Cream explains: 'No Lowell use a name. Each Lowell calling by their task and rank within – be Second Plumber or First Gardener or Thirteenth Custodian' (Newman 2014: 44). This naming system is a direct reflection of the Lowells' way of life. The 'Army' is a group in which girls have no agency, being relegated to something like a harem, and any female child born in the community is exchanged with another group. In the Army, girls have no names, a direct reflection of their lack of agency and importance to those who hold power. One of Newman's characters from Lowell was 'born an Army girl without a name' (Newman 2014: 85) but was sent to Lowell Mill, and Ice Cream knows her as *First Runner*. She has been adopted into the Lowell community and bears a name that reflects this.

The extreme nature of the imposed naming practices presented in *Ice Cream Star* may appear unrealistic, particularly given the relatively brief time-lapse between the present of the narration and the preceding disaster. However, it should be noted that the surviving characters in Ice Cream's part of the east-coast USA are all children, thus eighty years spans at least four generations, speeding up the rate of change and loss of cultural memory. Coupled with the intended young-adult audience, for whom the author might have made more explicit world-building choices, the names fit plausibly into the linguistic environment.

'in your mynd places be come the name of what happent in them'

Riddley Walker (Hoban 2012) likely needs little introduction for readers of this book. Like *Ice Cream Star*, its protagonist is an adolescent in a post-apocalyptic future world, in which they and their community speak a familiar but distinct dialect recognisable as rooted in present-day English. *Riddley Walker* is set more than two thousand years into the future, in what used to be Kent in the south-east of England. 'Riddleyspeak' (Hoban 2012: 225), the name used paratextually for the dialect of the book, is a fictional dialect which purportedly reflects what might happen to English if a community were cut off from wider contact with the world, with little access to literacy or education. As Gordin and Katz (2018: 71) put it, 'The transformations are not the product of language contact but of internal developments within an isolated speech community.' As an experiment in extrapolated dialect, *Riddley Walker* is rightly lauded as groundbreaking. However, both the place- and personal names in the novel sit oddly alongside Riddleyspeak, presenting 'less convincing markers of authentic linguistic development' (Norledge 2022: 45).

Hoban (2012: 225) explains that 'the place names came to [him] without much trouble', presumably on the basis of the same 'breaking down and twisting' that he applied in creating Riddleyspeak. Hoban's comment suggests an off-handedness to place-naming, which perhaps explains why his toponyms do not follow expected naming patterns. A typical development of place-names over time is that they are simplified and lose their lexical transparency. *Fathers Ham* for Faversham raises no objection, and *Fork Stoan* for Folkestone is plausible, although in both cases we might question whether two thousand years of linguistic change and oral transmission of names would result in more significant alteration. By contrast, Dover has gained two syllables to become *Do It Over*, Herne Bay becomes the peculiar *Horny Boy*, and Ashford is for some reason reinvented to *Bernt Arse*. For those who have a familiarity with English place-names, these names and others might chafe against the linguistic realism Hoban is aiming for. As in present-day England, where most names are fossilised and opaque, some degree of folk etymology or reinterpretation of names is to be expected; but folk etymology does not usually result in the addition of extra syllables, merely a reinterpretation of names along the lines of phonetic similarity and a desire to make sense of meaningless sounds.

In defence of these toponymic peculiarities, storytelling and double-meanings are certainly central to the plot of *Riddley Walker*, and an interest in the origins of places and people is explored in several places, such as Riddley's recollection of a story explaining the change of the name *Hogmans Kil* to *Hagmans Il*:

> He said, 'Hogman had a fight with his wife and she kilt him.'
> I said, 'O that musve ben why they callit Hogmans Kil then.'
> He said, 'No it ben callit Hogmans Kil before she done him in. After she done it they callit Hagmans Il. Becaws she ben a rough and ugly old woman and it come to il he marrit her.'
> I said, 'Then whered the other story come from? The 1 of the bloak as got on top of Aunty.'
> He said, 'It come into my mynd.'
> I said, 'You mean you made it up.'
> He said, 'Wel no I dint make it up [. . .] That story cudnt come out of no where cud it so it musve come out of some where. Parbly it ben in that place from time way back or may be in a nother place only the idear of it come to me there.'
> (Hoban 2012: 93–4)

Although place-names in the real world are 'resolutely practical' and 'tend to designate historically important features of a place', it is also true that 'these denotations are quickly lost and overlaid with the accidental associations of history' (Cavill 2016: 357), perhaps rendering the names of *Riddley Walker* more socially authentic, with Hoban's odd reinterpretation and reconstruction of place-names reflecting a society focused on myth-making and interpretation.

The same might be said for the personal names the reader encounters. The complexity and formalisation of the anthroponymic system in English has, broadly speaking, increased with the size of the speech community, with surnames needed to differentiate people with the same given name, and with surnames themselves having arisen from originally meaningful bynames which described a person, their profession, or their locale. In Riddley's Kent, where the community is small and isolated, we might expect a regression away from formalised surnaming practices, and perhaps a change in the kinds of names being used – the personal names used in England today, after all, bear little resemblance to those used two thousand years ago.

Contrary to these expectations, the personal names we encounter in *Riddley Walker* look very like those found in England in the twentieth and twenty-first centuries, but for the fact that we see little evidence of names with non-English origins. Of the men at the quarry who we meet early in the novel, we have *Fister Crunchman, Durster Potter, Jobber Easting, Straiter Empy, Chalker Marchman, Skyway Moates, Leaster Digman, Brooder Walker*, and *Reckman Bessup*. Morphologically these look like typical English surnames, with *-er* and *-man* suffixes suggesting occupational names, and *Bessup* and *Easting* perhaps deriving from locations. The likelihood of these being recently formed occupational names is low, as neither *Walker* nor *Potter* has those occupations in the novel. The only man whose surname might be appropriate to his current vocation is *Digman*. Many of the given names (*Jobber, Reckman, Fister, Durster, Straiter, Brooder*) are morphologically similar to the surnames, lacking the inventiveness we see in *Ice Cream Star*. Hoban takes some opportunities here, as in the place-names, to imbue the personal names with additional meaning (as in the protagonist's name itself), but a more inventive naming system in line with the linguistic developments Hoban portrays through Riddley's dialect would have allowed this just as well.

Creating an 'authentic' past

Constructing, or reconstructing, a historical version of English is not a feat for the faint-hearted. In Traxel's (2022: 114) recent examination of language in historical fiction, he emphasises that 'the construction of a believable and comprehensible linguistic past' is a relatively recent aim for authors, resulting in fiction which is experimental and innovative. Just as in writing a future dialect of English, 'The technical challenges of verisimilitude or characterization across centuries of linguistic change are enormous' (Holsinger and Trigg 2016: 179), with various approaches available to authors. The two novels in this section employ two contrasting techniques: *The Wake* immerses its reader in a reconstructed pseudo-Old English; *To Calais, in Ordinary Time* (hereafter, *To Calais*) does not recreate Middle English, but instead provides a peppering of linguistic features that create a medieval feel in a contemporary novel. The challenge in both is to walk the fine line between familiar and alien, between present and past: 'historical otherness' (Matthews 2023: 453) versus comprehensibility.

'i is buccmaster son of ascetil son of leofric'

The Wake (Kingsnorth 2015) is written in a 'shadow tongue', designed to immerse the reader in the mind and perspective of its protagonist, Buccmaster. Buccmaster lives in eleventh-century England, where his home and family are destroyed in the aftermath of the Norman Conquest. He takes to the woods and fens, enacting guerrilla warfare against the French ('frenc') while calling on the 'old gods' to aid him in his quest to take back 'angland' from the invaders. It has been convincingly argued elsewhere (see Traxel 2022) that Kingsnorth's 'shadow tongue' fits the criteria of a conlang, as it constitutes an English that is neither Old English nor modern In fact, 'in many ways, the language Kingsnorth invents for Buccmaster is Hoban's Riddleyspeak turned on its head' (Gordin and Katz 2018: 77), a linguistic regression of modern English into something comprehensible but difficult to process. Others have explored the linguistic plausibility of Buccmaster's fictional dialect (e.g. McCulloch and Wiles 2016, Traxel 2022); in brief, Kingsnorth's experiment is not as internally coherent as a linguist might hope, but it certainly achieves its end of being simultaneously familiar and strange.

Unlike Hoban, Kingsnorth has the option of using historical place-name forms, and opts to do so throughout the narrative. The spellings are not always eleventh-century ones (e.g. *Lincylne*, spelled as such in Bede rather than Domesday), but local and linguistic variation allows some flexibility here in any case. These historical spellings render Buccmaster's Lincolnshire unfamiliar even to a modern reader familiar with the area (excepting e.g. *Lundun* and *Lincylene*), and some names (e.g. *the brunnesweald*) refer to places now lost. The geography is so challenging to decipher that readers have created lists to help one another navigate this historical-fictional world (e.g. Tia 2020).

There are relatively few named characters in *The Wake*, and from these only a few patterns can be observed. Aside from the protagonist, all the personal names are recognisably late medieval, and fit their fictional context. Of *Buccmaster*, Kingsnorth (2015: 359) notes: 'it is not an Old English name.

But it came to me and refused to yield to anything more historically correct, and so, it stays.' Although apparently inadvertent, naming Buccmaster so differently from other characters has the effect of isolating him from his surroundings, an ongoing theme.

Although we see only a few anthroponyms within *The Wake*, in more than one case a point is made out of them:

> tofe saes grimcell at last to the cilde this is a denisc name is it not tofe he locs afeart then but he saes in a small way yes it is denisc thy folcs then was denisc saes grimcell to him but he saes it lic a freond my grandfather saes tofe again for we is in the danelaugh is we not before the anglisc cyngs toc baec this place it was under rule of north cyngs there is many here of denisc stocc but they is anglisc now we is all anglisc now is this not so.
>
> (Kingsnorth 2015: 127)

Here Buccmaster and a companion meet a child named Tofe, whose name is 'denisc'. Buccmaster makes a point of being able to recognise a 'foreign' name, but considers past Scandinavian settlers 'anglisc' now, in contrast to the Norman French incomers: 'our cildren will haf frenc names they will spec frenc words' (Kingsnorth 2015: 197). We also see Buccmaster's instinct for othering in his introduction to another character: 'his nama he telt us was wluncus though i has nefer hierde an anglisc nama lic this it was as dumb as the man what held it' (Kingsnorth 2015: 223).

The function of names in *The Wake* is varied: the place-names in their Old English spellings create a world linguistically different from our own even where locations have real-world counterparts. The personal names follow Kingsnorth's attempted linguistic immersion but are also used as tools for characterisation and world-building, adding a limited but effective accompaniment to the 'shadow tongue' of the novel's faux-medieval world.

'Ne speak his name'

To Calais (Meek 2019) is set in fourteenth-century England amidst the Black Death. Meek does not attempt to recreate Middle English, nor even a pseudo-Middle English in the style of *The Wake*, but uses its braided narrative (toggling between narrative storylines, see Bancroft 2018) with multiple first-person narrators to allude to a trilingual linguistic environment, 'setting discourses against one another and constantly drawing attention to them' (Matthews 2023: 452). Meek mainly achieves this through vocabulary used by his characters, which emphasises words in the languages they are most familiar with. Bernadine, a noblewoman, uses French-derived vocabulary, while the lower-class bowmen do not. The priest they travel with intersperses his narrative with Latin, as would be expected from his education. Through this linguistic differentiation, which results in Meek's characters sometimes struggling to understand one another, he immerses the reader in a quasi-medieval linguistic environment while maintaining a mostly modern pattern of grammar and syntax, albeit with a few exceptions, such as the *ne* + *verb* method of negation.

Unlike *The Wake*, the place-names in *To Calais* predominantly take their modern forms (e.g. *Dorset, Wiltshire, Melcombe, Warminster*), so are immediately accessible to a modern reader. The personal names in the novel settle in the linguistic space Meek creates between the familiar and the unfamiliar, with his characters' given names being recognisable (e.g. *Rob, Tom,* and *Bob*), but existing within a medieval-looking system of surnaming. In the novel's fourteenth-century setting, Meek's characters are firmly within the surnaming period, wherein individuals acquired additional names (bynames), which might be derived from occupation, location, or nickname. Gradually, these names would become fixed into hereditary surnames, a process which took place at different rates in different parts of England and at different levels of society, generally happening faster in the south and among the wealthy (see Hanks and Parkin 2016). In *To Calais* we see a flexibility in naming which reflects this historical period, and which simultaneously allows Meek to provide the reader with information about his characters. We learn most about the English bowmen and the Outen Green villagers, and the remainder of this section will focus, therefore, on these 'English' characters.

Meek capitalises the surnames of some of his English characters as if to label them as a permanent fixture, as with *Hayne Attenoke, Ness Muchbrook*, and *Bob Woodyer*. These surnames look like plausible Middle English names, the first two locational and the third occupational. Meek (2019: 33) also refers to 'the Quates' and 'the Muchbrooks' as family groups, confirming that some characters share a – presumably hereditary – family name. It is notable that *Bob woodyer* also appears with a lower-case *w* in the novel, where he is named alongside *Rob deacon* and *Tom smith*. This combination of capitalised given name and uncapitalised second name indicates a choice on Meek's part to represent a difference in naming: again, from an informed perspective, we could infer that the names without a capital represent bynames, names which are not yet fixed, 'proper' nouns.

The flexibility in naming demonstrated in *To Calais* can be read as a playfulness on the part of the author and of the characters as they get to know one another. Some characters have established nicknames which function as bynames, such as 'the bowman they called Sweetmouth' (Meek 2019: 60), a clearly ironic name for a man whose utterances include 'May the fiend fuck me in the arse till my eyes weep shit' (Meek 2019: 61). Meek uses the Middle English term 'ekename' for 'nickname' to describe this kind of naming elsewhere too: 'His name is John Fletcher. He goes by the ekename Softly' (Meek 2019: 58). Softly is then known as Softly John Fletcher and Softly John at various points in the narrative, employing this onomastic flexibility in context.

The process of nicknaming is also seen in the novel, with Will Quate being mocked for a mistake, and for his good looks: "'He mistook the players for us", he said. "Maybe you were better as a player than a bowman. You've the face for it'" (Meek 2019: 56). Will is later introduced to another character thus: 'Behold, Cess, Player Will Quate' (Meek 2019: 72), and the joke continues further into the novel as 'Sweetmouth said Will was a player. Will said it was but an ekename' (Meek 2019: 173). Nicknaming can function as an in-group marker (Adams 2009), with the acquisition of a nickname being both an important aspect of belonging, and also a marker of power on the part of the interlocutor. Those who understand and use the name are part of the group, and a distinction is drawn between the bowmen and the character to whom the nickname must be explained. In the case of *To Calais*, a modern reader can recognise this process taking place, as Will is adopted into the group of bowmen and recognised as part of their social group.

Despite being less linguistically immersive than *The Wake*, *To Calais* embeds characters within an authentic-feeling late medieval naming system, even using some modern expectations around naming practices to aid in character and plot development. Alongside the 'exuberant heteroglossia' (Matthews 2023: 453) of *To Calais* and its multiple narrators, the personal names provide a further feeling of a society and language related to, but different from, our own.

Extra-terrestrial naming

In science and speculative fiction, languages used on extra-terrestrial worlds fall broadly into one of two categories. Either they are languages used by humans living away from Earth, or they are languages used by non-humans. In the former case, we might expect fictional societies to have naming systems akin to our own, serving similar purposes and taking similar forms. In the latter case, it is more likely that an 'alien' language will have a naming system distinct from those the reader may recognise, with differences in everything from phonology to pragmatics. In this section we find one novel from each alien category. The characters in Le Guin's (1974) *The Dispossessed* are certainly human, albeit living in a galaxy far, far away. In Faber's (2015) *The Book of Strange New Things*, by contrast, we encounter an indigenous community on the planet Oasis (a human name, not an alien one) who have their own names as well as names they use to communicate with humans, both of which we make sense of through the lens of English-speaking human interlopers.

'What is more personal than a name no other living person bears?'

The Dispossessed (Le Guin 1974) is a science fiction novel based on a planet (Urras) and its moon (Anarres). The moon's inhabitants are descendants of a group of revolutionary settlers – who call themselves Odonians, after their founder – who left Urras to begin a new life on Anarres. Anarresi society is the *Ambiguous Utopia* to which the novel's subtitle refers. The protagonist of the novel is Shevek, a physicist who has travelled from Anarres to Urras, and the narrative is told in alternating chapters between Shevek's present on Urras and his past in Anarres. The Odonians created a new (and thus entirely artificial) language to use in their society: Pravic. Le Guin presents little of the language itself in the novel save for a few translations (e.g. '*kleggich*, drudgery' [Le Guin 1974: 75]), but provides snippets of insight into its characteristics. Pravic apparently makes no use of possessive pronouns, for example, reflecting the lack of individual property ownership on Anarres: instead of *my mother*, an Anarresi would say 'the mother', although a later explanation indicates that the word 'my' does *exist* but is not used (Le Guin 1974: 46). Pravic lacks words for some concepts the Anarresi do not have or believe in and does not differentiate between ideas in the same ways: Pravic 'used the same word for work and play' (Le Guin 1974: 75), for instance.

This section focuses on the names of Anarres, as insight into Urrasi naming is necessarily limited due to Shevek's limited exposure to that world. Unlike other languages discussed in this chapter, Pravic is explicitly artificial, and the names of Anarres are therefore bestowed in a systematic and intentional way which does not display the diachronic evolution we might find in other linguistic contexts. Le Guin gives her reader a very clear explanation of how personal naming works on Anarres:

> The five- and six-letter names issued by the central registry computer, being unique to each living individual, took the place of the numbers which a computer-using society must otherwise attach to its members. An Anarresti needed no identification but his name. The name, therefore, was felt to be an important part of the self, though one no more chose it than one's nose or height.
> (Le Guin 1974: 201)

Anarresi anthroponyms are meaningful in that they identify an individual uniquely, but they carry no lexical sense or connection to a name-giver. There is no system of family naming, reflecting both the fact that unique given names negate the need for additional identifiers, but also that the family is not a central part of Annaresti culture, with monogamous relationships being optional and flexible, and children living away from their birth parents from a young age.

Robinson (2011: 132) has noted that many Annaresti place-names take similar forms to personal names: these include *Chakar*, *Holum*, and *Keran*. We might surmise that these are randomly generated names bestowed upon new, planned settlements at the time of colonisation. Elsewhere we are presented with a contrasting group of toponyms which are semantically transparent (e.g. *Uttermost*) and presumably formed in Pravic. These perhaps represent an additional period of name coinage as new settlements were created in later stages of colonisation. On this basis, we can presume that the previous cluster (*Chakar*, etc.) are not names in Pravic left untranslated for the reader, but names which are opaque to both reader and narrator.

In Annares, despite the attempt to divorce place- and personal names from lexical meaning, evidently the Pravic language does generate its own names, for places (as seen above) and for people. We see this in Shevek's description of nicknames he bestows upon his baby daughter: 'An alert, responsive baby, she gave Shevek the perfect audience for his suppressed verbal fantasies [...] He gave extravagant and ever-changing nicknames to the baby, and recited ridiculous mnemonics at her' (Le Guin 1974: 200). It is notable, too, that Shevek refers to his daughter as 'the baby' here and on numerous other occasions, indicating that he dislikes her computer-generated name, which to him 'sounds like a mouthful of gravel' (Le Guin 1974: 201).

In earlier scholarship, attempts have been made to understand elements of the Pravic language through its onomastics. Meyers (1977), for example, attempted to use the store of Annaresi names included in *The Dispossessed*, along with their orthography, to reconstruct the possible range of phonemes in Pravic (which is otherwise, of course, chiefly a concept rather than an actualised language). Meyers calculates that the personal naming system of Annares cannot possibly generate enough new names for its population, but does so based on a likely incomplete understanding of the range of phonemes available and with no reference to the likelihood of close similarity between names illustrated in Shevek's hostile encounter with 'a man in camp whose name, spoken, sounded like Shevek's: Shevet' (Le Guin 1974: 38). It might be argued here, too, that the practicalities of the naming system are less important to Le Guin's fictional world than its fitness for the society and language from which it comes. As ever, we walk the fine line between the needs of the fictional world and attempts to render it 'realistic' or 'plausible' under linguistic scrutiny.

'What do animals care if a place has a name?'

The Book of Strange New Things (Faber 2015) takes place largely on the planet Oasis, which is inhabited by a human delegation as part of an Earth-based resource-mining corporation, along with a 'native' group known to us as the Oasans. The Oasans are described as roughly humanoid, but with noticeable differences in their bodies. They have faces without discernible humanoid features, vocal organs which produce sounds differently, and reproductive organs which expel newborns through the head. Faber's protagonist is Peter Leigh, a Protestant minister dispatched to Oasis at the request of the Oasans, some of whom have already converted to Christianity via a previous missionary preacher. The novel unfolds chiefly through a third-person narrative taking Peter's perspective, but also includes correspondence between Peter and his wife Beatrice, still living on Earth. The linguistic interest of the novel is in the Oasans' language, and their understanding of the English used by Peter.

Faber has rendered the strangeness of the Oasans' language through novel symbols representing phonemes, some of which are also used in substitute of *s* and *t* when the Oasans are conversing in English, these sounds being impossible for them to pronounce. We are introduced to this impediment in Peter's first encounter with the Oasans, where he is introduced to them by a colleague:

> 'You, here, now ...' he said. 'A ᶊurpriᶎe.' His voice was soft, reedy, asthmatic-sounding. Where the 's's should have been, there was a noise like a ripe fruit being thumbed into two halves.
> 'Not a bad surprise, I hope,' said Grainger.
> 'I hope ᵵogether with you.'
> The Oasan turned to look at Peter, tilted his head slightly so that the shadows from the hood slid back. Peter, having been lulled by the Oasan's familiar shape and five-fingered hands into expecting a more-or-less human face, flinched.
> Here was a face that was nothing like a face. Instead, it was a massive whitish-pink walnut kernel. Or no: even more, it resembled a placenta with two foetuses – maybe three-month-old twins, hairless and blind – nestled head to head, knee to knee. Their swollen heads constituted the Oasan's clefted forehead, so to speak; their puny ribbed backs formed his cheeks, their spindly arms and webbed feet merged in a tangle of translucent flesh that might contain – in some form unrecognisable to him – a mouth, nose, eyes.
> (Faber 2015: 120–1; the symbols here and in later quotations are a substitute for Faber's hand-drawn phonetic notation rather than resembling it exactly)

This depiction of the Oasan is visceral and uncomfortable for the reader. Peter describes both the Oasan's appearance and the sound of his attempt at pronouncing the letter *s* in terms of tangible, concrete objects, attempting to interpret the alien via very human metaphors.

The Oasans with whom Peter interacts – those who consider themselves Christians – introduce themselves to him by their Christian names. These adopted names are very simple, as we see in 'the four who called themselves Jeᶊuᶊ Lover One, Jeᶊuᶊ Lover Fifᵵy-Four, Jeᶊuᶊ Lover ᶊevenᵵy-Eighᵵ and Jeᶊuᶊ Lover ᶊevenᵵy-Nine' (Faber 2015: 182). The Jesus Lovers, as Peter often refers to them, have numbers to differentiate them from one another rather than individually meaningful names. This numbering system is chronological, with Jesus Lover One being the first convert, thus creating an implicit hierarchy with Christian worship at its centre. It is only much later in the novel when Peter begins to learn the sounds of the Oasans' language that he discovers that their own (pre-Christian) method of naming is quite different. Peter is invited to witness the birth – and naming – of an Oasan child:

> 'สคฉัร,' she announced. Another great cheer went up.
> 'What did she say?' Peter asked Lover One.
> 'สคฉัร,' said Lover One.
> 'Is that the baby's name?'
> 'Name, yeส,' said Lover One.
> 'Does that name have a meaning, or is it just a name?'
> 'Name have a meaning,' Lover One replied. Then, after a few seconds: 'Hope.'
>
> (Faber 2015: 313)

In the Oasans' society, personal names are (or can be) lexically transparent, even aspirational, and it is notable that 'Hope' is a name that would not be out of place in Peter's own culture and language. It is perhaps also of note that Jesus Lover One's translation of the name as 'hope' contradicts one of Peter's earlier comments that 'As for "ฉันณ", the word for faith [...] its meaning was not what you'd call precise. Faith, hope, intention, objective, desire, plan, wish, the future, the road ahead [...] these were all the same thing, apparently' (Faber 2015: 439). Despite this assertion from Peter, Jesus Lover One is able to select the word 'hope' rather than 'faith' to translate the name of the newborn, indicating a differentiation between the two terms; perhaps the Oasans have a better understanding than Peter of how to translate these concepts.

In this example we also see Peter's tendency to abbreviate the Jesus Lovers' Christian names: he omits the 'Jesus' from *Jesus Lover One* and simply refers to them as *Lover One*. This instinct to adjust an unfamiliar naming system to fit Peter's expectations has the effect of the component of the Oasans' names which they themselves evidently consider the most important.

There are only two Oasan settlements in the novel, one of which is abandoned. Peter tries to find out the name of their current town, but has little success:

> He'd tried to find out what the Oasans themselves called it, so he could refer to it by that name, but they appeared not to understand the question, and kept identifying their settlement, in English, as 'here'. At first he assumed this was because its real name was unpronounceable, but no, there *was* no real name.
>
> (Faber 2015: 275)

What Peter does not seem to consider is that there is no need to name a place if you never need to differentiate one settlement from another. We learn nothing in the novel which suggests that the Oasans travel beyond their own homes with any regularity; Oasan society simply does not have a need for names in the way Peter expects.

As the novel progresses, Peter becomes increasingly familiar with both the Oasan language and way of life: in '[l]earning the language, Peter understood better how his new friends' souls functioned' (Faber 2015: 439). The text reflects the importance of language in understanding a society, and we are given hints at the ways Oasan naming practices might reflect their culture as part of their fictional language; alas, our discovery – and Peter's – is cut short by his return to Earth at the novel's conclusion.

A case for the conomasticon

Through the settings and languages above, I hope to have demonstrated the sheer variety of ways in which authors have employed names as part of their fictional languages. In some cases, names are deeply embedded in the workings of these languages, and they are a crucial component in our understanding of the characters and cultures we encounter as readers. In others, names do not gel as neatly with the language as it is constructed, creating linguistic obstacles to immersion in the fictional world. The question of linguistic plausibility is relevant for some readers, and not for others, and we have seen various approaches from authors in this chapter in terms of how 'authenticity' and world-building are achieved. To draw a very brief conclusion from this variety, I would like to close this chapter with a bid for names to be seen as just as fundamental a part of language creation and conceptualisation as any other of language's building blocks. I hope to have demonstrated how useful a tool carefully chosen names can be in building a fictional world, and how intriguing they can be as a means of analysing and understanding the worlds – and languages – of others.

References

Adams, M. (2009) 'Power, politeness, and the pragmatics of nicknames', *Names* 57 (2): 81–91.
Bancroft, C. (2018) 'The braided narrative', *Narrative* 26 (3): 262–81.
Bollinger, L. (2016) 'Figuring the other within: the gendered underpinnings of germ narratives', in K. Nixon and L. Servitje (eds) *Endemic: Essays in Contagion Theory*. London: Palgrave Macmillan, pp. 243–64.
Bramwell, E. (2016) 'Personal names and anthropology', in C. Hough with D. Izdebska (eds) *The Oxford Handbook of Names and Naming*. Oxford: Oxford University Press, pp. 263–78.
Cavill, P. (2016) 'Language-based approaches to names in literature', in C. Hough with D. Izdebska (eds) *The Oxford Handbook of Names and Naming*. Oxford: Oxford University Press, pp. 355–67.
Faber, M. (2015) *The Book of Strange New Things*. Edinburgh: Canongate.

Falck-Kjällquist, B. (2016) 'Genre-based approaches to names in literature', in C. Hough with D. Izdebska (eds) *The Oxford Handbook of Names and Naming*. Oxford: Oxford University Press, pp. 310–29.

Gordin, M. D. and Katz, J. T. (2018) '*The Walker* and *The Wake*: analysis of non-intrinsic philological isolates', in S. Gurd and V. W. J. van Gerven Oei (eds) *'Pataphilology: An Irreader*. Goleta: punctum books, pp. 61–92.

Hanks, P. and Parkin, H. (2016) 'Family names', in C. Hough with D. Izdebska (eds) *The Oxford Handbook of Names and Naming*. Oxford: Oxford University Press, pp. 214–36.

Hoban, R. (2012) *Riddley Walker* [original 1980]. London: Bloomsbury.

Holsinger, B. and Trigg, S. (2016) 'Novel medievalisms', *postmedieval: a journal of medieval cultural studies* 7 (2): 175–80.

Kingsnorth, P. (2015) *The Wake*. London: Unbound.

Le Guin, U. K. (1974) *The Dispossessed: An Ambiguous Utopia*. New York: Avon.

McCulloch, G. and Wiles, W. (2016) 'Two linguists explain pseudo Old English in *The Wake*', *the Toast*, 14 June 2016. <https://the-toast.net/2016/06/14/two-linguists-explain-pseudo-old-english-in-the-wake/>

Matthews, D. (2023) 'Medievalism', in R. Radulescu and S. Rikhardsdottir (eds) *The Routledge Companion to Medieval English Literature*. London: Routledge, pp. 445–54.

Meek, J. (2019) *To Calais, in Ordinary Time*. Edinburgh: Canongate.

Meyers, W. F. (1977) '*The Dispossessed* and how they got to be that way: Ursula K. Le Guin's onomastics', *Names* 25 (2): 115–18.

Newman, S. (2014) *The Country of Ice Cream Star*. London: Vintage.

Norledge, J. (2022) *The Language of Dystopia*. London: Palgrave Macmillan.

Robinson, C. L. (2011) 'Onomaturgy vs. onomastics: an introduction to the namecraft of Ursula K. Le Guin', *Names* 59 (3): 129–38.

Tia (2020) 'List of places in *The Wake* by Paul Kingsnorth', *Capture Curiosity*, 9 March 2020. <https://capturecuriosity.com/2020/03/09/list-of-places-in-the-wake-by-paul-kingsnorth/>

Traxel, O. M. (2022) 'Creating a "shadow tongue": the merging of two language stages', in R. A. Fletcher, T. Porck and O. M. Traxel (eds) *Old English Medievalism: Reception and Recreation in the 20th and 21st Centuries*. London: Boydell & Brewer, pp. 95–114.

CHAPTER 13

The language of Lapine in *Watership Down*

Kimberley Pager-McClymont

The anthropomorphised rabbits in Richard Adams' 1972 novel, *Watership Down* speak a language called Lapine. In this chapter, Kim Pager-McClymont shows how the structure, idioms, and conceptual patterning of Lapine are intricately bound up with the embodied rabbit experience. Drawing on the stylistics of foregrounding, Conceptual Metaphor Theory, and her own model of pathetic fallacy, she shows how the rabbits' worldview is embedded in the narrative and how Adams' technique generates empathy for the rabbits in the novel. The fictional language bridges the gap between the naturalistic realism of the rabbits' behaviour and the 'unnaturalness' of their consciousness.

Introduction

Watership Down (Adams 1972) is a novel featuring anthropomorphised rabbits as main characters. The rabbits have the ability to speak, and they also have their own language called Lapine, as well as another language, Hedgerow, which is employed as a *lingua franca* for the rabbits to communicate with other animals. The novel is set in south-east England's Hampshire Downs, and follows a colony of rabbits led by Fiver and Hazel as they flee their home, following the intrusion of humans onto their land, Sandleford Warren. Amongst the different characters, two rabbits (Fiver and Hyzenthlay) have the gift of seeing the future, and one of their visions is the starting point for their quest for a mysterious promised land. On their way to this more perfect society, the colony faces the dangers of predators, adversaries, and war over warrens and claimed territories. Critics such as Leatherland (2020) argue that throughout the novel, the different warrens represent different forms of human government: Efrafa symbolises totalitarianism, the warren of the snares represents socialism, and Hazel's warren reflects a democracy. As such, the anthropomorphic nature of the rabbits is not just reflected in their ability to speak (as this would be prosopopoeia, and not anthropomorphism, see Pager-McClymont 2021, Wales 2011: 347), but it is also present in their battle of good and evil, defending their colonies, and seeking a utopia. *Watership Down* has been discussed from a zoosemiotic lens (Leatherland 2020), as well as in narrative studies (Anderson 1993, Meyer 1994), and translation studies (Grider 2019). These works discuss the impact of the anthropomorphism of the rabbits (and consequently Lapine) on readers.

Meyer (1994: 139), in reviewing how Adams develops the rabbit characters in the novel, poses the question: 'exclusive of their level of realism, are Adams' rabbits principally figurative devices for representing the concept of humanity, or are they simultaneously full-blooded creatures?' He draws on Chapman's (1978) observation that a 'rabbit society [is] a metaphor for problems of human survival', as well as on Hough's (1963) narrative concept of 'incarnation' (when a theme and image are completely fused and the relation between them is only implicit) to demonstrate that despite the figurative and abstract nature of the anthropomorphised rabbits, Adams' characterisation technique is effective as it draws on rabbits' real nature to convey their fictional traits.

Grider (2019: iii) explores how *Watership Down* can be translated, particularly the Lapine language, and argues that

> we can use the principles of translation studies, content analysis, and animal science to shed new light on how we depict animal culture while encouraging a learning-driven empathy for the animal experience in the human reader.

Animal narratives (such as *Watership Down*) can challenge readers' sense of empathy because they portray events and characters alien to readers' personal experience (see Harrison and Hall 2010, Keen 2011, Airenti 2015). Weil (2012: 20) suggests that 'critical empathy' can limit the gap between animal perspectives and human experience whilst acknowledging their differences: 'we may imagine [others'] pain, pleasure, and need in anthropomorphic terms but must stop short of believing that we can know their experience'. While it is not the focus of this chapter to discuss narratology studies in depth, it is important to consider that animal narratives have been more and more researched in recent years (see Herman 2011, 2018, Caracciolo 2016, Norledge 2022, amongst others). The main issue noted by scholars is that a double dialectic distinguishes animal narration as the capacity to manage sophisticated verbal systems, which is typically regarded as being exclusively human (Bernaerts et al. 2014). Indeed, Caracciolo (2016: 144–5) argues that 'the animal body can take center stage because it is a material, living reminder of this divide: it can be considered incomprehensible, alien, abject, immoral, thus estranging audiences from the narrator at an epistemic and axiological level', and that through anthropomorphism 'readers are invited to categorize a fictional entity as a minded being, thus adopting a mimetic stance toward him or her'. Bekoff (2013: 63) explains that anthropomorphic language 'does not have to discount the animal's point of view' as it 'allows other animals' behavior and emotions to be accessible to us'. This shows that overall concept of anthropomorphism can generate discussion, as there can be different instances of this phenomenon.

Herman (2018: ix) aims to develop a cross-disciplinary approach to narratives concerned with animals and human-animal relationships, meaning that it derives from Darwin's deconstruction of the hierarchical distinction between human and non-human beings. Herman (2011, 2018) proposes a model of anthropomorphism based on a continuum of complexity and granularity in the degree to which animal minds are portrayed in narratives, from more or less 'coarse' to more or less 'fine-grained' representations of non-human experiences (see Herman 2018: 138, or Norledge 2022: 391 for figures). This model aims 'to map out the dialectical interplay between anthropocentric and biocentric storytelling traditions, and to explore how specific narrative practices shape and are shaped by this interplay' (Herman 2018: 7). On the 'coarse' side of the continuum are narratives in which animals are 'stand-ins' for humans and are labelled as *Animal Allegories*. The second category on the continuum is the *Anthropomorphic Projection* (also known as *Human-Source-Animal-Target Projections*): narratives in which animals are attributed with certain human qualities, which provides a deeper sense of animal experience than Animal Allegory, 'but human motivations and practices continue to be used as the template for interpreting nonhuman behaviour' (Herman 2011: 167). The third category is *Zoomorphic Projection* (also known as *Human-Source-Animal-Target Projections*), which provides human characters with animal traits, offering a closer understanding of animal experiences to an extent. Lastly, the category *Umwelt Exploration* is labelled after von Uexküll's (1957) concept (meaning 'lifeworld'):

> to suggest how the emphasis is less on mapping human-generated understandings of animal worlds back onto the domain of the human than on using narrative thought experiments to construct models of the lived, phenomenally experienced worlds of nonhuman animals themselves.
>
> (Herman 2018: 140)

In *Watership Down*, the rabbit characters maintain their rabbit lives and traits, but are attributed with the human quality of conversational speech (though some may argue that vocal communication is not exclusive to humans). Additionally, the rabbits in the novel can distinguish between and side with Good and Evil, and they try to escape to a utopia. As such, in terms of Herman's model of anthropomorphism, *Watership Down* is an instance of Anthropomorphic Projection. The rabbits have their own language (Lapine), and I describe below how the construction of this fictional language revolves around the rabbits' experiences in a holistic way.

Linguistic discussions of *Watership Down* describe how Lapine is constructed. For example:

> Lapine consists primarily of nouns (many of them descriptive, objects described through action or negation); it contains numerous multi-syllabic and/or compound words; it is vivid, imagistic, poetic (that is, aesthetic in nature); and it resembles human language in various respects.
>
> (Anderson 1993: 1)

Different levels of language in Lapine are discussed in literature, primarily focusing on phonetics, lexis, and syntax as Adams provides a glossary of Lapine terms as a preface to the novel (see also Leatherland 2020: 109–10). In Graphic 13.1 I provide a sample of some of the Lapine lexis.

Interestingly, in Lapine, some of the lexis is not always specific, for example, the term *hrair* which means 'a great many' or 'an uncountable number' refers to any number above four, most likely because rabbits only have four paws to count on. Similarly, *inlé* can refer to the moon in a literal setting but can also be used to refer to darkness and fear. This is logical as rabbits are prey animals, the obscurity of the night (when the moon is visible) presents a danger as they cannot see other animals hunting them.

Lapine also occurs on the syntactical level, as shown for instance by the way nouns are made plural, most often by substituting the word's last vowel for -il: one hrudud**u** and two hrudud**il**. This also applies to hless**i**/hless**il**, homb**a**/homb**il**, yon**a**/yon**il** (amongst others, see Graphic 13.1), and thus generates a rule. The last letter of the singular noun can vary (here i, a, u), but the rule still applies. Additionally, certain words are created as combinations of others, using suffixes. For example, 'rah' is a suffix that shows superiority. Throughout the novel, when rabbits accomplish a great task the suffix is added to their name by other rabbits to show their accomplishment is appreciated by others (e.g. *Hazel-rah, El-ahrairah, Frithrah*), and *flayrah* refers to food of greater quality than usual (*flay* being the word for food). New words can also be created by combining two existing ones. For instance, *silf* refers to outside when it is not underground in burrows; and *flay* refers to food. As such, *silflay* is the term used to refer to going above ground to feed (as a verb), or as food to be consumed above ground (as a noun). This is not always the case, however, as for example the noun *hraka* refers to droppings, but the action has a different lexeme: the verb *vair*.

Lastly, some phonetic aspects can be found in the creation of Lapine lexis. For instance, the Lapine word *hrududu* is a noun to mean a motor vehicle such as a tractor or a car, and the word's sound mirrors an engine's. The fricative sounds /h/, /θ/, /ð/, /f/ are frequently used in Lapine lexis (I use British English phonetics as this is the language the novel was written in, but arguably Lapine could have different pronunciation of those sounds). This could potentially be because fricative sounds are produced by severely

The language of Lapine in Watership Down

Lexis	Meaning
Elil	Enemies (of rabbits).
Flay	Food, e.g. grass or other green fodder.
Flayrah	Unusually good food, e.g. lettuce.
Frith	The sun, personified as a god by rabbits.
Frithrah!	Lord Sun; used as an exclamation.
Hlessi	A rabbit living above ground, without a regular hole or warren. (Plural, hlessil.)
Homba	A fox. (Plural, hombil.)
Hraka	Droppings, excreta.
Hrududu	A tractor, car or any motor vehicle. (Plural, hrududil.)
Hyzenthlay	Literally, 'Shine-dew-fur' (Fur shining like dew). The name of a doe.
Inlé	Literally, the moon; also moonrise. But a second meaning carries the idea of darkness, fear and death.
Lendri	A badger.
Owsla	The strongest rabbits in the warren, the ruling clique.
Rah	A prince, leader or chief rabbit. Usually used as a suffix. E.g. Threarah, Lord Threar.
Roo	Used as a suffix to denote a diminutive. E.g. Hrairoo means 'Little Thousand' and is Fiver's Lapine name.
Silf	Outside, that is, not underground.
Silflay	To go above ground to feed. Literally, to feed outside. Also used as a noun. Combination of 'Flay' and 'Silf'.
Thlay	Fur
Threar	A rowan tree, or mountain ash.
Thrennions	Berries of rowan tree.
Vair	To excrete, pass croppings.
Yona	A hedgehog. (Plural, yonil.)

Graphic 13.1 Selected examples of Lapine lexis

obstructing the airflow to cause friction, and rabbits use their nasal cavity to make sounds such as hissing, snorting, or snoring (stertor and stridor). This could be an illustration as to how rabbits' natural behaviour is incorporated into *Watership Down*. Leatherland (2020) uses Seton's (1898) work to explore how rabbits' natural traits of communication (such as thumping, whisker-touches, ear movement) are featured in the novel. Examples of rabbit behaviour included in the narration are briefly observed further in this chapter, primarily focusing on the rabbits' use of their noses for communication.

Although Lapine has been studied through varied lenses, the impact of figurative language (other than anthropomorphism) in Lapine's construction is not considered by scholars. I argue that figurative language is salient in constructing Lapine and embedding it in the narration. Thus, in this chapter, I aim to answer the following questions:

1. How do Lapine's levels of language work together to provide readers with a coherent and holistic representation of the narrative and characters?
2. How do Adams' stylistic choices impact the reading experience?
3. How does the integration of Lapine in the novel impact the reading experience?

I demonstrate throughout this chapter that analysing the novel through a stylistic lens allows for the answering of these questions. I first introduce the stylistic tools used in my analysis, namely, foregrounding theory, and Conceptual Metaphor Theory focusing specifically on a certain type of metaphor – pathetic fallacy. I then explore how certain types of figurative language in the novel can be associated with Lapine, followed by a textual analysis and a discussion on metaphor visibility.

Two key stylistic aspects

Foregrounding and Conceptual Metaphor Theory

To illustrate how Lapine is embedded on all levels of language, I will draw on the stylistic theories of foregrounding and conceptual metaphor in my analysis. Foregrounding underpins how linguistic elements stand out against the rest of the text (Mukařovský 1964, Miall 2007, Leech 2008, van Peer 2007). This prominence can occur by *parallelism* (through repeated terms or structure), or by *deviation*. Deviation can be internal when the text deviates from its own established pattern (e.g. a non-rhyming stanza in a poem that otherwise only features rhymes), or deviation can be external if it deviates from the norm of the language (e.g. idioms). The theory of foregrounding accounts for effects 'real' readers can perceive in a natural setting (Miall and Kuiken 1994). In this chapter, I draw on foregrounding theory to observe how stylistic choices embed Lapine in the narration and allow the building of mental representations of scenes or to empathise with animal characters.

Conceptual Metaphor Theory (henceforth CMT) claims that one concept (known as the target domain, typically an abstract concept) is understood in terms of another concept (the source domain, typically more concrete) (Lakoff and Johnson 1980, Kövecses 2002). The cross-domain mapping is the correspondence between those two domains, a conceptual metaphor which can be labelled simply as A IS B. For example, certain emotions such as ANGER are understood in terms of HEAT in metaphors such as 'you are hot-headed' or 'to blow off steam', thus generating the mapping ANGER IS HEAT.

The language of Lapine in Watership Down   201

The specific conceptual metaphor salient to *Watership Down* and how rabbit characters express themselves is pathetic fallacy (hereafter PF), which can be mapped as EMOTIONS ARE SURROUNDINGS. The section below presents Pager-McClymont's (2022) stylistic model of PF used in this chapter.

A stylistic model of pathetic fallacy

I define PF as a projection of emotions onto the surroundings by an animated entity (see Pager-McClymont 2021, 2022). The emotions and animated entity in question can be featured implicitly or explicitly in the text. For this definition to be fulfilled, three criteria must be present in a text: the presence of an animated entity showing sign of emotions (here anthropomorphised rabbits), presence of surroundings (indoors or outdoors), and presence of emotions. I define emotion as a 'response to an event, either internal or external, that has a positively or negatively valenced meaning for the individual' (Salovey and Mayer 1990: 186), and these emotions can be present explicitly (clearly expressed) or implicitly (required to be inferred through textual cues) (see Palmer 2004: 115). Based on its definition, PF's metaphorical mapping is EMOTIONS ARE SURROUNDINGS, and as its target domain is an emotion, it renders it a conceptual 'emotion metaphor' (Kövecses 2008: 382). Because the three criteria needed to fulfil PF's definition might be featured anywhere in a text, particularly as they might be implicit or explicit, PF is thus an extended metaphor. To determine if enough context is provided in an extract, prompt questions can be asked such as 'Is there an animated entity present in the text explicitly or implicitly (character, narrator, speaker)?', 'Is the animated entity named directly or referred to by pronoun or noun?', 'What situation is the animated entity in?' For a greater discussion on context and identification of PF's criteria, see Pager-McClymont (2022: 435–6).

As part of my model of PF, I identify three 'linguistic indicators' (Short 1996) of PF: repetition (lexical, syntactic), negation (syntactic, morphological, and lexical), and imagery, which I define akin to Dancygier (2014) as tropes drawing on the senses to allow readers to build rich and vivid mental representations of scenes. PF can have (at least) four effects on narratives. Firstly, PF can communicate implicit emotions that otherwise may not be perceived by readers. Emotions are expressed through surroundings (that may or may not be there in the text, but that are evoked by characters). This is the most common effect of PF. Secondly, PF can build *ambience* (a combination of atmosphere and tone, see Stockwell 2014), including suspense. In such instances, PF set the scene, and can signpost to conflict in a scene until a denouement is reached (see Carroll's 'suspense paradox' 1996: 147–50, Iwata 2009: 253). Thirdly, PF can foreshadow forthcoming events in the plot, and this temporal manipulation of discourse generates suspense, and this can happen through symbolism (Bae and Young 2008: 157). Lastly, PF can contribute to characterisation, the process of building characters (Culpeper

2001). PF as a type of figurative language is an implicit cue of characterisation as it offers readers a mental representation of characters' emotions.

Figurative language in *Watership Down*

Figurative language can convey emotions and contribute to characterisation (Citron et al. 2015). There are two specific types of figures of speech (other than anthropomorphism) that are featured in *Watership Down* and that showcase the rabbits' communication, and as such can be considered as aspects of Lapine: idioms and PF.

Idiomatic expressions can inform readers on characters' cultural background, psychological state, and personality. Because those expressions are embedded in the text, there is no glossary. They are an inherent part of the narration, and yet, they are specific to the rabbits' verbalisation and conceptualisation of their environment, rendering those expressions part of the Lapine language. For example:

> Human beings say, 'It never rains but it pours.' This is not very apt, for it frequently does rain without pouring. The rabbits' proverb is better expressed. They say, 'One cloud feels lonely': and indeed it is true that the appearance of a single cloud often means the sky will soon be overcast.
>
> (Adams 1972: 107)

In this extract, the third-person narrator contrasts the human expression 'it never rains but it pours' with the rabbit equivalent and more accurate idiom 'one cloud feels lonely'. This example shows that throughout the novel, the rabbits communicate not only through body language or Lapine lexis and syntax, but also through discoursal expressions they can relate to, articulated through idiomatic metaphors and viewpoint, based on their experience and surroundings.

Moreover, the tendency to draw on their surroundings to convey how they feel is natural for the rabbit characters, as they maintain their rabbit activities. In nature, all animals depend on food, water, and temperature to feel comfortable and happy (as do humans, see Cunningham 1979, Howarth and Hoffman 1984), and surroundings are their shelter. Rabbits being prey animals, this is particularly salient to their existence. This makes PF the most natural metaphor for rabbits to express their emotions in the novel, as it has the cross-domain mapping EMOTIONS ARE SURROUNDINGS. Although I detail below how PF is featured implicitly in the novel, here is an explicit example:

> To come to the end of a time of anxiety and fear! To feel the cloud that hung over us lift and disperse – the cloud that dulled the heart and

The language of Lapine in Watership Down

made happiness no more than a memory! This at least is one joy that must have been known by almost every living creature
(Adams 1972: 35)

Here, the clouds are associated with negative emotions (anxiety and fear), and their dissipation with happiness. In typical British weather, clouds are often synonymous with lower temperature, potentially rain and wind, and this is often thought of as bad weather in contrast to sunny days. The rabbits' quality of life, survival, and worldly experience relies on their surroundings, and cloudy or rainy weather deprives them of food or renders their habitat wet, and this presents a challenge to their survival. Thus, rabbits not only associate their surroundings with their emotions, but they also use the surroundings to mirror how they feel, and this is an explicit instance of PF. Indeed, although the element of surroundings used to express emotion is metaphorical in itself ('the cloud that hung over us [...] the cloud that dulled the heart'), the fact that the rabbit uses an element of surroundings to express its emotion (relief of anxiety) generates a mental representation of the emotion, and as such renders it an instance of PF.

I have illustrated so far how Lapine can be constructed on all levels of language, including figures of speech. The section below furthers this demonstration by showing how it works in a textual example, and the consequences this has for readers.

Analysis of a textual example

The following extract is taken from chapter 35, 'Groping', of *Watership Down*. It portrays Bigwig, a key character in the novel, who is a strongheaded rabbit with a tuft of hair on his head that gave him his Lapine name 'Thlayli' (meaning fur-head). Bigwig tried to convince Hyzenthlay to escape from Efrafa, a dictatorship-like warren. Hyzenthlay has the ability to see the future through visions, which she uses to decide if escaping Efrafa is possible. (Sentences have been numbered for ease of reference later.)

'You spoke of your friend – the one who knew that that warren was a bad place. He is not the only such rabbit.(1) Sometimes I can tell these things, too: but not often now, for my heart is in the frost.'(2)

'Then will you join me – and persuade your friends as well?(3) We need you: Efrafa doesn't need you.'(4)

Again she was silent.(5) Bigwig could hear a worm moving in the earth nearby and faintly down the tunnel came the sound of some small creature pattering through the grass outside.(6) He waited quietly, knowing that it was vital that he should not upset her.(7)

At last she spoke again, so low in his ear that the words seemed barely more than broken cadences of breathing.(8)

'We can escape from Efrafa.(9) The danger is very great, but in that we can succeed.(10) It is beyond that I cannot see.(11) Confusion and fear at nightfall – and then men, men, it is all things of men!(12) A dog – a rope that snaps like a dry branch.(13) A rabbit – no, it is not possible! – a rabbit that rides in a hrududu!(14) Oh, I have become foolish – tales for kittens on a summer evening.(15) No, I cannot see as I did once: it is like the shapes of trees beyond a field of rain.'(16)
(Adams 1972: 283; sentence numbering added)

The rabbits are anthropomorphised and maintain their rabbit traits in addition to being able to speak and think, akin to humans, as shown by the direct speech present in sentences (6) and (7). In the passage, the nouns 'rabbits' and 'warren' are the only two words that indicate that the characters in this passage are indeed rabbits. The ways rabbits and other animals are represented in the novel also differ as other creatures are not anthropomorphised. In sentence (6) a 'worm' is described as *'moving* in the earth' and a small creature as *'pattering* through the grass'; these are typical animalistic actions. This in itself reinforces the anthropomorphic qualities of the rabbits: not only are they given human attributes, but they are also superior to other creatures. The analysis below explores key themes in this extract focusing on lexis, syntax, and figures of speech which contribute to the portraying of the rabbits' emotions, as well as elements of the Lapine language.

Theme of 'danger'

The lexical field of danger is foregrounded by parallelism due to its prevalence: 'bad place', 'danger', 'escape', 'confusion and fear', 'rope', 'vital', 'dog', 'men', and 'upset'. Similarly, most of the adverbs in the passage refer to time: 'sometimes', 'again', 'often now', 'once'. This also foregrounds by parallelism, the repetition echoing and further illustrating the urgency of the rabbits' dangerous situation. Moreover, the nouns 'rabbits' and 'men' are the only two nouns repeated within the same sentences. 'Men' is repeated three times in sentence (12) and 'rabbits' twice in sentence (14). These nouns are foregrounded by parallelism because of their repetition, and they are also internally deviant as the only two nouns repeated. In the novel (and arguably in reality), men are a great threat to rabbits, and the repetition of the nouns in sentences close together conveys an opposition between the two: rabbits are prey and men are hunters. This adds to the sense of danger expressed by Bigwig and Hyzenthlay. Lastly, negation is equally present and foregrounded by parallelism. There is lexical negation ('bad', 'no', 'danger', 'escape', 'confusion and fear') and syntactic negation ('not', 'cannot'), reinforcing the negative situation and sense of danger. These elements illustrate the situation Hyzenthlay and Bigwig are facing: they must rally as many rabbits as they can to escape Efrafa because of the dictatorship-like society

The language of Lapine in Watership Down

it has become. If caught trying to escape, they will be killed, a theme that is conveyed by the atmospheric foregrounded lexical field of danger.

Theme of 'senses'

The lexical field of sound is also prominent, foregrounded by parallelism: 'spoke', 'silent', 'hear', 'quietly', 'low', 'ear', 'cadences'. Sentence (8) contains the metaphor 'the words seemed barely more than broken cadences of breathing', comparing Hyzenthlay's speech to hesitant breath. The effect is that readers can mentally represent how quiet Hyzenthlay is: it only sounds like she is breathing. This further contributes to the danger the rabbits are in and how scared Hyzenthlay is: she does not risk being heard by others. It also mirrors rabbits' behaviour generally, as they use their noses to communicate with one another. The emphasis on the sense of hearing is directly linked to the characters rabbits predominantly use their ears to orient themselves and assess their surroundings. Because Hyzenthlay and Bigwig are plotting to escape, they rely on their hearing to sense any immediate danger.

Syntactic structures

The passage features two simple sentences (out of 16), and they are therefore foregrounded by internal deviation. The sentences 'again she was silent' (5) and 'we can escape from Efrafa' (9) illustrate the outcome of Bigwig's persuasion of Hyzenthlay: after hours of convincing her to leave with him, she agrees to help him. The simple sentences convey the finality of Hyzenthlay's decision and emphasise the importance of the moment in the overall plot, thus further endangering them.

Sentences (12) to (15) employ dashes to separate its clauses, a foregrounding by parallelism as a recurrent structure in four consecutive sentences. The dashes emphasise Hyzenthlay's narration of her vision to Bigwig: the sentences are fragmented as the different elements she can see are introduced. Hyzenthlay provides the information in ascending order from an overview of what she sees ('confusion and fear at nightfall'), to something more focused ('and then men'), and then to specific details ('a rope that snaps', 'a rabbit that rides a hrududu'). Hyzenthlay's interjections and reaction to what she sees are separated from her narration of her vision by the dashes ('no, it is not possible!') and the use of exclamation. The fragmented aspect of those sentences by the dashes iconically conveys Hyzenthlay's panic and feeling of endangerment.

Figures of speech

Sentence (13) includes the simile 'like a dry branch' referring to the sound of 'a rope that snaps'. This simile is foregrounded by external deviation as a comparison is made between a rope and a branch for readers' mental representation of the sound the rope makes. It is also foregrounded by parallelism in the sentence: it is a visual representation following the auditory representation of the action provided by the onomatopoeic verb 'snaps'. In previous scenes of the novel, traps had been set by hunters accompanied by dogs to catch rabbits. Those traps were made of ropes and wood. Therefore, the use of the onomatopoeic verb 'snaps' and the noun 'rope' suggests that Hyzenthlay sees rabbits being captured in traps, thus further contributing to her feeling of danger and fear.

Sentence (14) contains the onomatopoeia *hrududu* (the Lapine word for vehicles with an engine such as cars or tractors) and is thus foregrounded by external deviation because it is not a word in the English language. The sounds of the term *hrududu* create parallel with the object it represents by mimicking the noise of a car's engine. This further illustrates the how the rabbits are anthropomorphised and how Lapine is built: not only do they talk like humans, but they also have their own language in which phonetics and lexis naturally mirror meaning.

Sentence (15) contains the phrase 'tales for kittens on a summer evening', which is foregrounded by external deviation as it compares Hyzenthlay's vision to children's stories. Although this is a metaphor, I consider it also an idiomatic expression in Lapine. As shown above, rabbits in the novel have developed their own language including lexis and syntax rules. It is possible for them to create their own idiomatic expressions too. The metaphor suggests that Hyzenthlay's visions are fables or children's stories, but other rabbits would not know what this means as they still have rabbit lives, despite being anthropomorphised. Thus, creating an idiom involving what rabbits can picture such as their own children ('kittens') and surroundings ('summer evening') ensures that other rabbits understand the phrase's meaning.

Sentence (16) features the simile 'it is like the shapes of trees beyond a field of rain', also including the metaphor 'field of rain' which can be mapped as PRECIPITATION IS SPACE. Overall, the independent clause is foregrounded by external deviation as it compares Hyzenthlay's vision to the trees and the rain. Hyzenthlay's emotions are tied to her vision, and to ensure Bigwig understands her, she uses the surroundings to portray her vision and feelings. Because emotions are unique and abstract, the use of shared experiences such as surroundings to convey those emotions to others (here Bigwig and the reader) allows for clarity. The simile describes the shape of trees in the rain, their shape being blurry, almost unknown. Hyzenthlay is scared not only because of the imminent danger the rabbits are in, but also because her vision is blurred, uncertain, like their fate. This is explicit PF: a direct comparison is made between Hyzenthlay's fear and the visual presentation of the trees in the rain – the surroundings. The metaphor 'field of rain' in this simile is an image metaphor (Lakoff and Turner 1989: 89) and presents the rain as a space ('field'). The metaphor depicts the thickness of the rain, as if it was taking up space in a field of vision. Since it is used to convey Hyzenthlay's blurry vision of the future, it portrays the shape of the trees as being hidden behind a close space.

Sentence (2) includes the metaphor 'my heart is in the frost' which links Hyzenthlay's 'heart' (a human-like metonymy for her emotions) to the 'frost'. The preposition 'in' suggests that the frost is a physical space, and since frost is mostly found on the floor (at least as far as rabbits are concerned), the metaphor suggests that Hyzenthlay feels low, aligning with Lakoff and Johnson's 'orientational metaphor' BAD IS DOWN. Interestingly, this could potentially contrast with the rabbits' nature: to them their burrow would be conceptualised as good, and the notion of UP represents the unknown or danger. However, using the metaphor GOOD IS DOWN would be counter-intuitive to readers as Lakoff and Johnson's (1980: 10–11) orientational metaphors (GOOD IS UP and BAD IS DOWN) are arguably universally shared. Inverting this orientation would generate an additional challenge: not only do readers find it difficult to empathise with non-human characters (Harrison and Hall 2010, Keen 2011, Airenti 2015), if accepted concepts are also challenged, readers could further disengage from the narration. In addition, since Hyzenthlay had lost hope of leaving Efrafa until Bigwig joined the warren, the cold aspect of the frost could represent the fear she felt, and as such the metaphor 'my heart is in the frost' could be mapped as FEAR IS COLD. The cold aspect of the surroundings represents the fear Hyzenthlay feels at the idea of not escaping Efrafa, rendering it an instance of PF. The metaphor creates links between Hyzenthlay's emotions and negative natural elements: the frost (and winter in general) is portrayed as a negative event for the rabbits, rendering the scene easier to picture mentally. This makes the use of PF natural in this instance and throughout the novel: the rabbits employ shared concepts to convey how they feel, which inherently streamlines the process of empathy for readers.

This section demonstrated that a stylistic analysis allows for a comprehensive portrayal of Lapine in an extract from *Watership Down*: from phonetics, lexis, syntax, figures of speech such as idioms or PF, and the rabbits' own body language. In the following section, I aim to explain how figurative language other than anthropomorphism is significant in *Watership Down*, drawing on the concept of metaphorical *visibility*.

Metaphor visibility in *Watership Down*

Visibility (or realisation) is the extent to which a metaphor is realised on the surface of the text and thus is linked to how effortlessly readers notice the use of metaphors during the reading process. According to Stockwell (1992, 2000, see also Goatly 1997), certain forms of metaphors are more visible and noticeable than others. For example, copula constructions following the pattern 'A is B' such as 'Juliet is the sun' (from Shakespeare's *Romeo and Juliet*) are more visible when reading than 'verb-metaphors' (Brooke-Rose 1958: 212) such as 'the wind roared'. Stockwell (1992: 2) suggests there is a cline of metaphoric forms, ranging from the most visible extended metaphors, analogies, similes, and copula metaphors, right through to the most invisible forms such as plain proverbs and fictional texts, where the source domain does not appear at all in the language. The cline also relates this visibility of metaphor to their level of reader effort required for their perception. The overall metaphor for *Watership Down* is linked to anthropomorphism which has for its metaphorical expression RABBITS ARE PEOPLE, mirroring Herman's mapping (2018: 139) of Human-Source-Animal-Target Projections for Anthropomorphic Projections on his continuum. The persistent and extended articulation of this metaphor across the novel reinforces its visibility, and its ease of mapping for readers. It becomes habituated and simple for readers to identify the human-like qualities of the rabbits.

On the other hand, other metaphors featured in the novel are generally idioms and emotion metaphors linked to the rabbits' environment, often instances of PF, as discussed above. PF's mapping is EMOTIONS ARE SURROUNDINGS, and it is most often an extended metaphor (Pager-McClymont 2021, Kövecses 2002: 51; see also 'conceit metaphor' in Wales 2011: 78) as it requires the presence of three criteria to occur (animated entities, emotions, surroundings). Because there is no guarantee of where in the text the criteria will be featured, it is not possible to specifically point out on each occasion where PF occurs and how much context to include, which renders the metaphor an extended one (for a detailed discussion on context, see Pager-McClymont 2022: 8–9). Overall, this makes PF a low-visibility metaphor, because of how scattered its criteria (and thus domains) can be, especially when they are featured implicitly and must be inferred. I argue that there is little research on metaphors and idioms in Lapine because they tend to be instances of PF, and are harder to discern, blending in the narration to allow for an embodied narration from the rabbits' perspective. Because the fictional aspect of the anthropomorphism is so foregrounded by external deviation, idioms that would otherwise not exist for humans and would typically also be foregrounded ultimately do not stand out as much in the readers' eyes.

Furthermore, the idioms and other metaphors in Lapine being instances of PF is what makes the language natural to readers: rabbits' comfort, survival, and experience are dependent on their surroundings. Their use of surroundings to communicate with other rabbit characters thus seems logical: they express abstract concepts such as their rabbit emotions (which readers might not be familiar with) through the shared concrete concept of their surroundings, known by readers and other rabbits. This allows for the representation of a story featuring characters that are more difficult to empathise with or understand.

Conclusion

The rabbits in *Watership Down* are anthropomorphised to some degree: they can speak like humans, but still live their rabbit lives and conceptualise the world as rabbits, including drawing on their surroundings to convey how they feel to other characters who share those surroundings. The use of pathetic fallacy to convey emotions in Lapine allows for readers (who are also likely familiar with these natural surroundings) to empathise. Lapine is embedded in the narration, appearing natural for the rabbits, which arguably allows for a richer mental representation of them in the novel.

In narratology studies, there is some criticism around giving animals speech or other human qualities as these are inherently informed by human motivations, or as humans perceive them (see Harrison and Hall 2010, Airenti 2015). Even though this is still the case in *Watership Down*, the stylistic way that the animals are anthropomorphised reflects the rabbits' nature. Indeed, one can argue that animals can differ between right and wrong (Rowlands 2015) – though maybe not between Good and Evil. The characters' quest for a better warren is not too far from genuine rabbit behaviour in the wild. Rabbits being territorial and being able to bond with others also shows that the friendships and rivalries in the novel (as exemplified in the analysis in this chapter) are equally quite natural. The way Lapine is constructed mirrors rabbit communication to an extent by using primarily fricative sounds in Lapine lexis or emphasising movement of the nose when they communicate. Lastly, the rabbits' emotions portrayed in the novel are basic emotions such as fear, excitement, sadness, love; all of which rabbits experience in the wild. Rabbits are bonded animals and thus experience love for their mate, and sadness if their mate dies. They experience fear of being hunted, and excitement if their needs are met (for instance shown by 'binkies' – rabbits' jumps of happiness). Typical, specifically human emotions are also not attributed to the rabbits in the novel, further showing a naturalistic approach to their portrayal.

This realistic portrayal of rabbits in *Watership Down* can be seen when compared to other animal narratives. For example, in *The Wind in the Willows* (Grahame 1908), characters are portrayed as stand-ins for humans (they drive cars, go boating), rendering the narrative an Animal Allegory. *Animal Farm* (Orwell 1945) equally stands as an Animal Allegory, with animals behaving like humans to the extent that some of them wear uniforms, within a hierarchical society. In *Hollow Kingdom* (Buxton 2019, see an analysis by Norledge 2022), the narrative not only features Anthropomorphic Projections where animals can converse and express emotions, but it is also an example of *Umwelt* modelling (Norledge 2022: 400) as the animals' lives and surroundings are thoroughly explained by the crow narrator's perspective. *Watership Down* does not feature *Umwelt* modelling because there is no clear commentary nor reflections from the rabbits on their experiences or habitat. Nevertheless, through authorial choices, including the way Lapine is constructed as a fictional language, readers can access a window into the rabbits' fictional world, rendered accessible to us because it is built bearing reality in mind.

References

Adams, R. (1972) *Watership Down*. London: Rex Collings.
Airenti, G. (2015) 'The cognitive bases of anthropomorphism: from relatedness to empathy', *International Journal of Social Robotics* 7 (1): 117–27.
Anderson, K. (1993) 'Shaping self through spontaneous oral narration in Richard Adams' *Watership Down*', *Journal of the Fantastic in the Arts* 6.1 (21): 25–33.
Bae, B. C. and Young, R. M. (2008) 'A use of flashback and foreshadowing for surprise arousal in narrative using a plan-based approach', in U. Spierling and N. Szilas (eds) *Joint International Conference on Interactive Digital Storytelling*. Berlin: Springer, pp. 156–67.
Bekoff, M. (2013) 'Animal consciousness and science matter: anthropomorphism is not anti-science', *Relations* 1 (1): 61–8.
Bernaerts, L., Caracciolo, M., Herman, L. and Vervaeck, B. (2014) 'The storied lives of non-human narrators', *Narrative* 22 (1): 68–93.
Brooke-Rose, C. (1958) *A Grammar of Metaphor*. London: Mercury Books.
Buxton, K. J. (2019) *Hollow Kingdom*. London: Headline.
Caracciolo, M. (2016) *Strange Narrators in Contemporary Fiction: Explorations in Readers' Engagement with Characters*. Lincoln: Nebraska University Press.
Carroll, N. (1996) 'The paradox of suspense', in P. Vorderer (ed.) *Suspense: Conceptualizations, Theoretical Analyses, and Empirical Explorations*. London: Routledge, pp. 147–88.
Chapman, E. L. (1978) 'The shaman as hero and spiritual leader: mythmaking in *Watership Down* and *Shardik*', *Mythlore* 5 (2): 7–12.
Citron, F. M. M., Cacciari, C., Kucharski, M., Beck, L., Conrad, M. and Jacobs, A. M. (2015) 'When emotions are expressed figuratively: psycholinguistic and affective norms of 619 idioms for German (PANIG)', *Behavior Research Methods* 48 (1): 91–111.
Culpeper, J. (2001) *Language and Characterisation: People in Plays and Other Texts*. Harlow: Pearson Longman.
Cunningham, M. R. (1979) 'Weather, mood, and helping behavior: quasi experiments with the sunshine samaritan', *Journal of Personality and Social Psychology* 37 (11): 1947–56.
Dancygier, B. (2014) 'Intensity and texture in imagery', in P. Stockwell and S. Whiteley (eds) *The Cambridge Handbook of Stylistics*. Cambridge: Cambridge University Press, pp. 212–28.
Goatly, A. (1997) *The Language of Metaphors*. London: Routledge.
Grahame, K. (1908) *The Wind in the Willows*. London: Methuen.
Grider, R. A. (2019) *Bilingual Rabbits, Bilingual Readers:* Watership Down *as a Case for Animal Texts in Translation* (unpublished master's dissertation). North Dakota State University.
Harrison, M. A. and Hall, A. E. (2010) 'Anthropomorphism, empathy, and perceived communicative ability vary with phylogenetic relatedness to humans', *Journal of Social, Evolutionary, and Cultural Psychology* 4 (1): 34–48.

Herman, D. (2011) 'Storyworld/*Umwelt*: nonhuman experiences in graphic narratives', *Substance* 40 (1): 156–81.
Herman, D. (2018) *Narratology Beyond the Human*. Oxford: Oxford University Press.
Hough, G. (1963) *A Preface to the Faerie Queene*. New York: Norton.
Howarth, E. and Hoffman, M. (1984) 'A multidimensional approach to the relationship between mood and weather', *British Journal of Psychology* 75 (1): 15–23.
Iwata, Y. (2009) *Creating Suspense and Surprise in Short Literary Fiction: A Stylistic and Narratological Approach* (unpublished doctoral dissertation). University of Birmingham.
Keen, S. (2011) 'Fast tracks to narrative empathy: anthropomorphism and dehumanization in graphic narratives', *SubStance* 40 (1): 135–55.
Kövecses, Z. (2002) *Metaphor: A Practical Introduction*. Oxford: Oxford University Press.
Kövecses, Z. (2008) 'Metaphor and emotion', in R. W. Gibbs (ed.) *The Cambridge Handbook of Metaphor and Thought*. Cambridge: Cambridge University Press, pp. 380–96.
Lakoff, G. and Johnson, M. (1980) *Metaphors We Live By*. Chicago: University of Chicago Press.
Lakoff, G. and Turner, M. (1989) *More than Cool Reason: A Field Guide to Poetic Metaphor*. Chicago: University of Chicago Press.
Leatherland, D. (2020) 'The capacities and limitations of language in animal fantasies', *Humanimalia* 11 (2): 101–30.
Leech, G. N. (2008) *Language of Literature: Style and Foregrounding*. London: Routledge.
Meyer, C. A. (1994) 'The power of myth and rabbit survival in Richard Adams' *Watership Down*', *Journal of the Fantastic in the Arts* 3 (4): 139–50.
Miall, D. S. (2007) 'Foregrounding and the sublime: Shelley in Chamonix', *Language and Literature* 16 (2): 155–68.
Miall, D. S. and Kuiken, D. (1994) 'Foregrounding, defamiliarization, and affect: response to literary stories', *Poetics* 22 (5): 389–407.
Mukařovský, J. (1964) 'The esthetics of language', in P. Garvin (ed. and trans.) *A Prague School Reader on Esthetics, Literary Structure, and Style*, Washington: Georgetown University Press, pp. 31–69.
Norledge, J. (2022) 'Experiencing dystopia through *Umwelt*: modelling the nonhuman animal in *Hollow Kingdom*', *English Studies* 103 (3): 386–406.
Orwell, G. (1945) *Animal Farm*. London: Secker & Warburg.
Pager-McClymont, K. (2021) *Communicating Emotions through Surroundings: A Stylistic Model of Pathetic Fallacy* (unpublished doctoral thesis). University of Huddersfield.
Pager-McClymont, K. (2022) 'Linking emotions to surroundings: a stylistic model of pathetic fallacy', *Language and Literature* 31 (3): 428–54.
Palmer, A. (2004) *Fictional Minds*. Lincoln: University of Nebraska Press.
van Peer, W. (2007) 'Introduction to foregrounding: a state of the art', *Language and Literature* 16 (2): 99–104.
Rowlands, M. (2015) *Can Animals be Moral?* Oxford: Oxford University Press.
Salovey, P. and Mayer, J. D. (1990) 'Emotional intelligence', *Imagination, Cognition and Personality* 9 (3): 185–211.
Seton, E. T. (1898) *Wild Animals I Have Known*. New York: Scribner.

Short, M. H. (1996) *Exploring the Language of Poems, Plays, and Prose*. Harlow: Pearson Longman.

Stockwell, P. (1992) 'The metaphorics of literary reading', *Liverpool Papers in Language and Discourse* 4: 52–80.

Stockwell, P. (2000) *The Poetics of Science Fiction*. London: Longman.

Stockwell, P. (2014) 'Atmosphere and tone', in P. Stockwell and S. Whiteley (eds) *The Cambridge Handbook of Stylistics*. Cambridge: Cambridge University Press, pp. 360–74.

von Uexküll, J. (1957) 'A stroll through the worlds of animals and men: a picture book of invisible worlds', in C. H. Schiller (ed. and trans.) *Instinctive Behavior: The Development of a Modern Concept* [original 1934]. New York: International University Press, pp. 5–76.

Wales, K. (2011) *A Dictionary of Stylistics* (3rd edn). Harlow: Pearson Longman.

Weil, K. (2012) *Thinking Animals: Why Animal Studies Now?* New York: Columbia University Press.

CHAPTER 14

Unspeakable languages

Peter Stockwell

In the final chapter in this *Reading Fictional Languages* volume, Peter Stockwell considers those fictional languages that are difficult or impossible to represent in the language of fiction. These *nonlangs* appear in various indirect forms: as minimal illustrative elements, as gestures towards a language that cannot be comprehended by human minds, or by simple metalinguistic and abstract description. Often, the conceptually ineffable is realised iconically in literary fiction as the prose is rendered poetically into syntactic or semantic fractures. The different functions of fictional languages are presented in correspondence with stylistic realisations and with embodied forms from the humanoid to the ethereal.

A scheme for the unspeakable

In his *Chronicon Anglicanum*, Ralph of Coggeshall (c. 1225) recounts the legend of the green children of Woolpit, a boy and a girl with green skin who appeared from a cavern near the village of Woolpit in Suffolk, eastern England, at some time in the twelfth century. They seemed disorientated, were frightened of the sun, did not understand the food they were given and refused to eat it even though they were clearly hungry. As mystifying as their green hue was the fact that they spoke a language that no one in Woolpit could understand. The boy soon died, but the girl survived, learned English, and told the tale of how they came from an underground civilisation of green people called St Martin's Land, where it was permanently twilight (Stevenson 1875: 118–20). Coggeshall was recounting the story first recorded by William of Newburgh (c. 1197) whose account is framed as a miracle of Christian redemption (Walsh and Kennedy 1988: 114–17). Coggeshall tones down the religious framing a little, humanises the children, and wryly characterises the girl in later life as somewhat loose in her conduct! Both accounts are framed as historical events. The origins of the green children have been variously hypothesised through the centuries as being foreign

Flemish-speakers suffering from iron deficiency, as supernatural fairies or escaped demons, or as extra-terrestrials (see Harris 1998, Clark 2006). All of the original and later sources are tales of tales, indirect recounts of the story that William of Newburgh even says he was reluctant to believe. No sources actually give any examples of the language that the green children spoke, so it is impossible to say whether they were indeed foreign visitors, supernatural beings, or aliens cast away on the strange planet of Earth.

The speculative, fantastical, and science fictional tradition has often gestured in this way towards languages that are not actually articulated in the text. Instead of *conlangs* we have *nonlangs* – communication systems that cannot be exemplified but can only be referenced or pointed towards, or are cited mystically, mysteriously, or vaguely. These are the unspeakable languages of fiction.

In this chapter, I consider how science fiction has dealt with the linguistically ineffable, and how writers in the genre have imagined futuristic, alternate, or alien languages in different ways and for different purposes. The key to understanding language and cognition is the notion of *embodiment* (Shapiro 2011, Varela 2017). This is the thesis that language, perception, cognition, and consciousness – all the paraphernalia of mind – are related and defined by the fact that they originate in an integrated body, interacting with other embodied minds. For example, it is argued, any apparent universals in structure, metaphor, sense, or typology across the world's languages can be understood to be founded on the fact that humans share a basic bodily experience of the world (Lakoff and Johnson 1999). When those bodies are altered in fiction, either because they are technologically augmented, or evolved by deep time, or cast into mechanical or software forms, or are imagined as aliens or monsters, or have even become disembodied and ethereal altogether, then it is clear that the language of those bodies must be affected too.

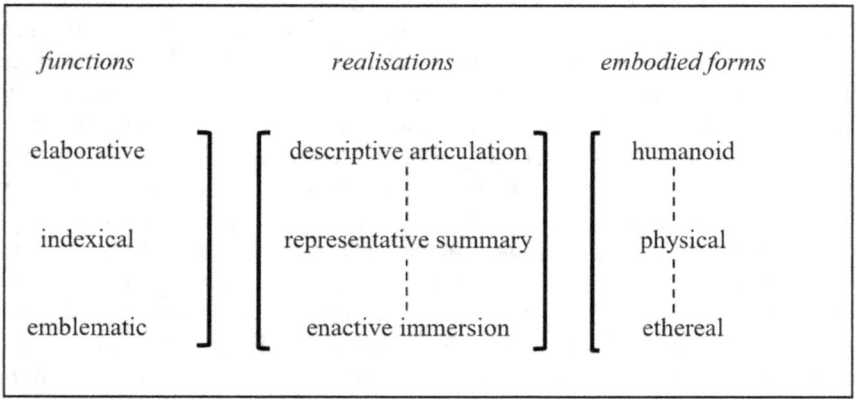

Graphic 14.1 Correlations of function, realisation, and embodiment

The language of a fictionalised altered body can be understood along three dimensions or broad functions as I have briefly outlined elsewhere (*elaborative, indexical,* and *emblematic* functions, Stockwell 2005, and see Noletto, Chapter 10 this volume): the language can simply elaborate the richness of the imagined world; it can indicate the disjunction and counterparts between the imagined world and our own; and language can itself serve a thematic role in the literary work. (The last of these has been expanded more granularly by Noletto [2022: 22] as *rhetorical, diegetic,* and *paratextual* functions.) These functions can be broadly correlated with three stylistic forms of realisation by which the imagined language can be manifest. First, in order to work as a world-builder at all, the imagined language has to be directly described or articulated. This articulation can range from extremely thorough, rich, and highly developed conlangs right through to the odd word or single utterance reproduced in the text. Second, the newly imagined language can be outlined or described in summary, as if at one remove, as it were. It is not necessary to reproduce or represent the language itself, but simply set out its principles, mechanism, and characteristics. Third, the language can be gestured towards without being actually represented at all. This often takes the form of a poetic enactment of the sensation or essence of the language for a reader, as if a reader is immersed in the sense and feeling of the language without being exposed to it directly with a simple example or translation. Note that these three functions and three stylistic mechanisms are only rough correlations.

In the rest of this chapter, I will show – also broadly – how these functions and manifestations are used to fictionalise the languages associated with three different bodily forms of the human and humanoid, the non-human but physically monstrous or alien, and finally the disembodied and ethereal form of alien life. In spite of my 'broad' disclaimer, it is noticeable that where the elaborative function is prominent in an sf text, the invented language tends to be described directly, and the users tend to be human or recognisably humanoid (Tolkien's Elves being an example). Similarly, where language is prominently thematically emblematic, it tends to be realised iconistically so that a reader has to enter into its stylistic forms; often the source of this type of language is non-human and often not even physically embodied (the heptapods and their language in Ted Chiang's [2002] 'Story of your life' is a rough example of this). It is important to emphasise that these correlations are loose tendencies and shade into each other though. (Nadsat in Burgess' [1962] *A Clockwork Orange* is prominently indexical as a political satire, yet it is directly described and its users are human – though arguably animalised and brutish, even there).

Fully described and articulated imaginary languages are actually less common across literature and film, which is partly why those fully worked-out and rich conlangs (as featured across this book) are so widely studied and prominent. For the most part, the fictional languages that feature across all literary fictions are not rich conlangs but are more sketchy, minimal, or illustrative in nature. However, this is not to diminish their significance nor utility: the sociolinguistic principle that all varieties of language are at least adequate for their cultural purpose seems generally to apply in the literary context too.

There are very many examples in fiction where the imagined language is directly articulated in the text. This *Reading Fictional Languages* book mentions or explores several of them: Quenya, Sindarin, Klingon, Dothraki, Valyrian, Na'vi. These are not simply gestured towards but actually appear in their 'authentic' form in the text or on-screen. As we can see from these and others, many conlangs are exuberantly over-engineered for their functional requirements in their fictional worlds. Tolkien's families of Elvish languages and dialects are thoroughly worked out far beyond their instrumental value in his novels (Weiner and Marshall 2011, and see Beinhoff, Chapter 6 in this volume, and Mooshammer et al., Chapter 7 in this volume), but *The Lord of the Rings* also features Entish, the language of the tree-creatures known as Ents. Almost no words in Entish appear in the novels because its sonorous and long-winded phonology cannot be represented in writing, and no non-Ents have been able to learn it. Only the phrase 'a-lalla-lalla-rumba-kamanda-lind-or-burúmë' appears (in *The Two Towers*, Tolkien 2005: 465), where it is roughly glossed as meaning 'hill', but even this translation is presented as being doubtful. Entish consequently appears not in any sort of descriptive articulation but simply as a representative summary. It is not only unspeakable but literally unreadable.

Unreadable languages

Where an imagined language is simply pointed at, rather than appearing in full, the stylistic format tends to be at a more distanced form of generalisation. Instead of specific quoted utterances of actual words and phrases, the narrative will explain the imagined language almost as if in a general encyclopaedia. In Robert Heinlein's (1949) short novella, 'Gulf', for example, 'Speedtalk' is an imagined language invented for advanced 'New Men', in which 'one phonetic symbol was equivalent to an entire word in a "normal" language; one Speedtalk word was equal to an entire sentence. The language consequently was learned by letter units rather than by word units – but each word was spoken and listened to as a single structured gestalt' (Heinlein 1949b: 66). Of course, for obvious reasons of impossibility but also because the reader is a not a New Man, no actual translated examples of Speedtalk can be given. Only this mysterious exchange is reproduced early on in the novella, without explanation:

Male: 'tsʉmaeq?'
Female: 'nø!'
Male: 'zUlntsɨ.'
Female: 'ɨpbit' New Jersey.'

(Heinlein 1949a: 84)

These sounds purport to be what the protagonist, Gilead, hears outside his room. But of course they are narratorialised very strongly in the written form of the strikethrough accents on 'o', 'i', and 'u', and the capitalised 'U' in what is presented as if it is in fact authentic direct speech. It is not certain what these sounds mean, though it is evident that the pragmatics of a question and an exclamation are still carried even in Speedtalk by intonation (marked here by '?' and '!').

In Roger Zelazny's (1971) 'A rose for Ecclesiastes', the only Martian language word that appears (twice) directly is 'M'narra' (Zelazny 1971: 79 and 83) – which is not translated but is, in context, evidently a greeting. This story is about a linguist who learns both the Martians' vernacular and their 'High Tongue' and is allowed to read their sacred texts, written in the latter. He masters some pragmatic features, such as 'their Eleven Forms of Politeness' (Zelazny 1971: 73), but the crux of the story arises because he arrogantly assumes his expertise in their intercultural norms and is proven badly wrong at the end, in an unrequited love affair. The only description of the language that otherwise appears is as follows:

> The High and Low Tongues were not so dissimilar as they had first seemed. I had enough of the one to get me through the murkier parts of the other. I had the grammar and all the commoner irregular verbs down cold; the dictionary I was constructing grew by the day, like a tulip, and would bloom shortly [...]
>
> They wrote about concrete things: rock, sand, water, winds; and the tenor couched within these elemental symbols was fiercely pessimistic.
>
> (Zelazny 1971: 78)

Aside from the greeting 'M'narra' and the name of the Martian matriarch 'M'Cwyie', the reader is given no further examples of either of the diglossic forms of Martian. Instead, the gesture towards the language is presented in summary, where the function of this style is not so much any elaborative world-building as to indicate the difference between the Martians and the Earth humans. In this case, the Martians are sufficiently humanoid for the linguist, Gallinger, to be able to mate with a Martian female, manipulated into doing so by the Martians themselves. Again, though, the fact that the Martians are not seen speaking their own language serves to remove some of their human-like autonomy: Gallinger speaks their language and mistakes them for human in belief and emotions, but the reader, without access to their actual language forms, is kept at a distance. This empathetic divergence, iconically carried in the stylistic formal difference for Gallinger and the reader, carries the emotional punch at the end of the narrative. In short, Gallinger is in an elaborative relationship with the Martians, while we readers are in an indexical relationship with them through their language presentation.

In Greg Bear's (1985) *Eon* and its sequels, the humans are future versions of us, returned to Earth orbit in a modified asteroid called the 'Thistledown', with an internal chamber that is infinitely long through time. The future humans augment their spoken language with 'picts':

> The President's advocate was not pleased with the news Olmy brought.
> 'The P.M. had no suspicion of this when you alone were sent?' Toller picted. The symbols that flashed between the two men came from pictor torques around their necks, devices which generated and projected the graphicspeak that had developed over the centuries in the Thistledown and in the Axis City. [...]
> Toller picted an unpleasant image of a roiling nest of snake-like creatures. [...]
> Toller raised his eyebrows and picted four orange rectangles of surprise.
> (Bear 1985: 258–9)

Clearly the pict system here is both iconic (distaste via snake images) and symbolic (surprise as an orange rectangle). Other than this mention, though, graphicspeak itself is never used nor illustrated directly. As in the excerpt above, the meaning of the pict sequence is rendered in English in direct speech form as if narratorially translated, or as a narrative report of the speech act (unpleasantness, or surprise).

These three examples feature humanoid characters altered from us by evolution. In H. G. Wells' (1895) *The Time Machine*, the Traveller arrives in the year 802,701 to find that the human class system has resulted in speciation into the placid surface-dwelling Eloi and the more monstrous subterranean Morlocks. No examples of either of their languages are directly reproduced; instead the Time Traveller narrates his sense of the Eloi's speech as 'a strange and very sweet and liquid tongue', 'speaking in soft cooing notes to each other' (Wells 1895: 37, 39), and soon his 'first attempts to make the exquisite little sounds of their language' meant that 'presently I had a score of noun substantives at least at my command; and then I got to demonstrative pronouns, and even the verb "to eat". But it was slow work' (Wells 1895: 44). The grotesque Morlocks' language represents their inhumanity even more distantly: 'I tried to call to them, but the language they had was apparently different from that of the Over-world people' (Wells 1895: 91). In spite of the speciation, the Morlocks are presented as cannibals, farming the Eloi for food. In different ways, then, the Eloi and the Morlocks are animalised, literally and morally, respectively, and the different representations of their language reflect this.

Where the body is different, so too must be the cognitive embodiment of language. In George Lucas' *Star Wars* films (1977ff.), the humanoid android C3PO can speak in English, but he has to translate the beeps and whistles of the barrel-shaped droid R2D2. In Ursula K. Le Guin's (1983:

11) imagined 'therolinguistics', the language of ants is written 'in touch-gland exudation on degenerated acacia seeds [...] No known dialect of Ant employs any verbal person except the third person singular and plural and the third person plural.' At the conceptual metaphor level, GOOD IS DOWN, contrary to most human languages, because 'down is where security, peace and home are to be found' (Le Guin 1983: 13). Her story ends imagining 'the still less communicative, still more passive, wholly atemporal, cold, volcanic poetry of the rocks' (Le Guin 1983: 19): no example of the rocks' speech is given, because we would not be able to understand it. In China Miéville's (2011) *Embassytown*, the double-voicedness of the extremely alien aliens, the Arieki, can only be articulated by humans by cloning twins to speak each side of the alien conscious mind. Throughout the novel, the aliens' bodies themselves are represented in highly vague, fluid, edge-less descriptions, as if their bodies themselves cannot be separated perceptually from the environment of their planet. In Alastair Reynolds' (2021) *Inhibitor Phase*, the narrator Warglass attempts to bluff his way into an alien starship:

> I dabbed my hands against the surface. I made a series of precise gestural strokes, using the heels of my palms to imitate the narrow but elongated contact area of a Nestbuilder secondary appendage. I worked quickly, since I had to emulate the effect of four limbs with only two of my own [...] The surface blistered and darkened in definite geometric patches, indicating a query as to my credentials and intentions. It was no small thing to demand admittance to a Nestbuilder ship, even in the language of their kind.
> (Reynolds 2021: 424)

Once inside, he discovers that the Nestbuilders have been taken over by a second parasitical species: 'They have a name for themselves, but it would break our sanity to utter it. Call them *Slugs* [...] They haunt the bodies of the Nestbuilders, running a zombie civilization that only looks like the Nestbuilders from outside' (Reynolds 2021: 431). He tries to communicate with a 'mass of pseudopods' or fronds:

> The fronds were stimulating my suit with chemical and electrical signals and expecting the suit to respond in kind, just as if it were a Nestbuilder's sensory appendage. Cautiously, following a set of pre-programmed decision steps, my suit reciprocated the contact. It was generating localised electrical and chemical emissions at the points where the fronds touched it: attempting a kind of deeper, more intimate form of the gestural grammar.
> In a manner the frond terminal was talking to me, or at least attempting to talk. The impulses picked up by the suit were packaged and translated into forms compatible with my neural systems. But that

did not mean that I understood them. It was a discussion going on at a level beyond my own direct comprehension.

(Reynolds 2021: 436)

In each of these examples, the language of the non-humans (droids, ants, slugs) cannot be articulated directly and can only be translated for the reader. In general in sf, there is a correlation between the articulated readerly accessibility of the imagined capacity for language and the projection of consciousness, civilisation, intelligence, and morality of the imagined species. Monstrous aliens are animalised, and their brutishness is often reflected in the aesthetic or cognitive distance of their language compared with the English of the surrounding narrative.

Suzette Haden Elgin's (2019a) novel *Native Tongue*, first published in 1984, is most famous for her invention of Láadan, a conlang developed by the oppressed women in the novel as a secret language grounded in feminine experience. Láadan is a full-spectrum conlang, with a fully worked out phonology, morphology, grammar, and rich lexis (see Elgin 1988, and Norledge, Chapter 11 in this volume). However, there are other languages in the novel which are not articulated at all. Radical Linguists in the story have successfully trained babies to acquire extra-terrestrial languages for trade purposes. Government agents set themselves against these radicals whom they scornfully term 'Lingoes' and conduct their own experiments on babies in an effort to enable them to acquire these alien languages as native speakers. However, one of the 'nonhumanoid' alien languages proves deadly for the babies to learn, as one of the agents explains:

'The cognitive scientists tell us that whatever the hardwiring is in Terrans, it's reasonably close to whatever it is in humanoid Aliens, because the brains and sensory systems are similar enough, even if there's tentacles coming out of one humanoid's ears and not of some other's [...] There's something about the way the nonhumanoid Aliens perceive things, something about the "reality" they make out of stimuli, so impossible it freaks out the babies and destroys their central nervous systems permanently [...] We've tried putting the baby in the Interface for just a fraction of a second... makes no damn difference. Come the time that the baby somehow gets an Alien perception, it self-destructs, all the same.'

(Elgin 2019a: 155–6)

This particular alien language is never directly articulated in the novel at all, presumably because the reader would suffer the same fatal consequence as the babies. It is therefore simply gestured towards very indirectly, as above. By stark contrast, Láadan is represented in the novel and especially its sequels (Elgin 2019a, 2019b, 2019c), and it exists outside its fictional context in dictionaries, grammars, and a rich set of language-learning resources (see

Elgin 2019d). The Alien language is named Beta-2, a name that encapsulates its deflected, indirect, and secondary nature. It retains the function simply of indexing the radical difference between our human languages and the aliens, and also the emblematic function of thematising the malignancy of the (male) government agents.

These issues concern the extent to which an alien or imagined language is translatable or even thinkable. '[N]o human mind can view the universe as it is perceived by a nonhumanoid extraterrestrial and not self-destruct [...] No human being, so far as he knew, could share the worldview of a nonhumanoid' (Elgin 2019a: 71–2). Human(oid) languages can be translated into each other because we all share a fundamental physical experience. However, as Wittgenstein (2009: 235 [fragment 327]) asserted, 'If a lion could talk, we wouldn't be able to understand it.' What he means here, it is generally accepted, is that a lion's worldview is so embodied in lionness that the essential structure of its thinking and therefore its language would be incomprehensible to us (see also Nagel 1974). In *Native Tongue*, the 'Aliens-in-Residence' (AIRYs) often have immaterial, even imperceptible bodies:

> Sometimes Showard wasn't sure he saw the AIRY, really; the way it flickered (??), and never any pattern to the flickering (??), it drove the Terran eye to a constant search for order until there were great flat spots of color floating in the air between you and the source of the sensory stimulation. And then there were other times when you profoundly wished that you *couldn't* see it.
> (Elgin 2019a: 50)

Compared with this immateriality, the essentials of a lion's experience and embodiment are probably not too different from a human's, but if Wittgenstein's lion had been an alien, that would have been a better instance of the key notion of *ineffability*.

> Why think that the kinds of representations that are available in human languages and to human minds are good enough to represent all facts and truths? We can say that a fact is structurally ineffable if the source of its ineffability is the required structure of a representation of it, i.e. a structure we do not have access to. Structural ineffability gets at the heart of the matter. Any limitation of this kind would pass the incommunicability test: if there are facts that cannot be represented by representations available to the human mind then aliens who do not have this limitation could not communicate them to us. These facts would be in principle beyond us, not just due to our location, our access to objects, but due to the nature of our minds. These facts would be ineffable for us in the sense that matters.
> (Hofweber 2017: 142)

What Hofweber here calls 'structural ineffability' goes beyond a mere untranslatableness of words and instead concerns concepts, relationships, and complex systems of thought that are not articulatable because they are beyond our ability of mind to grasp. His analogy is that of a honeybee which can communicate the location of nectar but is mentally incapable of representing a fact such as an economic crisis in another, distant country. 'We can imagine that there are vastly superior aliens or gods, say, who look down at us like we look down at the honeybee' (Hofweber 2017: 133).

H. G. Wells uses the same perspectival analogy at the beginning of *The War of the Worlds*, imagining the Martians looking down on humanity 'almost as narrowly as a man with a microscope might scrutinise the transient creatures that swarm and multiply in a drop of water'. These 'minds that are to our minds as ours are to those of the beasts that perish, intellects vast and cool and unsympathetic' (Wells 1898: 3) are revealed eventually to be monstrous within their heat-ray machines. And aside from their distress cry 'Ulla, ulla', they seem to have no language at all. Not only are no words of Martian ever represented, but the narrator suggests they communicate by telepathy: 'I am convinced – as firmly as I am convinced of anything – that the Martians interchanged thoughts without any physical intermediation' (Wells 1898: 211). The Martians' lack of spoken language representation aligns with their monstrousness, but there is no suggestion that their motives and mindsets are ineffable. These are plain to deduce from their invasive murderous actions.

The imperialistic Martians in *The War of the Worlds* are all too human, in many ways, but it is their lack of an articulated language that helps to render them animalistic and monstrous. Their actions suggest that the content of their telepathic communication is at least knowable, for a human mind, even if their actual language does not appear. In the next section, I will consider cases where the language of the aliens is absent because it is unknowable to the merely human mind of the reader.

Unknowable languages

Malmgren (1993) differentiates between 'human aliens' and 'alien aliens', and the distinction is not just between human and non-humanoid but sets up a scale of strangeness away from the human. At the furthest extreme are aliens who have become disembodied, ethereal, or have transcended our reality completely. In the 'Culture' universe of Iain M. Banks, advanced civilisations move through a period of technological supremacy to the point at which many of them decide to 'sublime'. This involves every individual in that civilisation agreeing to leave the physical universe and move to a set of higher dimensions. The Culture itself is an advanced technological anarchist utopia that has persisted for so long that other civilisations that have sublimed cannot understand why the people and artificial intelligences

('Minds') that comprise the Culture have not also sublimed. However, the Culture seems to view subliming as an immoral rejection of responsibility for the material universe (see Clarke 2018).

The ineffability of the Sublime is gestured at but cannot be articulated:

'[... I]t's all very ... inchoate. Inexplicable. Hard – impossible – to translate back into here, the here-and-now.'
'Try.'
The *Zoologist* sighed, put its long-fingered hands to its face and made a sort of patting motion. 'You still don't get it, do you?'
'What? How intrinsically ungraspable it all is?'
'Pretty much. See that insect? [...]
(Banks 2012: 143)

The *Zoologist* Mind then goes on to use the same insect analogy used by Hofweber (2017) above to try to explain how far above our puny minds the ungraspable concept is.

The Real – with its vast volumes of nothing between the planets, stars, systems and galaxies – was basically mostly vacuum; an averaged near-nothing incapable of true complexity due to its inescapable impoverishment of structure and the sheer overwhelming majority of nothingness over substance. The Sublime was utterly different: packed with existence, constantly immanentising context, endlessly unfolding being-scape.
(Banks 2012: 149)

The stylistic shift here from describing the Real universe to trying to describe the ineffable Sublime demonstrates a reliance on broken syntax, new coinages, and poetic forms to capture its ungraspability. A reader might expect a clause with a main verb after the colon, or a list of noun phrases in a parallel structure, instead of a mixture of appositions, continuous verb forms, and ambiguous agency in 'immanentising' and 'unfolding'. 'Immanentising' reaches for an obscure word from political theology meaning to create heaven on earth, and the explanation ends in a coinage, 'being-scape'. These sorts of stylistic patterns are highly characteristic literary devices when trying to gesture towards the ineffable.

The Culture does also have a common language, Marain, which is a complex computer code-based system. It is available to humans in both spoken and written form but is ultimately based on a glyph composed on a 3x3 grid to create angular 'letters', some of which correspond with thirty-two phonemes. However, the artificial intelligence Minds also extend this grid into cube form, and then into eleven higher dimensions so that Marain is massively articulatable. Needless to say, this super-dimensional extension of the language is not accessible to human readers of the novels.

Banks (1994) set out the principles of Marain in a short descriptive essay that describes the language; and though there are brief lines in the Marain script in *The Player of Games* (Banks 1988) and elsewhere, the language itself never directly appears, other than in translation to English direct speech. The Minds chat to each other in a highly idiomatic and casual register that is written in English, though is presumably 'actually' conducted in Marain. Aside from its emblematic theme around the notion that the Culture is highly advanced compared with the reader's world, it is asserted 'that when Culture people didn't speak Marain for a long time and did speak another language, they were liable to change; they acted differently, they started to think in that other language, they lost the carefully balanced interpretative structure of the Culture language, left its subtle shifts of cadence, tone and rhythm behind for, in virtually every case, something much cruder' (Banks 1988: 29).

This hard connection between the complexity of language and the complexity of possible thought is a consistent thread in the popular understanding of language across science fiction (as a strong version of the 'Sapir-Whorf hypothesis', see Noletto and Lopes 2020, Koparan 2020). It also underlies the thesis that our conceptualisation is limited by our physical and experiential condition, so that the limits even of our imaginable languages are the outer limits of what we can ever know (see Moro 2016, Miller 2021). It finds its correlate in a literalisation of the cognitive body in the popular pulp-sf imagery of super-intelligent aliens possessing massive heads. In Banks' Culture, the Minds are artificial intelligences that occupy ten-metre-long hardware ellipsoids, but whose microcircuitry extends down to the quantum scale and also into several higher dimensions (Banks 1987: 89) – in effect, their massive super-intelligent heads are extended into hyperspace.

The effect of such extrapolation is a foregrounded diminishment of the human reader. We are well and truly put in our place by the sense of the infinite, or at least the ungraspably large, complex, and inaccessible. This thrilling vertigo is a key poetic feature of science fiction, of course (see Benford 1987). The ineffable is a stylistic emblem for the vast realms of higher and larger complexity that we cannot understand but which the narrative can gesture towards in various different stylistic ways.

The stylistic shift in gear can be represented subtly. In Frank Herbert's (1972) *Whipping Star*, mysterious aliens called Calebans have provided humans and other sentient species with 'jumpdoor' technology that allows them to travel instantaneously across the universe. The Calebans 'speak' partly telepathically:

> The Caleban radiated. Its communication registered in the sentient mind as sound, but the ears denied they had heard anything. It was the same order of effect that Calebans had on the eyes. You felt you were seeing something, but the visual centers refused to agree.
>
> (Herbert 1972: 28)

The actual speech of the Calebans is presented in plain English direct speech in the narrative, though the register is punctuated and telegrammatic:

> 'That thing talks like a computer,' Furuneo said.
> 'Let me handle this,' McKie ordered.
> 'Computer describes mechanical device,' the Caleban said. 'I live.'
> 'He meant no insult,' McKie said.
> 'Insult not interpreted.'
> 'Does the flogging hurt you?' McKie asked.
> 'Explain hurt.'
> 'Cause you discomfort?'
> 'Reference recalled. Such sensations explained. Explanations cross no connectives.'
>
> (Herbert 1972: 34–5)

The Calebans are thus presented as slightly non-human, but as if they are simple-minded. Their stripped-down idiom and lack of idiomatic knowledge and odd attraction to being whipped makes them appear strange but not utterly alien. However (and the spoiler is, unaccountably, apparent in the novel's title!), it is revealed near the end that the Calebans are the consciousness of stars, and so are much vaster and incomprehensible than was imagined. The novel ends with the Caleban destroying its sadistic antagonists, Cheo and Abnethe. In the closing description, the telegrammatic style becomes more poetic:

> Cheo experienced the instant of Abnethe's death as a gradual dissolution of substance around and within him [...], a formless void possessed of no qualities.
>
> The moment passed abruptly, and Cheo ceased to exist. Or it could be said that he discontinued in becoming one with the void-illusion. One cannot, after all, breathe an illusion or void.
>
> (Herbert 1972: 221–2)

Here, the experience of death mixes the style of the Calebans ('discontinued in becoming one with the void-illusion') and the conversational human idiom ('it could be said', 'after all'). The ineffability of death, along with apocalypses, advanced science beyond our understanding, and mystical transcendence in science fiction are all often articulated through such poetic stylistic effects. The failure of the reader's own standard language forms, at such moments, emblematises the smallness of our comprehension, while gesturing towards the unknown.

The trope of stars and planets with consciousness is a feature also of Stanisław Lem's (1970) *Solaris*, which displays a similar stylistic pattern for the ineffable. The ocean of the planet is conscious, and it seems to shift its tidal forces to keep Solaris in a stable orbit in spite of its complex double-star solar system. It becomes clear that the ocean can communicate with the humans on the scientific station in orbit, delving into their memories and embodying copies of people on the station who have previously died. Though there is communication, there is no language. The terms that the scientists have used to name parts of the ocean show their primitive confusion in mixing up impressionistic words with a range of scientific registers: they

> devised a plain descriptive terminology, supplemented by terms of [their] own invention, and although these were inadequate, and sometimes clumsy, it has to be admitted that no semantic system is as yet available to illustrate the behavior of the ocean. The 'tree-mountains,' 'extensors,' 'fungoids,' 'mimoids,' 'symmetriads' and 'asymmetriads,' 'vertebrids' and 'agilus' are artificial, linguistically awkward terms, but they do give some impression of Solaris to anyone who has only seen the planet in blurred photographs and incomplete films.
> (Lem 1970: 111)

Again, the human reader is aligned with the observing, focalising characters, and again we are positioned in a diminished role in relation to the inexpressible and ineffable:

> We observe a fraction of the process, like hearing the vibration of a single string in an orchestra of supergiants. We know, but cannot grasp, that above and below, beyond the limits of perception or imagination, thousands and millions of simultaneous transformations are at work, interlinked like a musical score by mathematical counterpoint. It has been described as a symphony in geometry, but we lack the ears to hear it.
> (Lem 1970: 171)

The stylistic patterns at work here are some of those same features we have seen across the literary grasping towards the ineffable: an analogy in which human consciousness is small and aliens are huge; dissonant and surrealistic metaphors ('a symphony in geography'); a blend of scientific terminology and common idiom ('transformations ... mathematical counterpoint' to 'lack the ears') that suggests a desperate and wide-ranging attempt to comprehend the incomprehensible.

Returning to Alastair Reynolds' *Revelation Space* series, ineffable and incomprehensible communication is a feature of the recurring species of the 'Pattern Jugglers' across several novels. These are aliens who live in the oceans and collect the consciousnesses and memories of any individual of any other species who swims there. The Pattern Jugglers are never described directly, but the planetary ocean, as on Solaris, is sketched out by one of the characters as if it is a distributed network or a physical mind:

'It's a messenger sprite, flying between two nodes. Packaged with information at its point of origin, sent off to be received and digested by the recipient node. They send information by other means, including biochemical signals in the water'
[...]
'Don't be alarmed by these cross-connections: they're just to enable the node to communicate with itself. Think of us as a cell moving through the commisural gap between brain hemispheres.'

(Reynolds 2021: 331, 335)

The Jugglers and their patterns of communication are ultimately unknowable. They reconfigure people's personalities, and even blend them with other people, or people from within their memories. Though it is clear the ocean is organic, the novels present the Pattern Jugglers in shifting metaphors: a distributed consciousness, a hive mind, a complex computer circuit, an ecology of bacteria, a virtual network, a brain. And of course, like *Solaris*, the oceanic image serves as an emblem that is restless, deep, and mythologically unknowable for us.

The positive absence of nonlangs

Unknowable, unreadable, and unspeakable languages, in science fiction, ultimately gesture towards the ineffable. Linguistically, they represent the strongest possible forms of both the Sapir-Whorf principle and also the principle of cognitive embodiment, taken to their logical and extreme fictional conclusions. The correlations that I set up at the beginning of this chapter – between the functions of imagined languages, their typical stylistic realisations, and the nature of their embodied human/alien forms – are tendencies that I have observed across the literary worlds, rather than hard alignments. But in general it seems fair to notice that where the imagined language mainly serves a descriptive function, elaborating its world, then it is more likely to be fully worked out as a conlang, and placed into the mouths of a recognisable body. By contrast, immaterial and imperceptible alien bodies and minds tend to possess what I have called nonlangs, and the presence of a nonlang principally serves an emblematic, thematising purpose.

Nonlangs are referentially there but simultaneously asserted to be not there: a positive absence that is inaccessible to the human reader. In the field of cognitive poetics, such gaps, negations, or indeterminacies have been understood as *negative figures* – objects that are characterised by their absence, and that can only be delineated by their edges (Stockwell 2009: 31–43). Such conceptual *lacunae* cannot be directly and explicitly described, but can only be articulated by negation, by analogy, simile, or metaphor, by circumlocution, synonymy, or imprecision, or by enactive poetic forms.

All of these patterns of articulation have been in evidence in the examples mentioned in this chapter.

At the level of apparent authorial motivation, a reader of course can understand that a nonlang can be compositionally present but cannot be perceived directly; an author has no other choice than to gesture towards it and around it, without actually reproducing it. In this sense, a reader must perceive that the author – for all their authority – is in the same embodied human and inadequate situation as the reader, faced with the utterly alien.

It is striking how many inarticulatable and unnameable languages occur at narrative points of death, mental derangement, apocalypse, radical transformation, or transcendence – as if the exhaustion of our language capacity represents the end of all possible thought. As we have seen, such narrative moments are often enacted for a reader rather than denoted descriptively, in the stylistic form of fragmentation, impressionistic analogy, or dissonant metaphor, or simply by the silent page that follows the end of the book.

References

Banks, I. M. (1987) *Consider Phlebas*. London: Orbit.
Banks, I. M. (1988) *The Player of Games*. London: Orbit.
Banks, I. M. (1994) 'A few notes on Marain', posted on Ken MacLeod's defunct newsgroup <rec.arts.sf.written>. Now available at: <https://trevor-hopkins.com/banks/a-few-notes-on-marain.html>
Banks, I. M. (2012) *The Hydrogen Sonata*. London: Orbit.
Bear, G. (1985) *Eon*. New York: Bluejay.
Benford, G. (1987) 'Effing the ineffable', in G. E. Slusser and E. S. Rabkin (eds) *Aliens: The Anthropology of Science Fiction*. Carbondale: Southern Illinois University Press, pp. 13–25.
Burgess, A. (1962) *A Clockwork Orange*. London: William Heinemann.
Chiang, T. (2002) *Stories of Your Life and Others*. New York: Tor.
Clark, J. (2006) '"Small, vulnerable ETs": the green children of Woolpit', *Science Fiction Studies* 33 (2): 209–29.
Clarke, J. (2018) 'The Sublime in Iain M. Banks's Culture novels', in N. Hubble, E. MacCallum-Stewart and J. Norman (eds) *The Science Fiction of Iain M. Banks*. Canterbury: Gylphi, pp. 211–26.
Elgin, S. H. (1988) *A First Dictionary and Grammar of Láadan*. Madison: Society for the Furtherance and Study of Fantasy and Science Fiction.
Elgin, S. H. (2019a) *Native Tongue* (2nd edn) [original 1984]. New York: Feminist Press.
Elgin, S. H. (2019b) *The Judas Rose* (2nd edn) [original 1987]. New York: Feminist Press.
Elgin, S. H. (2019c) *Earthsong* (2nd edn) [original 1994]. New York: Feminist Press.
Elgin, S. H. (2019d) *A Third Dictionary & Grammar of Láadan* (eds J. Gomoll and D. Martin). Morrisville: Lulu Press.
Harris, P. (1998) 'The green children of Woolpit: a 12th century mystery and its possible solution', *Fortean Studies* 4: 81–95.
Heinlein, R. (1949) 'Gulf', *Astounding Science Fiction* [in two parts] (a) November XLIV (3): 53–90 and (b) December XLIV (4): 54–79.

Herbert, F. (1972) *Whipping Star*. London: New English Library.
Hofweber, T. (2017) 'Are there ineffable aspects of reality?', in K. Bennett and D. W. Zimmerman (eds) *Oxford Studies in Metaphysics, Vol. 10*. Oxford: Oxford University Press, pp. 124–70.
Koparan, C. (2020) 'Subversion and the Sapir-Whorf hypothesis in contemporary science fiction', *Journal of Science Fiction and Philosophy* 3: 1–19.
Lakoff, G. and Johnson, M. (1999) *Philosophy in the Flesh*. New York: Basic Books.
Le Guin, U. K. (1983) 'The author of the Acacia Seeds and other extracts from the *Journal of the Association of Therolinguistics*', in *The Compass Rose*. London: Gollancz, pp. 11–19.
Lem, S. (1970) *Solaris* (trans J. Kilmartin and S. Cox). London: Faber and Faber.
Malmgren, C. D. (1993) 'Self and other in SF: alien encounters', *Science Fiction Studies* 20 (1): 15–33.
Miéville, C. (2011) *Embassytown*. London: Macmillan.
Miller, J. T. M. (ed.) (2021) *The Language of Ontology*. Oxford: Oxford University Press.
Moro, A. (2016) *Impossible Languages*. Cambridge: The MIT Press.
Nagel, T. (1974) 'What is it like to be a bat?' *The Philosophical Review* 83 (4): 435–50.
Noletto, I. A. C. (2022) *Language Extrapolation: Glossopoesis in Science Fiction* (unpublished PhD thesis). Federal University of Piauí, Teresina.
Noletto, I. A. C. and Lopes, S. A. T. (2020) 'Heptapod B and whorfianism. Language extrapolation in science fiction', *Acta Scientiarum. Language and Culture* 42 (1). <https://www.redalyc.org/journal/3074/307464863008/307464863008.pdf>
Reynolds, A. (2021) *Inhibitor Phase*. London: Gollancz.
Shapiro, L. (2011) *Embodied Cognition*. London: Taylor and Francis.
Star Wars (and sequels) (1977ff.) G. Lucas (executive director). Lucasfilm.
Stevenson, J. (ed.) (1875) *The Chronicon Anglicanum* of Ralph of Coggeshall [edited from the Latin ms, c. 1225]. London: Longman.
Stockwell, P. (2005) 'Invented language in literature', in K. Brown (ed.) *The Encyclopedia of Language and Linguistics, Vol. 6* (2nd edn). Cambridge: Elsevier, pp. 3–10.
Stockwell, P. (2009) *Texture – A Cognitive Aesthetics of Reading*. Edinburgh: Edinburgh University Press.
Tolkien, J. R. R. (2005) *The Two Towers* (rev. edn) [original 1954]. London: HarperCollins.
Varela, F. J. (2017) *The Embodied Mind: Cognitive Science and Human Experience* (rev. edn). Cambridge: The MIT Press.
Walsh, P. G. and Kennedy, M. J. (eds) (1988) The *Historia Rerum Anglicarum* of William of Newburgh [edited from the Latin ms, c. 1198]. Warminster: Aris and Phillips.
Weiner, E. S. C. and Marshall, J. (2011) 'Tolkien's invented languages', in M. Adams (ed.) *From Elvish to Klingon: Exploring Invented Languages*. Oxford: Oxford University Press, pp. 75–109.
Wells, H. G. (1895) *The Time Machine: An Invention*. London: Heinemann.
Wells, H. G. (1898) *The War of the Worlds*. London: Heinemann.
Wittgenstein, L. (2009) *Philosophische Untersuchungen/Philosophical Investigations* (4th edn) (trans. G. E. M. Anscombe, P. M. S. Hacker and J. Schulte) [original German 1953]. Oxford: Wiley-Blackwell.
Zelazny, R. (1971) 'A rose for Ecclesiastes', in *The Doors of his Face, the Lamps of his Mouth, and Other Stories* [original November 1963, *The Magazine of Fantasy and Science Fiction*]. London: Doubleday, pp. 71–106.

Index

ʃUiʃuid, 93, 97, 99–101, 109

Âliya, 49–61
Âliyan dialects, 51–61
A Clockwork Orange, 4, 146–7, 162, 215
A Feminist Dictionary, 165–6, 220
'A rose for Ecclesiastes', 217
'A spot of Konfrontation', 9, 145–60
Abkhaz, 49–50
Adams, Richard, 10, 195–212
Adûnaic, 3, 96, 101, 107
Advanced Conlang, 42
Aldiss, Brian W., 9–10, 144–60
alien, 5–6, 63–75, 87–9, 139, 164, 179–80, 185, 187, 191–3, 214–27
    alien alien, 222
    human alien, 222
alphabets, 32, 36, 63–75
    Cyrillic, 71–3
    fictional, 63–73
    Latin, 36, 70–3
Always Coming Home, 96–7
anglicisation, 44–5, 150
Animal Allegory, 195–7, 208
animal narratives, 195–210
Anthropomorphic Projection, 197
anthropomorphism, 196–210
a posteriori conlang, 5–6, 21, 22–3, 42, 180
a priori conlang, 5–6, 21, 22, 42–3, 180
Arabic, 66, 68, 72–3, 88, 102
Aristophanes, 2

Armenian, 102
artlang, 7, 62, 133, 161–2, 165
A Song of Ice and Fire, 24, 26
Atala, 51–61
Aterra, 44
Atlantean, 96, 101, 107–8
audio recordings, 80–1
Aurebesh, 68–70, 73
authenticity, 4, 10, 33, 47, 179, 184, 188, 193, 216
author–conlanger collaboration, 17–31, 32–46
authorial intention, 8–9, 76–92, 115–32, 228
Avatar, 5, 8–9, 18, 31, 66, 76, 78–9, 96

Bacon, Francis, 3
Banks, Iain. M., 4, 222–4
Bardugo, Leigh, 23, 27
Barefoot in the Head, 146–7, 155–6
Basic Conlang, 42
Basic English, 156
Bear, Greg, 218
Beta-2, 221
Blackfoot, 50–1
blending, 151
Brithenig, 21
Brooding, 33
Burgess, Anthony, 4, 146, 162, 215

cacophony, 9
cannibalese, 9, 133–41
Chiang, Ted, 215

Index

children's literature, 133–41
Chinese, 3, 67–8, 73, 138
Chronicon Anglicanum, 213–14
colonialism, 5, 65–7, 73, 87, 134–5, 145, 157
conceptual metaphor, 10, 174–5, 205–8, 219
Conceptual Metaphor Theory, 10–11, 172–5, 195, 200–1, 205–7
Conlang Sketch, 42
conlanging, 17–31, 32–46, 49, 61–2, 72, 148–9, 157
conlanging community, 72
conlects, 49, 53
conscripts, 8, 63–75
contracts, 35–8
copyright, 37, 40–1
Crane, Stephen, 69–70

Danish, 48, 149–51, 155, 158
Defiance, 22, 30
design aims, 8, 63–4, 76–91, 93–109
deviation, 200, 205–8
dialect, 4, 8–9, 29, 47–62, 69, 129, 138, 144–60, 179–80, 182–5, 216, 219
dialect coach, 29–30
dialect continuum, 48, 61–2
dialect variation, 8, 47–62, 69
dialectal extrapolation, 196–7
Dickens, Charles, 9, 133–41
Disney, 20, 28
Dothraki, 5, 8, 19, 22, 24–6, 41, 96–7, 99–101, 108, 216
Dune, 5, 8, 23, 66–7, 70–3
Dutch, 48, 149–51, 155, 158
dystopia, 8, 10, 145, 154–7, 161–76, 180

Earthsong, 164, 176
Elgin, Suzette Haden, 10, 161–76, 220–1
Elvish, 3, 8–9, 76–91, 94–109, 115–31, 216
Embassy Town, 219
embodiment, 208, 214–22, 227–8
empathy, 195–7, 200, 207–10, 217
Encoding, 171–3
English, 4–5, 9, 21–2, 25, 27, 30, 33, 44–5, 49–50, 59, 69, 73, 79–80, 88–91, 94–105, 116, 121, 124, 138, 144–59, 164, 168–71, 182–8, 191–3, 224–5
Entish, 118, 216
Eomentesa, 42
Eon, 218
Esperantido, 156
Esperanto, 3, 5, 41, 43, 148, 155–7
estrangement, 66, 148, 150, 153, 158, 162, 196
euphony, 6, 9, 94
exoticism, 4, 8, 21, 63–7, 70–3
exotification, 67–8, 70–3
experimental literature, 9, 144, 146–7, 153, 185
extra-terrestrial, 10, 42, 63, 188–93, 214–28

Faber, Michael, 10, 188, 190–3
Farsi, 88, 102
feminism, 165–76
Finnish, 24, 78, 83, 93, 94, 102
Fjerdan, 96, 99, 101, 109
foregrounding, 10, 147, 195, 200–8, 224
Fremen, 5, 68, 70–3
French, 22, 33, 42, 53, 57, 82, 130, 148–51, 158, 181, 186
Frommer, Paul, 76–81, 86, 88, 96
function, 6–7, 64–5, 214
  descriptive, 6–7, 144, 157, 216, 227–8
  diegetic, 6, 71, 158, 215
  elaborative, 6, 64, 146, 214–15, 217
  emblematic, 6, 64–5, 70–1, 214–15, 221, 224–5, 227
  indexical, 6, 64–5, 214–15, 217, 221
  paratextual, 6–7, 163–4, 182, 215
  rhetorical, 6–7, 179, 214
  speculative, 6–7, 179, 214
Futhark, 69
Futhork, 63, 68–73

Galach, 70–3
Game of Thrones, 5, 8, 19, 22, 23, 26, 96

German, 9, 24, 33, 48, 50, 69–70, 86, 93–105, 147, 149–55, 158
glossopoesis, 1–11, 64–6, 69, 72–3, 144–50
Gödel's Theorem, 166
graphicspeak, 218
Greek, 79, 83, 93, 123, 130, 135, 156
'Gulf', 216–17
Gungans, 69

hanzi, 67, 73
Hebrew, 102, 122–3
Hedgerow, 195
Heinlein, Robert, 216–17
Heptapod B, 5, 215
Herbert, Frank, 23, 66–7, 70–3, 224–5
Hergé, 68
Hindi, 102
Hoban, Russell, 4, 10, 146, 182–5
Holiday Romance, 9, 133–43
Hollywood, 7, 17–20
Horn, 97, 99–101, 109
Hungarian, 102

Icelandic, 102
Idealised Cognitive Model (ICM), 161, 165, 172–5
identity, 47–8, 78, 181
idiom, 10, 44, 49, 68, 195, 200, 202–3, 206–8, 224–6
Ido, 3, 156
ineffability, 10–11, 213–28
Inhibitor Phase, 220–21
Imperial *see* Modern Standard Imperial
imperialism, 65, 71, 139–41, 157, 222
intellectual property, 38, 40
International Auxiliary Language (IAL), 3, 5, 9–10, 43, 155
International Phonetic Alphabet (IPA), 22
Irish, 102
Italian, 42, 84, 149, 151, 154, 158

Jackson, Peter, 76
Japanese, 66–73
Japonisme, 66–7

Kanson, 53–61
katakana, 68, 70–3
Kesh, 97–8, 99, 101, 108
Khandaq'i, 5
Khoekhoe, 102
Khuzdul, 3, 96, 100, 101, 106
Kingsnorth, Paul, 10, 185–6
Klingon, 4–5, 19–20, 40, 63, 93, 96–7, 99–105, 107, 176, 216
Kurosawa, Akira, 68

L1, 93, 95–6, 98, 105
L2, 95–6
Láadan, 10, 161–76, 220–1
Language Creation Society (LCS), 19–20, 35, 41
Lapine, 10, 195–210
Latin, 3, 21, 36, 53, 57, 70–3, 79, 128, 134–5, 137, 148, 150
Le Guin, Ursula K., 10, 96–7, 108, 188–90
legendarium, 47, 116, 124
Lem, Stanislaw, 225–6
lingua franca, 3, 71, 118, 131, 155, 157, 195
linguistic determinism, 4, 62–3
linguistic relativity, 6, 162–3, 166
loanwords, 123, 145, 150–1, 156
loglang, 6, 40
Lucas, George, 66, 68, 70, 218

Marain, 223–4
Marquesan, 158
Martin, George R. R., 23–6
Meek, James, 10, 179, 186–8
Méníshè, 22
Merineth, 42
Metaphoric ICMs, 174–5, 201–3
Miéville, China, 219
Modern Standard Imperial, 44–5
More, Thomas, 4
Motherland: Fort Salem, 8, 22
mu' tetlh, 230

Na'vi, 5, 8–9, 19, 76–91, 96–105, 108, 216
Naboo, 69–70
Nadsat, 4, 146–7, 162, 215
Nahuatl, 50

Index

Naming Language, 42
native script, 44–5, 69
Native Tongue, 10, 161–76, 220–21
Natlang, 98
neographies, 64
neologism, 72, 144, 145, 163, 171
neosemes, 145, 147, 151–2, 154
Newman, Sandra, 10, 179–82
Newspeak, 4, 10, 162–4, 176
Nineteen Eighty-Four, 4, 162–4
nonlang, 10, 213–28
Novial, 3, 156
novum, 7, 163

Occidental, 156
onomastics, 7, 69, 179–93
Orientalism, 8, 63–73
Orkish, 96–7, 99–107
Orwell, George, 4, 10, 162–4, 209

parallelism, 200–1, 204–5
paratext, 6–7, 163–5, 182–3, 215
perceptual dialectology, 48
personal names, 179–93
Peterson, David, 7–8, 17–31, 72, 96–7
phonaesthetics, 39, 93–111, 140
phonology, 22, 24–5, 42–3, 45, 49, 52–5, 61, 80, 93–109, 136, 150, 188, 216, 220
picts, 218
pidgin, 69, 138, 154–8
Pitona, 54–61
place-names, 6–7, 43, 117, 120–24, 129, 131, 179–93
proto-language, 38, 53–5, 58

Quenya, 3, 9, 76–91, 93–106, 118–23, 128–31, 216

Ravkan, 27
reduplication, 4, 57, 135, 137–40, 151, 154, 157
relativisation, 58–60
Reynolds, Alastair, 219–20, 226–7
Riddley Walker, 4, 10, 146, 148, 156, 180–5
Rohirric, 3, 94, 117–18, 129
romanisation, 24, 44–5
Russian, 27, 50, 71, 102, 146, 156

Sapir-Whorf hypothesis, 4, 6, 162–3, 166, 175, 224, 227
Scandinavian, 48, 69–70, 102, 186
science fiction, 4, 6, 8, 11, 23, 34, 42, 63–73, 82, 96, 145–5, 152, 164–5, 180, 188, 214–28
Scope of Work, 37
Serbian, 102
Shadow and Bone, 23, 96
Sindarin, 3, 9, 76–91, 96–106, 118–30, 216
Solaris, 225–7
sound symbolism, 6, 77–91, 93–109
Spanish, 22, 33, 42, 82, 102, 146, 149–50, 158, 180–1
SpEEC (Speech of the European Economic Community), 9–10, 144–59
Speedtalk, 216–17
Star Trek, 4–5, 46, 96
Star Wars, 8, 66, 68–70, 73, 218
Swahili, 102
Swedish, 48, 102, 148–9, 155

Tahitian, 158
Tamil, 51
Tanol, 49
television, 4, 17–31, 47, 76, 134, 140
Tenibvreth, 42
The BFG, 140
The Book of Strange New Things, 10, 180, 188–93
The Country of Ice Cream Star, 10, 179–82, 184
The Dispossessed, 10, 180, 188–93
The Dune Encyclopedia, 68, 72
The Hobbit, 3, 76, 116–17, 124
The Judas Rose, 164, 166, 174–5
The Lord of the Rings, 3–5, 9, 46, 76–91, 93–109, 115–31, 216
The Player of Games, 224
The Shannara Chronicles, 28
The Silmarillion, 3, 116
The Time Machine, 218
The Wake, 10, 180, 184–8
The War of the Worlds, 222
therolinguistics, 218–19
Tlagan, 51–4, 59, 61

To Calais, in Ordinary Time, 10, 179–80, 184–8
Tolkien, J. R. R., 3–4, 6, 8–9, 23, 34, 47, 76–91, 93–109, 115–31, 133, 135–6, 215–16
toponymns, 179–93
transliteration, 32, 44–5, 117, 123
Tuamotuan, 158
Turkish, 102
typography, 63–75

Umwelt Exploration, 197, 209
Utopia, 4, 7
utopia, 4, 162, 166, 189, 196–7, 222–3

video games, 20
visibility (of metaphor), 10, 174, 200, 207–8
Volapük, 3, 5
von Bingen, Hildegard, 2
Vulcan, 96, 101, 107

Watership Down, 10, 195–210
Webster's First Intergalactic Wickedary of the English Language, 165–6
Wells, H. G., 218, 222
Welsh, 86, 89, 102
Wenedyk, 21
Westron, 116–18, 121, 124–5
Whipping Star, 224–5
world-building, 4, 10, 33, 36, 38, 43–4, 47, 49, 66, 115–16, 130–1, 164, 179–82, 186, 193, 217
writing systems, 3–5, 8, 35–6, 42, 63–4, 67–73, 95, 121, 130

Xhosa, 102

Yumin, 51–2, 54–5, 59, 61

Zelazny, Roger, 217
zeugma, 147
Zoomorphic Projection, 197

EU representative:
Easy Access System Europe
Mustamäe tee 50, 10621 Tallinn, Estonia
Gpsr.requests@easproject.com

www.ingramcontent.com/pod-product-compliance
Lightning Source LLC
Chambersburg PA
CBHW070345240426
43671CB00013BA/2402